Singing the Law

Postcolonialism across the Disciplines 24

Postcolonialism across the Disciplines

Series Editors
Graham Huggan, University of Leeds
Andrew Thompson, University of Exeter

Postcolonialism across the Disciplines showcases alternative directions for postcolonial studies. It is in part an attempt to counteract the dominance in colonial and postcolonial studies of one particular discipline – English literary/cultural studies – and to make the case for a combination of disciplinary knowledges as the basis for contemporary postcolonial critique. Edited by leading scholars, the series aims to be a seminal contribution to the field, spanning the traditional range of disciplines represented in postcolonial studies but also those less acknowledged. It will also embrace new critical paradigms and examine the relationship between the transnational/cultural, the global and the postcolonial.

Singing the Law

Oral Jurisprudence and the Crisis of Colonial Modernity in East African Literature

Peter Leman

Liverpool University Press

First published 2020 by
Liverpool University Press
4 Cambridge Street
Liverpool L69 7ZU

British Library Cataloguing-in-Publication data
A British Library CIP record is available

ISBN 978-1-78962-113-6 cased

Typeset in Amerigo by Carnegie Book Production, Lancaster
Printed and bound by CPI Group (UK) Ltd, Croydon CR0 4YY

Contents

Acknowledgments

As much as I enjoy the process of archival research and textual analysis and discovery, one of the most fulfilling aspects of this project was the opportunity to work with many remarkable people, to learn from and be supported by friends and scholars from all over the world. I have tried my best to remember everyone who has helped me in some way, but this has been a long process, so if in that time I have forgotten someone's contribution, please forgive me.

This book began as a dissertation at the University of California, Irvine, and I am still deeply grateful to the mentors and friends there who supported me and provided invaluable guidance and encouragement. In particular, I will forever be indebted to Laura O'Connor, Brook Thomas, Ngũgĩ wa Thiong'o, Rajagopalan Radhakrishnan, Sanjay Krishnan, Catherine Liu, R. John Williams, Annie Moore, and Julia Obert, some of whom have continued to be sources of support and friendship at critical points in this project's development as a book.

I have worked at Brigham Young University since 2011 and received extraordinary support from wonderful colleagues, administrators, and staff, including John Rosenberg, J. Scott Miller, Edward Cultler, Phil Snyder, Lance Larsen, Kristin Matthews, Aaron Eastley, Robert Colson, Brian Roberts, Jason Kerr, Jamie Horrocks, Mary Eyring, Jarica Watts, Miranda Wilcox, Kimberly Johnson, Matthew Wickman, Nicholas Mason, Heather Hammond, Wendy Cloutier, and Tessa Hauglid. For the kind of support that only they can provide and appreciate, thank you to Matthew Ancell, Mike Pope, and Seth Jeppeson.

I am grateful to the many students I have worked with over the years at UC Irvine and BYU—in particular, Candice Stratford and Kylie McQuarrie, who both wrote MA theses on African literature and joined me for a memorable directed study on East African literature. And thank you to Matthew Fellows, my undergraduate research assistant for a brief period, who was particularly helpful in researching important legal cases in East Africa.

I am extremely grateful to the many individuals who have read or listened to portions of this work in its rough forms and provided feedback at conferences, workshops, and other events. I am sure there are many more than I can even remember, but, in particular, I would like to thank Stephanie Jones, Ambreena Manji, Awol Allo, Joey Slaughter, David Babcock, Lasse Horne Kjælgaard, Sidonie Smith and other members of the University of Michigan English Department, James Chandler, Elizabeth Anker, Jonathan Goldberg-Hiller, Eve Darian-Smith, and Anne W. Gulick. Special thanks to Gaurav Desai, who reviewed the entire manuscript at an early stage and has always been a source of encouragement and inspiration; John Lonsdale who hosted me and provided access to some of his personal research materials at Cambridge University; and those who responded with such kindness and generosity when I sought them out for guidance on specific issues, including Richard Ireland, Edward Cheng, Ronald Atkinson, Thomas Spear, Chris Wanjala, Benjamin Kirato, Mary Llewelfryn Davies, and Juliane Okot Bitek.

As a graduate student, I received funding for this project in its dissertation form from the Jacob K. Javits program, the UC Irvine Humanities Center, and the UC Irvine Department of English. The BYU English Department and College of Humanities provided much-needed financial support for research and conference travel since 2011, and the BYU Humanities Center coordinated a manuscript workshop and supported the African Worlds Faculty Research Group, which I co-directed with Robert Colson. As part of that group's work, we brought Gaurav Desai and Ngũgĩ wa Thiong'o to the BYU campus and both were extremely generous in helping me with different aspects of my research. I am also grateful to the administrators, librarians, and archivists where I have done archival research including the Aberystwyth University Department of Law, the Karen Blixen Archive at the Royal Library in Copenhagen, Cambridge University and the Wren Library, Oxford's Bodleian Library, and the British Library.

Early versions of a portion of Chapter 1 (on Jomo Kenyatta) and Chapter 2 appeared in *Law and Literature* and *Research in African Literatures*, respectively. I am grateful to Taylor & Francis and Indiana University Press for permission to include them here.

My sincerest thanks to Liverpool University Press for giving this book a chance and to the editors of the Postcolonialism Across the Disciplines series, Graham Huggan and Andrew Thompson. I am incredibly proud to be part of the LUP family through this series. Thank you to the anonymous reviewers, the designers, and copy-editors who have made this book better with their insight and creativity. I am particularly grateful to my editor, Chloe Johnson, for her enthusiasm for this project, her intelligence and professionalism, and the care she has taken to see this project through to the end. I couldn't have asked for a better editor.

I first became interested in East Africa when I spent nearly two years in Uganda and Ethiopia as a young man—it has been quite a while since that time, but I think of my experiences there often and continue to be grateful to the many people who helped me develop a better understanding and appreciation of their cultures and histories. I would like to thank my family, including my parents, Thomas and Rosalie Leman, who have given me such encouragement and have always shown interest in the work I'm doing even when it gets a bit drawn out and obscure. And, lastly, I am most grateful to my best friend and spouse, Christi, and my children, Caleb and Clara—their love, patience, and endless support are more meaningful to me than I can find words to express. I dedicate this book to them.

Introduction: Temp/orality in Law and East African Literature

Speaking before Parliament in 2013, British Foreign Secretary William Hague announced the end of *Mutua & others* v. *The Foreign & Commonwealth Office* (2012). In the case, a group of elderly Kenyans alleged that Britain's current government was responsible for acts of torture (including castration and sexual assault) committed by the colonial government during Kenya's State of Emergency (1952–59). Since the case began in 2009, the government tried to assert that liability for the crimes had transferred to the Kenyan government at independence in 1963, but the High Court disagreed. Unable to have the case dismissed, the British government finally settled with the claimants, agreeing to "pay compensation [...] as well as gross costs, to the total value of £19.9 million and finance the construction of a memorial in Kenya to the victims of colonial era torture" ("The Mau Mau Claims"). In addition to announcing this settlement, Hague also offered the following acknowledgment, a much-needed moment of clarity and confession after the government's many rhetorical and legal maneuvers to deny liability:

> However I would like to make clear now and for the first time, on behalf of Her Majesty's Government, that we understand the pain and grievance felt by those who were involved in the events of the Emergency in Kenya. The British Government recognises that Kenyans were subject to torture and other forms of ill treatment at the hands of the colonial administration. The British government sincerely regrets that these abuses took place, and that they marred Kenya's progress towards independence. Torture and ill treatment are abhorrent violations of human dignity which we unreservedly condemn. (Hague, "Statement to Parliament")

One must note, of course, that this expression of understanding, recognition, and regret is still not an admission of legal liability. In fact, Hague goes on explicitly to deny liability and assert that the financial settlement reached with the claimants was part of a process of reconciliation and future-oriented healing between the two nations rather than of admitting actual legal responsibility for something that happened in the past. Hague announces confidently that the agreement now reached between the government and Leigh Day (the solicitors representing the Kenyan claimants) represents a "full and final settlement of their clients' claims." Furthermore, Hague asserts that the case, because its resolution was driven by humanitarian and diplomatic reconciliation rather than legal liability, has set no precedent and cannot be the basis for further claims against the British government for acts committed by the colonial administration. A little over a year later, on October 29, 2014, the following headline appeared in the *Guardian* newspaper (online): "40,000 Kenyans Accuse UK of Abuse in Second Mau Mau Case" (Engelhart).[1]

This flood of new accusations suggests that, from the perspective of the Kenyan people, at least, *Mutua* did in fact set a precedent.[2] Troubling Hague's desire for closure and containment, the new claims also draw our attention back to the first Mau Mau case and to the letter that initiated the proceedings in 2009. The letter, drafted by the five original claimants and addressed to Gordon Brown, MP, opened with the following Gikuyu proverb and its English translation:

> "Muingatwo na kihoto dacokaga; muingatwo na njuguma niacokaga."
>
> He who is defeated with unjust force will always come back, he who is dealt with justly will never come back.

The fact that over 40,000 Kenyans came back despite the British government's insistence that the first case did not set a precedent suggests that the Kenyan people have not been dealt with justly. It perhaps even suggests that the denial itself is unjust, a failure to admit actual liability despite offering recognition of and regret for past injustices. Even if many of these claims are motivated by the possibility of financial remediation, there is at least symbolic value in the return of so many accusations as a challenge to the government's desire for closure without liability.[3]

1 In May 2016, the High Court in London began hearing arguments; in 2018, the case was dismissed on the grounds that, according to the Limitation Act, too much time had passed for a personal injury claim to be made. See *Kimathi & others* v. *The Foreign and Commonwealth Office* [2018] EWHC 2066 (QB).

2 On the question of precedent, see Gogineni, "Mau Mau Ruling Sets Legal Precedent" (2012) and Paramaguru, "Justice for the Mau Mau: Court Case in the U.K. Sheds Light on Grim Colonial Past" (2012).

3 It may seem cynical, but it is important to note the possibility that some of these plaintiffs are motivated by financial gain rather than questions of justice and morality. There are, of course, many who were dealt with unjustly and who have legitimate cases to make, but there are certainly others who see this as an opportunity that might be exploited for personal gain. For example, the Law Society of Kenya (LSK) has reported that, following the *Mutua* judgment, "a number of elderly people had been targeted by imposter lawyers, some claiming

Though brief and only the first step in a complex case, the *Mutua* proverb is significant for a number of reasons, not least of which is the way it temporalizes justice, simultaneously foreshadowing the outcome of the case it initiates and encapsulating the history of British colonial law to which it is a direct response. It invites a meditation on open-endedness and closure in the context of the law. Our return, the proverb says, is evidence of a past injustice and, furthermore, promises perpetual return until justice is done. The effect of this proverb and its implicit temporal narrative is all the more profound when we understand, first, that orature in many African societies, including that of the Kikuyu, is a medium of legal, not only aesthetic, expression: oral myths, songs, poems, stories, histories, and, of course, proverbs collectively archive normative wisdom and play a role in legal procedures. This is no mere epigraph, in other words, but an act of framing the international claim within the authority, and normative temporality, of indigenous law.[4] Second, the proverb's temporality is significant because the system of law that perpetrated the past injustice—half a century earlier—was itself deeply informed by and dependent upon narratives of time. At the heart of the British colonial response to Mau Mau, a response that included the torture of the five original *Mutua* claimants, was a narrative or myth about Africans and modernity: more specifically, a myth that explained the apocalyptic violence of Mau Mau by asserting that Africans were experiencing a crisis of modernity, or a psychological retreat into the "primitive" past brought on by an inability to cope with the rapidly advancing pace of the modern world. It was upon the accepted authority of this narrative that a State of Emergency was declared, laws were passed, suspects detained, detainees tortured and killed. To respond to this history, therefore, by means of a legalistic proverb that leverages a kind of messianic time in pursuit of justice is to address and

to represent British firms, and defrauded of savings" (Engelhart). The LSK has even alleged that Leigh Day took advantage of Kenyan citizens for financial gain. See Ochieng, "Lawyers Battle It Out for Mau Mau Billions" (2015).

4 I discuss this phenomenon in greater detail below and through specific cases in subsequent chapters, but it is worth noting Stephen Morton's discussion of this proverb in his book *States of Emergency: Colonialism, Literature and Law* (2013). Morton correctly observes that the proverb frames the claimants' charges against the British government with the authority of Gikuyu traditional law. "In doing so," Morton writes, "the proverb legitimates the detainees' claim with reference to the legal values and codes of Kikuyu society and culture, and defines the authority of the former detainees as legal subjects with the right to address the figure of British parliamentary sovereignty, the prime minister" (119). Morton uses the example of the proverb to introduce his chapter on fictional responses to Kenya's State of Emergency, particularly with regard to torture and indefinite detention, and his book as a whole offers an important contribution to the conversation about law and literature in colonial/postcolonial contexts. However, he leaves unexamined the implications of the fact that the proverb is part of a much larger and more complex tradition and history of African oral law that, as I will show, is intimately tied to literature in the postcolonial era.

authoritatively challenge the very myths that made colonial law possible and that still make possible modern forms of law and legal discourse, if William Hague's desire for closure is any evidence.[5]

The *Mutua* case and its initiative proverb exemplify the core concern of this book, which is about the relationship between law and cultural narratives of time in colonial and postcolonial literature and history. Recent scholarship has significantly enhanced our understanding of law's relationship to and central role within the British Empire, and, separately, scholars have revealed the important role of time in the imperial project.[6] The deep connection between the two has received much less attention. In terms of law's centrality, Gary Boire has argued that "colonialism's first language is law" (231), a phenomenon that has not until recently been substantially examined in postcolonial studies.[7]

5 In addition to, and by way of, seeking closure, Hague also insists on looking to the future—i.e., closing the door on the past and moving ahead in terms of a neo-liberal narrative of progress. He concludes his speech saying, "Although we should never forget history and indeed must always seek to learn from it, we should also look to the future, strengthening a relationship that will promote the security and prosperity of both our nations. I trust that this settlement will support that process. The ability to recognise error in the past but also to build the strongest possible foundation for cooperation and friendship in the future are both hallmarks of our democracy" (Hague, "Statement to Parliament"). Futurity, obviously, is also important in the *Mutua* proverb, and, as we will see, in many of the postcolonial literatures I examine that seek to challenge colonial law; the difference, however, is in the basis, objective, and meaning of futurity: for Hague, the future is a way to move beyond and no longer be liable for the past; for the *Mutua* claimants, the future offers the promise of vindicating the past; for others, the future may mean both or something else entirely.

6 The question of temporality has, in a sense, been central to postcolonial theory for years, particularly in how theorists have addressed issues such as historicism, nationalism, and the tradition vs. modernity binary. Dipesh Chakrabarty's *Provincializing Europe* (2000) may be the most obvious example, although many years earlier, Franz Fanon, in *Black Skin, White Masks* (1952), asserted, "Every human problem cries out to be considered on the basis of time, the ideal being that the present always serves to build the future" (xvi). More recently, scholars such as Adam Barrows, in *The Cosmic Time of Empire: Modern Britain and World Literature* (2011) and Giordano Nanni, in *The Colonisation of Time: Ritual, Routine, and Resistance in the British Empire* (2013), have addressed the problem of time in relationship to imperialism much more directly.

7 Of course, law is tied to culture, language, and politics in nearly every context, not only the colonial. However, the conventional themes of postcolonial studies, at least as approached through critical theory and the humanities, have tended not to prioritize the law as a central discourse. Although there are certainly legal implications to concepts and theories such as Said's Orientalism, Bhabha's hybridity and mimicry, Spivak's subaltern, and Fanon's critique of the psychological and physical violence of colonialism, the law has only figured occasionally and typically as a marginal feature of colonial administrative structures. Scholars in law and political science, such as Peter Fitzpatrick, Lauren Benton, Eve Darian-Smith, Nasser Hussein, and others, have, of course, demonstrated the

I agree with Boire but wish to take his claim a step further and assert that if colonialism's first language is law, the law's first language is narrative, and the most basic narratives of colonial law have to do with time.

In developing and exploring this claim, this book offers three primary arguments: first, it argues that colonial law grew out of but also gave life to narratives of temporality. Colonial law, in a sense, was both child and parent of colonial time. It formally enacted the normative force of conventional narratives of colonial modernity (e.g., that the "uncivilized" world was temporally stunted when compared to the West), but it also produced new forms of regulated temporality (e.g., work and court schedules, sentencing, land claims in perpetuity, etc.) in the lives of colonized subjects. To understand the workings and legacies of colonial law, in other words, we must understand colonial time (or *times*, as colonial temporality was hardly homogeneous despite claims or aspirations to the contrary).

Second, this book asserts that there was inevitably a gap between the aims and ideals of colonial time and lived realities of its subjects, or what some have called the "*heterotemporalities* that the British aimed to repress [but] often escaped regulation" (Mawani 78). Essential for my purposes are the heterotemporalities embodied in and expressed through oral jurisprudence: like the *Mutua* proverb, various forms of juridical expression found in East African orature and orature-infused literatures also frequently rely upon and confront questions of temporality and, in particular, the promises and problems of futurity. How do we account for this coincidence? Why do oral jurisprudence and questions of time recur so often in East African legal and literary history? In short, many writers recognized what Renisa Mawani calls the "temporalizing forces of legality" (69), and they sought to leverage the authority and unique temporalities of oral jurisprudence to resist, manipulate, and even replace such forces. Understanding the legal capacities of African orature ultimately enables radical re-readings of literary texts that draw on oral conventions to address questions of law and modernity within a framework of critical or experimental temporality.

Finally, this book offers a more general argument about what East Africa can contribute to our understanding of modern/global law and not just the history of colonialism as such. A recognition of the legal dimensions and

---

centrality of the law in colonial culture and history, and more recently scholars in the humanities have begun to examine such issues, particularly in relationship to postcolonial literatures. See, for example, the 2004 special issue of *ARIEL: A Review of International English Literature* on "Literature, Law, Postcoloniality"; Steven L. Bishop, *Legal Oppositional Narrative: A Case Study in Cameroon* (2008); Elizabeth Anker, *Fictions of Dignity: Embodying Human Rights in World Literature* (2012); Stephen Morton, *States of Emergency: Colonialism, Literature and Law* (2013); Anne Gulick, *Literature, Law, and Rhetorical Performance in the Anticolonial Atlantic* (2016); and, among others, the 2019 special issue of the *Journal of Commonwealth and Postcolonial Studies* on "Law and Literature from the Global South."

temporal orientations of African orature thus opens one of many possible doors for doing what Jean Comaroff and John Comaroff call "theory from the south" (1). In other words, the local cultures and literary/legal discourses of the global south, so long disregarded by imperial ideology and neo-liberal universalism as overly particular, exceptional, or of limited juridical significance, actually offer "privileged insight into the workings of the world at large" (1). If "[m]odern law itself is a creature of colonialism" (Merry 19), as several notable scholars have argued,[8] then that which challenges colonial law also has the potential to challenge modern law. Thus, if oral jurisprudence offers privileged insight into the temporal workings of colonial law, then, I propose, it offers privileged insight into the temporal workings of modern law as well. In its myriad interrogations of the temporal foundations of colonial law (manifest, as we will see, on a variety of fronts including contracts, evidence, emergency law, labor law, indirect rule, etc.), the story of oral jurisprudence functions as a kind of "theory from the south" by inviting us to ask what modern law would—and may yet—look like were it attentive to or founded upon the heterotemporalities of the formerly colonized world rather than upon the residues of colonial temporality. Ultimately, the texts, histories, and cultural–legal phenomena I examine in this book provide compelling examples of how the apparently local and particular of the global south

8 Peter Fitzpatrick has been particularly influential in demonstrating the colonial foundations of modern—or "occidental," as he often calls it—law. See, in particular, *The Mythology of Modern Law* (1992) and *Modernism and the Grounds of Law* (2001). In the latter, he argues that "occidental law is imperial 'in itself' and not only in some remote or passing application of it in the colonies 'out there'" (*Modernism* 146). Sally Engle Merry builds on Fitzpatrick's work in making a similar claim at the outset of *Colonizing Hawai'i: The Cultural Power of Law* (2000) and Antony Anghie (*Imperialism, Sovereignty and the Making of International Law* [2007]) takes the claim a step further in asserting that international law, in particular, has deep roots in colonial history: "colonialism was central to the constitution of international law in that many of the basic doctrines of international law—including, most importantly, sovereignty doctrine—were forged out of the attempt to create a legal system that could account for relations between the European and non-European worlds in the colonial confrontation" (3). My own approach is generally influenced by Fitzpatrick, although, like Anghie, I am particularly interested in the connection between colonial law and modern international law; unlike Anghie, I do not focus on a single doctrine as he does with sovereignty, but on the deeper relationship between *nomos* and narratives of time, which translate into or are manifest within a range of legal devices, doctrines, and institutions that either explicitly or implicitly enforce or depend upon the fiction of temporal difference between the so-called developed and developing worlds. Again, William Hague's temporally reactive rhetoric illustrates this, as does international human rights law in a broad sense, inasmuch as it projects an ideal narrative of "free and full human personality development," something Joseph Slaughter has so influentially studied in relationship to the *Bildungsroman*. See Slaughter, *Human Rights Inc.: The World Novel, Narrative Form, and International Law* (2007).

are tied to global flows of history, culture, and justice, and, like the *Mutua* proverb, can authoritatively speak to and reorient perspectives on modernity and modern law as we understand them today.

Although variations on these issues can certainly be found in many parts of the African continent and, indeed, the world, this book focuses on several countries and cultures within East Africa. My choice to do so is motivated, in part, by a critical shift away from the nation as the analytical baseline for historical and cultural inquiry: in other words, a regional framework offers one way of thinking beyond the nation and attending instead to cultural commonalities, historical resonances across borders, as well as the diversity of responses to shared historical experiences. Furthermore, given the richness of its oral traditions and the dramatic ways in which colonial law took root, East Africa provides a crucial case study in the legal effects of colonial time and the many forms of oral jurisprudence that rose up to "rival" the colonial and postcolonial state "in articulating the laws, moral or formal, that regulate life in society" (Ngũgĩ, *Penpoints* 37). At the same time, however, I see East Africa as more than a case study; indeed, despite some tendencies to treat the region as marginal,[9] it has been and continues to be politically, historically, and culturally central, a site of events and cross-currents of the global that have played a constitutive role in the developments and definitions of modernity in (relatively) recent history.[10] Evidence of this fact will become clear through the

9 Introducing his provocative analysis of the limits of globalization theory and the continued need for the postcolonial, Peter Kalliney writes ("East African Literature and the Politics of Global Reading" [2008]), "East Africa is an ideal site to perform this kind of cultural scholarship because it is at once historically and manifestly global—it has a long history of trade and migration throughout the Indian Ocean before and during the colonial period—and also marginal within the auspices of North American academy—East Africa is one of the places that literary theory attuned to globalization promises to open up for study" (3–4). Later, he points out "the more general subordination of Africa, *and particularly East Africa*, in both the global culture industry and also postcolonial studies in the North American academy" (18–19; emphasis added).

10 To say nothing of the region's deep history as the place of origin for modern *Homo sapiens*. This would seem to be so temporally distant as to be irrelevant, but several major archaeological discoveries were made in East Africa during the colonial period, many by the famed archaeologist Mary Leakey and her husband Louis Leakey, whom John Lonsdale and Bruce Berman describe as Jomo Kenyatta's intellectual rival and who was a translator during Kenyatta's trial in 1952–53 (discussed in Chapter 1). Furthermore, the narrative postulating the origin of modern humans in East Africa is called the "Out of Africa" hypothesis, putting it in dialogue with Karen Blixen/Isak Dinesen's famed memoir (also discussed in Chapter 1). Finally, these discoveries and their significance have emerged in discussions about "deep time": Henry Gee, for example, begins his book *In Search of Deep Time: Beyond the Fossil Record to a New History of Life* (1999) in Kenya. See my conclusion, "Temp/orality and Law in the End Times," for some additional thoughts on East Africa, deep time, and the Anthropocene.

course of this introduction and throughout the book more generally, although the nature and significance of the tension between East Africa's marginality vs. centrality is something that deserves much more investigation than one work can provide. My hope, then, is that this book will not only tell a story about East Africa, orature, and modern law that has not been told before, but also contribute to growing interest in the region and encourage more work, particularly in law and the humanities, to account more fully for East Africa's important place in global culture, history, and futurity.

Colonial Law, Time, and History's Dirty Joke

In *Heart of Darkness* (1899), Joseph Conrad's narrator famously captures the most prominent temporal narrative at the heart of colonial ideology. Describing his journey into the continent via the Congo and its tributaries, Marlow states, "Going up that river was like travelling back to the earliest beginnings of the world" (33); and, later, "We were wanderers on a prehistoric earth, on an earth that wore the aspect of an unknown planet" (35). For European colonizers, to travel to Africa was not only to travel in space, but also backward in time. Within a colonial imagination that associated civilization and modernity with futurity, the evolutionary model of progressive time allowed colonizers to divide the world temporally and move backward on a continuum from present to past by moving spatially from Europe to Africa. This contrast between the pre-modern and the modern in temporal terms—what Johannes Fabian calls the "denial of coevalness" (31)—took various forms in colonial Africa, from the broad contrast between European civilization and African primitivity, to more specific contrasts or binaries between law and custom, contract and status, literacy and orality, techno-supremacy and techno-infancy. The implication always was that Africa existed in the past and that Europe represented its possible future, or a future toward which it could potentially evolve with sufficient guidance. As a cultural narrative, the contrast between modernity and pre-modernity provided the primary justification for the colonial project, at least in its early stages. This was particularly evident in the development of colonial law. Indeed, as Mahmood Mamdani has written, "Civilization here [in Africa] meant the rule of law" (*Citizen and Subject* 109).

Temporality in all of its protean forms is a longstanding concern among scholars in multiple disciplines, and there continue to be innovative approaches to the subject and its varied manifestations, constructions, adaptations in a range of media and social phenomena. In this book, however, my goal in terms of temporality is not to provide a new theory as such, but to account for the frequent coincidence of different forms of law and questions of time in colonial and postcolonial literature and history in East Africa. Colonial/imperial time has been examined at length, but much less has been said about the relationship between such time(s) and law and, further, what the complex forms of temporality we find in certain works of literature might offer our understanding of colonial law and its still resilient residues. It is my contention that colonial temporality finds its most rigorous and consequential manifestation in the underlying philosophy and concrete instruments of the law. Thus, to adapt Robert Cover, I maintain that "no set of [colonial] legal institutions or prescriptions exists apart from the narratives [of time] that locate it and give it meaning" (4).

Beyond the colonial context, there has been a growing interest in the relationship between law and time.[11] Although *time* has, in the past, been privileged over *space* in critical theory,[12] the law seems more naturally attentive to and defined by spatiality—e.g., boundaries, borders, jurisdictions, zones of regulation, private vs. public spaces, etc. Time, it would seem, is a law unto itself, or at the very least is a better fit for the speculations of scientific inquiry and theorization rather than the normative concerns of the law. Recent studies have begun to alter this perception, but they also reveal that the law's dependence upon, movements through, and production of temporalities of different kinds are certainly nothing new. Particularly those legal systems within or modeled upon the Anglo-American common law tradition have long been sensitive to and in tension with temporality, turning to the past in the form of precedent in order to maintain stability and continuity while also making sense of the future by adapting to new circumstances and setting new precedents for future decisions. Peter Fitzpatrick describes the qualities of "determination and responsiveness" between which the law moves and, in the process, is ultimately constituted (*Modernism* 6). This tension, however, is only one of the myriad ways in which law negotiates with, controls, or is controlled by time. Renisa Mawani argues that "law is fundamentally about time" (71), noting through a variety of examples how "juridical concepts, legal discourses, and legal authority are underwritten by and draw their

11 Among others, see Greenhouse, "Just in Time: Temporality and the Cultural Legitimation of Law" (1989); Kahn, "Temporality of Law" (2008); Richland, "Sovereign Time, Storied Moments: The Temporalities of Law, Tradition, and Ethnography in Hopi Tribal Court" (2008); Birla, "Performativity between Logos and Nomos: Law, Temporality and the Non-Economic Analysis of Power" (2012); Wistrich, "The Evolving Temporality of Lawmaking" (2012); Fitzpatrick, "Marking Time: Temporality and the Imperial Cast of Occidental Law" (2012); Castillejo-Cuéllar, "Historical Injuries, Temporality and the Law" (2014); and Mawani, "Law as Temporality: Colonial Politics and Indian Settlers" (2014).

12 Foucault famously begins his essay "Of Other Spaces: Utopias and Heterotopias" (1984; based on a lecture from 1967) declaring, "The great obsession of the nineteenth century was, as we know, history: with its themes of development and of suspension, of crisis, and cycle, themes of the ever-accumulating past, with its great preponderance of dead men and the menacing glaciation of the world. The nineteenth century found its essential mythological resources in the second principle of thermodynamics. The present epoch will perhaps be above all the epoch of space" (22). The larger "spatial turn" in critical theory has explored (and, certainly, challenged) this distinction and its many implications. See, for example, Crang and Thrift, *Thinking Space* (2000).

meanings from the production, specification, and arrangement of time." Crucially, although she makes these observations about law broadly speaking, she ultimately focuses her attention on a colonial problem (the legal status and temporal claims of Indian settlers in South Africa), suggesting, again, that the colonial/imperial is not an exception or aberration in the development of modern law (including in the development of modern law's temporalities), but is, in fact, a constitutive phase.

Mawani argues that "time is integral to the ontology and epistemology of law," generally, and further that it is "equally significant to law's organization of social and political life" (71). This significance becomes even more pronounced in the colonial context. In India during the nineteenth century, "British time became a critical foundation of British law," imposing and regulating temporality in the day-do-day operations of courts and administrative offices (75). Furthermore, "British law and legality substantiated and legitimized its authority through its promises for the future" (76). The conventional narrative justifying colonialism asserted that although the "uncivilized" societies of the world existed in an undeveloped, pre-modern state—the perspective Conrad expresses so vividly—the gift of modernity would enable such societies to progress toward the very future inhabited and exemplified by the West. Writing in 1875, James Fitzjames Stephen, the Victorian judge, legal theorist, and former legal member in India, offered a particularly dramatic version of this narrative. Discussing the need for governance by "sensible laws" in India—many of which, as we will see, were later imported into East Africa—Stephen declared,

> [T]he establishment of a system of law which regulates the most important part of the daily life of the people, constitutes in itself a moral conquest more striking, more durable, and far more solid, than the physical conquest which renders it possible. It exercises an influence over the minds of the people in many ways comparable to that of a new religion. [...] Our law is in fact the sum and substance of what we have to teach them. It is, so to speak, the gospel of the English, and it is a compulsory gospel which admits of no dissent and no disobedience. (168–69)

In other words, whatever else colonialism offered its subjects, law was the most significant and meaningful, apparently surpassing even that of religion (to the point of metaphorically colonizing it here in Stephen's language). Law, thus, was not merely a technical means of governing time or a concrete embodiment of colonial temporal ontology; more importantly, it was both means and end of modernity itself. The religion of law had the power to change minds and regulate lives, but it also represented an ideal future: a society governed by this "compulsory gospel" was, like Augustine's City of God, the ultimate telos of colonial rule.

Such, at least, was the ideal or the claim. Mawani's approach to "law as temporality" ultimately "points to a doubling of time through the tensions between law's time and the multiplicity of lived times," but one of the most important outcomes of this doubling, the creation of indirect rule, falls outside the scope of her analysis (80). Like Mawani, Mahmood Mamdani notes a similar kind of doubling in his discussion of law in colonial Africa: "Civilization here meant the rule of law. The torchbearers of that civilization were supposed to be the colonial courts. The courts were intended neither just as sites where disputes would be settled nor simply as testimony to effective imperial control; rather, they were to shine as beacons of Western civilization" (*Citizen* 109). As Mamdani's language here suggests, however—i.e., "supposed to be," "were intended," "were to shine"—the reality of legal conditions on the ground in Africa differed from the intended ideal, requiring a different approach to the rule of law. In *Alibis of Empire: Henry Maine and the Ends of Liberal Imperialism* (2010), Karuna Mantena articulates this approach as it was first developed in India and later exported to Africa. Mantena argues against the common assumption that the "progressive civilizing mission" was the "paradigmatic ideological form of nineteenth-century empire" (8), demonstrating instead that although the progressive mission was paradigmatic prior to the mid-nineteenth-century, crucial events thereafter, such as the Sepoy Mutiny in India, the Morant Bay Rebellion in Jamaica, and, among others, the Fenian Rising in Ireland, dramatically disrupted and reoriented ideas "about the meaning, character, and future trajectory of the British Empire" (1). Colonial subjects' resistance to civilization led to new beliefs about "deep-seated 'cultural' differences between peoples" and the harm that contact with modernity would cause those considered to be pre-modern. Colonial administrators in India, most prominently Henry Maine (who was James Fitzjames Stephen's predecessor), argued that contact with modernity had created a crisis in "traditional" societies that led to instability and disaffection. Such societies were said to be so far back on the timeline of human progress that they were unable to cope with the demanding pace of modernity and, in a state of crisis—indeed, a crisis of modernity—retreated into the past, lashing out in violent resistance to the empire. Maine and others came to believe that preserving native social order served the interests of imperialism more than modernizing did. Through the second half of the nineteenth century, the model of direct rule, the justification for which was founded upon the future-oriented narrative of colonial time, was replaced by the model of indirect rule, which aimed to absorb native institutions into the colonial framework and, thereby, protect them from the negative consequences of modernity (and protect the empire from the negative consequences of rebellion). When the idealistic form of law failed, in other words, Maine changed the underlying temporal narrative, which then provided the basis for a new legal system. Indirect rule is, thus, one of the most significant examples of the relationship between colonial law and an uncertain, changeable colonial time.

Mantena's important revision of the conventional narrative of imperial justification lays the groundwork for also revisiting this narrative in Africa. She does not analyze indirect rule in Africa in detail but does observe that "in colonial Africa [...] indirect rule reached its zenith in terms of the breadth of application, institutional articulation, and theoretical elaboration" (173) largely thanks to Frederick Lugard's influential *The Dual Mandate of British Tropical Africa*, published in 1922. In contrast to India, however, the policy of indirect rule in Africa was implemented not as a response to specific acts of violence, but as a means of preventing them. When colonialism in Africa was in its early stages, the crisis of modernity had not yet taken place, and indirect rule, by allowing "native institutions" to remain intact under the watchful eye of the empire, was supposed to keep that crisis at bay. In this way, indirect rule was a kind of emergency law, suspending the conventional rule of law in favor of a legal system designed to avert crisis. "The preventative or preemptive aspect of the policy," Mantena claims, "attests to how deeply indirect rule was implicated in a transformed ideological framework that predicted social trauma and upheaval as the inevitable consequences of modern imperial rule" (173). In his own words about the "present task in Africa," Lugard writes, "It becomes impossible to maintain the old order [of direct rule]—the urgent need is for adaptation to the new—to build up a tribal authority with a recognised and legal standing, which may avert social chaos" (217). This authority was to be founded upon and representative of "native habits of thought" and would leave Africans "free to manage their own affairs through their own rulers, proportionately to their degree of advancement, under the guidance of the British staff, and subject to the laws and policy of the administration" (94). Lugard then outlines the procedures for establishing chiefs and a larger Native Authority to oversee groups of "tribes," with direct involvement from British officers dictated by the people's degree of "backwardness"—i.e., how far back they were on the measuring stick of Western progressive time. Some amount of "direct rule," Lugard admits, is "at first temporarily unavoidable among the most backward of all," but as the Native Authority demonstrates that it can act independently, Lugard says British involvement would become less and less direct and "the community will acquire a legal status" (218). The hope, again, was that this procedure would "avert social chaos."

Among the most obvious problems with indirect rule as Maine and Lugard defined it are, first, that the crisis narrative displaced blame for disruption and social chaos from colonialism itself onto the very societies experiencing disruption. "Indirect rule," Mantena writes, "functioned to decisively shift the burden of imperial legitimation onto native societies" whose tendency toward instability and even violence against the empire was described as the product of an inability to cope with modernity (177). A second problem with indirect rule was that the very idea of "native society" was an imperial invention. Indeed, as Mamdani observes,

> Unlike what is commonly thought, native does not designate a condition that is original and authentic. Rather, as in Maine, the native is the creation of the colonial state: colonized, the native is pinned down, localized, thrown out of civilization as an outcast, confined to custom, and then defined as its product. (*Define* 2–3)

Ultimately, indirect rule was not a system that functioned according to African modes of thought as it claimed but was in fact a "highly circumscribed affair" (Mantena 174). Lugard himself cites Lord Milner who "emphasizes the absolute necessity of supervision and control over native officials" (227). Though Lugard attempts to assert that indirect rule avoided the problems he saw with the imposition of direct rule through an "alien system" (217), indirect rule was in fact an alien system.

In addition to invented concepts like "native," "traditional," and "tribe," what colonialists identified and attempted to codify as customary law was one of many systems of law in a given region. "The tradition that the colonial powers privileged was the one with the least historical depth," Mamdani explains (*Citizen* 22). This meant that custom "was state ordained and state enforced." (This fact was important, I argue, in the evolution of orature as a counter-authority to colonial law, as I will explain below.) Furthermore, in addition to appointing chiefs to administer customary law (such as Isak Dinesen's friend Chief Kinanjui, discussed in Chapter 1), even when chieftaincies were foreign to a particular ethnic group, the colonial administration also imposed English procedure. A 1953 report on customary law in Africa insists that "the improvement [i.e., Anglicization] of procedure is more important than that of substantive law" ("Native Courts" 30). Though procedure may have been important, substantive law was also "improved" through the widespread application of the repugnance rule, which stipulated that native courts may only administer those aspects of customary law not "considered to be repugnant to the principles of 'natural justice, equity and good conscience'" (Elias 20–21). Lugard perhaps alludes to this rule when he observes that colonialism's "disintegrating effect on tribal authority" was due, in part, to "unavoidable restrictions imposed" on African leaders who could "no longer inflict barbarous and inhuman punishments on the individual, or take reprisals by force of arms on aggressive neighbors or a disobedient section of the community" (215). This clearly illustrates Mantena's claim that for figures such as Maine and Lugard, "empire could be simultaneously cause and cure for the crisis of native society" (177).

However, despite indirect rule's supposed promotion of African progress only "along indigenous lines," thus theoretically making the future-oriented narrative of colonial time unnecessary at least as a strategy of justification, Lugard continues to emphasize that narrative with evident fervor (Lugard 229). For this reason, I argue, Lugard's writings and the trajectory of indirect rule in Africa require closer attention.[13] As quoted earlier, Lugard

13 Mamdani (*Citizen and Subject: Contemporary Africa and the Legacy of Late Colonialism* [1996]) accounts for the continuation of the narrative of progress by observing that although "the accent shifted from direct to indirect rule, the two continued in tandem: the civilizing mission (assimilation) existed alongside the management of difference (pluralism)" (45). However, in Lugard's text, as in later uses of the crisis of modernity discourse during the Mau Mau war, assimilation and pluralism appear less complementary than contradictory.

recognizes that colonialism's impact made it "impossible to maintain the old order," and therefore "the urgent need is for adaptation to the new" (217). And although he clearly states at certain points in *Dual Mandate* that what is best for the African population is the freedom "to manage their own affairs" (94), he frames his entire book with the justification narrative. In his introduction, Lugard briefly narrates the history of European contact with Africa and at one point pauses to testify of the virtues of the British Empire:

> It was the task of civilisation to put an end to slavery, to establish Courts ofLaw, to inculcate in the natives a sense of individual responsibility, of liberty, and of justice, and to teach their rulers how to apply these principles; above all, to see to it that the system of education should be such as to produce happiness and progress. I am confident that the verdict of history will award high praise to the efforts and the achievements of Great Britain in the discharge of these great responsibilities. For, in my belief, under no other rule—be it of his own uncontrolled potentates, or of aliens—does the African enjoy such a measure of freedom and of impartial justice, or a more sympathetic treatment, and for that reason I am a profound believer in the British Empire and its mission in Africa. (5)

Here, the principles Lugard celebrates are precisely the principles of liberal imperialism that were supposedly no longer used to justify empire by the late nineteenth century. Mantena claims, in fact, that with the ideological shift toward the indirect rule model, "the moral foundations of empire [were] evacuated" (177). This is evidently not the case, at least not in Lugard's discourse about Africa. In the conclusion to *Dual Mandate*—i.e., after he has thoroughly detailed the system of administration meant to protect Africans from modernity—Lugard reiterates these principles in terms that even more clearly embrace the moral justification of the imperial project:

> As Roman imperialism laid the foundations of modern civilisation, and led the wild barbarians of these islands [i.e., the British Isles] along the path of progress, so in Africa to-day we are repaying the debt, and bringing to the dark places of the earth, the abode of barbarism and cruelty, the torch of culture and progress, while ministering to the material needs of our own civilisation. [...] British methods have not perhaps in all cases produced ideal results, but I am profoundly convinced that there can be no question but that British rule has promoted the happiness and welfare of the primitive races. Let those who question it examine the results impartially. If there is unrest, and a desire for independence, as in India and Egypt, it is because we have taught the value of liberty and freedom, which for centuries these peoples had not known. *Their very discontent is a measure of their progress.* (618; emphasis added)

This is an amazing statement. To say nothing of the uncanny and revealing resemblance between Lugard's language and that of characters in *Heart of*

Darkness,[14] Lugard also appears to contradict himself in a most serious way. Before, Lugard characterized discontent and social upheaval as evidence of the trauma of Africa's contact with Western civilization, a crisis of native society that could be averted through the principles and procedures of indirect rule. Now, in his conclusion to a book outlining those very principles and procedures, he is taking credit for that discontent, domesticating resistance by saying it is evidence that the British Empire has "taught the value of liberty and freedom." Apparently, discontent can signify, at once, both the failure and success of "primitive races" in coping with modern progress. One thinks of Shabine's observation in Derek Walcott's "The Schooner *Flight*": "Progress is history's dirty joke" (356).

This dirty joke, I argue, is evidence not of a crisis of modernity among Africans, but of a crisis of colonial modernity, a crisis within colonialism itself in its need for and fear of modernity that led to long-standing "regimes of intelligibility" (Mbembe 339). The myth of native crisis that became the basis of indirect rule was a fiction that enabled colonial administrators to reconcile the contradiction between the core temporal narrative that justified colonialism—i.e., the narrative of progress—and the reality of native resistance to that project. Rather than admit that the project was flawed, the crisis led to narratives of time and native culture and, thus, to a new regime of intelligibility formalized in the system of indirect rule. Of course, indirect rule is only one of many instances in which colonial temporalities influenced or provided the basis for British colonial law, and throughout this book I examine other configurations of the law/time relationship, including those found in contracts and evidence law in colonial Kenya (Chapter 1), international law and post-conflict reconciliation in Northern Uganda (Chapter 2), labor and emergency law in postcolonial Kenya (Chapter 3), and *lex talionis* and the legalities of dictatorship in Somalia (Chapter 4). The legal scope of this book, in other words, extends far beyond indirect rule, but I narrate a portion of its history not only because it often formed the larger legal context in which many of these other laws were written and implemented, but more importantly because it provides us with an initial understanding of a key aspect of the relationship between law and time in colonial culture that will enable us to understand further how and why so many leaders and writers in East Africa address colonial law and its legacies by turning to questions

14 For example, Marlow also compares the British Empire to that of Rome, saying that "this [the British Isles] also [...] has been one of *the dark places of the earth*" (5; emphasis added). And the company Manager similarly uses the term "method" euphemistically saying that Kurtz had done great harm to the company despite having gathered great quantities of ivory because "the method is unsound" (62). Comparisons of the British Empire to Rome were, of course, quite common throughout the former's history, but the coincidence of all of these terms—i.e., Rome, "dark places," "method," etc.—in Lugard's text is quite interesting in light of their use and significance in Conrad's.

of time. Furthermore, the history of indirect rule enables us to identify the changing contexts that transformed aspects of African orature from being legal to illegal, legitimate to subversive.

Before examining postcolonial engagements with these questions, I first look at some of the variations on as well as consequences of the contradictory temporal narratives during the colonial period. Chapter 1, "Catching History by the Tail: Colonial Non-Fiction, Aristocratic Atavism, and the Crisis of Modernity in Kenya," reveals how the crisis of modernity that the architects of indirect rule attributed to colonized peoples was actually experienced by the colonizers themselves. The nature and implications of this crisis become particularly clear in two trials that correspond to significant moments—one early, the other late—in colonial Kenya. The first section of the chapter takes Isak Dinesen's *Out of Africa* (1937) as its central text, discussing the extent to which Dinsen's memoir exemplifies the crisis of modernity among Kenya's aristocratic settlers who justified colonialism through the narrative of modernity but came to Africa precisely to escape modernity in Europe. However, when faced with an unsettling crisis on her farm that results in a complicated trial, Dinesen resorts to the unfair use of modern contract law to bring the crisis to an end. The myth of modernity justifies an escape from modernity that can only be preserved through a contradictory use of modern law. The trial also reveals colonial anxieties about African orature and its ability to unsettle and exploit the weaknesses of colonial law: although Dinesen discursively incorporates African orality within a colonial myth that equates literacy with modernity, oral law's open-endedness resists her attempts to assert closure through the *written* device of contract. Orature's insistent contemporaneity and futurity ultimately reveal the deep temporal contradiction at the heart of colonial law.

The second section of Chapter 1 turns to the obsessive colonial accounts of Mau Mau's violence as evidence of a crisis of modernity, a peculiar iteration of the discourse used to justify indirect rule. Indeed, the discourse was reified in a particularly powerful form as colonial leaders hired a psychiatrist—Dr. J.C. Carruthers—who actually diagnosed Mau Mau as a psychic disease brought on by a rushed confrontation with modernity. This pathological narrative was central to emergency laws that emerged at this time, and in the inaugural event of the emergency, the arrest and trial of Kenya's future president Jomo Kenyatta, we see a heated contest between the temporally based narratives of colonial law and the counter-narratives of African orality. My argument focuses, in particular, on another work of non-fiction, Montagu Slater's *The Trial of Jomo Kenyatta* (1955), which presents a selective retelling of the trial in order to reveal how African orature adapted more quickly to modern culture (through audio and video recordings), contrary to colonial expectations. Furthermore, Slater's emphasis on the tension between African orality and colonial literacy in the trial shows how orature challenged the laws of evidence in the context of emergency and, like the Kikuyu court on Dinesen's farm, demonstrated the extent to which the colonial use of the crisis discourse was actually evidence of an ongoing crisis within colonial culture itself. Ultimately, I argue that these two trials form an important part of and enable necessary perspectives on the larger picture of Mau Mau's impact on colonial and, therefore, modern law, an impact with effects witnessed as recently as 2012 in *Mutua & others* v. *The Foreign & Commonwealth Office*.

Law, Orature, and Postcolonial Futurity

Both Dinesen's and Kenyatta's cases in Chapter 1 also illustrate an important by-product of the temporalizing forces of colonial law: the criminalization of African orature. This criminalization was not universal, of course, but colonial law maintained that there were aspects of African oral law that could not be integrated into the framework of indirect rule and, therefore, needed to be banned. The infamous repugnance rule, versions of which were used throughout the British colonies, banned those aspects of "customary" law that were identified as "repugnant to the principles of 'natural justice, equity and good conscience'" (Elias 20–21), and, as Mamdani noted, the architects of indirect rule were myopic and/or self-interested in their identification of what laws constituted "native institutions" worth preserving: some traditions were favored more than others and some were invented entirely. This meant that a large portion of indigenous law was either ignored or explicitly proscribed. In her microcosmic way, Dinesen illustrates the tendency to proscribe orality by using a written contract to force closure upon the oral procedures of the Kikuyu court (an objective that fails, as we will see). The Mau Mau oath (also discussed in Chapter 1) was also banned by colonial law, and because of its subversiveness became one of the most feared and hated symbols of Mau Mau authority. There are other instances in both the colonial and postcolonial periods that I examine, but it is important here to consider why oral jurisprudence repeatedly appears in key moments in the history of the crisis of colonial modernity and why it presented such a threat.

One reason is that orature, in a sense, is explicitly bound up in that very crisis. Indirect rule sought to resolve the colonial crisis of modernity by presuming to prevent the crisis of native society, but in so doing it rendered large portions of indigenous law illegitimate. However, because that law was oral and because orality is fluid and highly adaptable, it did not cease to exist; rather, it often went underground, responding with resilience to the shift in the context of its authority from legitimate to illegitimate, normative to subversive. Ngũgĩ wa Thiong'o, as quoted earlier, captures this shift in his description of a "rivalry" between African artists and the state: laws and moral codes, Ngũgĩ writes, were traditionally expressed by African artists through "narratives, dances, theater, rituals, music, games, and sports"; but then, "[w]ith the emergence of the state, the artist and the state became not only rivals in articulating the laws, moral or formal, that regulate life in society, but also rivals in determining the manner and circumstances of their delivery" (*Penpoints* 37). The image of "rivals" suggests that indigenous forms of law continued to exist throughout the colonial and postcolonial periods and continued to resist colonial law in presenting alternative claims to authority, jurisdiction, and cultural and political legitimacy. In fact, Ngũgĩ later argues that orature "played the most important role" in anti-colonial struggles (105). "Not surprisingly," he observes, "it is the only tradition against which the colonial state often took firm measures, banning many of the songs and performances, and gaoling the artists involved." Colonial law's most crucial vulnerability was the crisis of modernity, and it attempted to obscure that crisis through myths characterizing African resistance as evidence that Africans were not yet (and may never be) ready for modernity. The legal edifice built upon this unstable foundation tried both to domesticate and alienate different aspects of oral law; however, oral law returned (in the sense expressed by the *Mutua* proverb) to respond to the injustices of colonial rule. And because oral jurisprudence is sensitive to and voiced through narratives of different kinds, it was particularly well suited to critiquing the foundational narratives of colonial law. Thus, it is not a coincidence that the moments of crisis I examine in this book witness a convergence of the rival forms of colonial and African authority over questions of time and modernity; orature (associated with pre-modernity in the colonial imagination) played an important part in the construction of colonial authority and, thus, came to play "the most important role" in that authority's (still ongoing) de-construction (Ngũgĩ 105).

I recognize, of course, that there is a danger here of essentializing orature as a coherent body of legal discourse fully oriented toward and capable of challenging colonial and post/neocolonial oppression. Indeed, I share Ruth Finnegan's concern that privileging the oral as more "quintessentially human" (or African) than the written risks reinforcing "the recurring binary oppositions" that pin "'Africa' with an enduring badge of difference" (222). Finnegan insists that we must maintain a "critical awareness" of the "limiting and perhaps ethnocentric connotations" of conventional approaches to oral forms in Africa and, instead, situate such forms in relationship to the "full range of human media." In my effort to do this with respect to oral jurisprudence in East Africa, I take cues from Finnegan as well as from other influential scholars of orature/oral literature, including Isidore Okpewho, Abiola Irele, Liz Gunner, Eileen Julien, and others, who approach the subject with critical awareness, countering in particular the conventional perspective that sees orature in evolutionary terms: i.e., as less developed than written forms of literary expression.[15] This is, of course, another version of the narrative(s) of

15 Of course, the question of whether orality or literacy is superior is one that has been addressed in a variety of ways throughout history. As we know, Socrates considered speech to be superior to writing, as did Rousseau, Levi-Strauss, and others, and this debate entered the realm of critical theory in the twentieth century in a particularly influential form with Jacques Derrida's discussion, and

temporality we find within colonial law, a fact that encourages us to attend more closely to the normative implications of debates about orality vs. literacy. Irele, for example, in responding to the "extreme valorization of writing," describes "the distinctive contribution of African orality to the experience of literature: the reminder it provides that the use of language for imaginative purposes represents a fundamental component of the symbolic structures by which the individual relates to society and by which society itself relates to its universe of existence" (77). There is a normative pull at the heart of this idea, suggesting that orality's distinctive contribution may have implications for our understanding of law, of the rules and normative expectations that govern relationships between individuals and society, society and the universe (understanding, of course, that for many African cultures the law is something that depends upon and has consequences for worlds beyond material reality). Despite Irele's gesture toward the normative, however, the question of law has not figured prominently in most literary approaches to African orality, although authors like Ngũgĩ wa Thiongo, Mĩcere Githae Mugo, Okot p'Bitek, and others examined in this book have made explicit connections between orature and law: in a late essay, for example, Okot declared that the African artist "expresses the law but in the most indirect language, through metaphor and symbol, image and fable. He sings and dances his laws" (*Artist* 39).[16] Taking

deconstruction, of the speech/writing binary in *Of Grammatology* (1967) and other works. This debate is also one that has figured in legal history, and one suspects that the legal variation is a product of the tendency in Western culture to privilege (or claim to privilege) speech over writing. In the English common law tradition, in particular, orality has long been seen as superior to writing. As Mark R. Kravits writes ("Written and Oral Persuasion in the United States Courts" [2009]), "The English judicial tradition has been described as one of 'comprehensive orality,'" with oral arguments, judgments, and witness testimony being much favored over written ones (250). See also Heerey, "Aesthetics, Culture, and the Whole Damn Thing" (2003) and Ehrenberg, "Embracing the Writing-Centered Legal Process" (2004). Like the tension between "determination and responsiveness" in the temporal orientations of common law (Fitzpatrick, *Modernism* 6), the tension between orality and writing is characteristic of the tradition but it takes an unusual form in the colonial context: because African orality is associated with pre-modernity in the colonial imagination and becomes the object of proscription, literacy is emphasized as the superior form of civilized expression toward which orality must evolve. Thus, the English preference for orality in law finds itself in tension with the colonizing imperative to suppress orality and elevate the written word. This tension, as I demonstrate in Chapter 1, becomes particularly dramatic and important in the trial of Jomo Kenyatta.

16 I discuss Okot's work in detail in Chapter 2. Mĩcere Mugo was a colleague of Ngũgĩ's at the University of Nairobi and his co-author of the play *The Trial of Dedan Kimathi* (1976), which I discuss in Chapter 3. In addition, Mĩcere would go on to explore the orature/law connection in much more detail in two books: *African Orature and Human Rights* (1991) and *African Orature and Human Rights in Gikuyu, Shona, and Ndebele Zamani Cultures* (2004).

such statements seriously, I argue, enables us not only to maintain a critical awareness of the limitations of certain approaches to orature in Africa, as Finnegan recommends, but more importantly to identify the ways in which authors like Okot draw on the authoritative spirit and letter of orature to challenge colonial law and its residues and ultimately articulate temporal paradigms and normative visions that have the potential to speak to questions of law far beyond local and even national contexts.

Of course, these paradigms and visions bring with them the distinctiveness and specificities of their cultures of origin, and this is one of the reasons I examine a range of cases of oral jurisprudence from throughout East Africa. As Mĩcere Githae Mugo asserts in her discussion of orature's relationship to human rights, "if we are to understand African Orature and the philosophy that shapes it, we must place the particular Orature being examined within the context of the specific mode of production from which it is generated" (11). At the same time, however, there are enough commonalities that we can bring Kikuyu, Somali, Acholi, and other oral traditions into conversation with one another and see their respective engagements with a shared history of colonial law as part of a larger story of law and modernity in East Africa and beyond. One of the most crucial points of overlap among the different cultures has to do with time or a recurring preoccupation with or demonstration of unusual forms of temporality. Of course, orature and its adaptations are used to approach the question of temporality because, as argued above, colonial law depends upon narratives of time and many African leaders and writers recognized, or at least intuited, this fact. Because orature represents an alternative form of authority, it directs its powers of critique toward the temporal foundations of the law. Like modern law generally, however, orature also demonstrates the alternating impulses of "determination and responsiveness" (Fitzpatrick, *Modern* 6). Although orature is, at the most basic, phenomenological level, tied to the present moment—as Walter Ong observes, "the oral utterance has vanished as soon as it is uttered" (39)—the larger movements and objectives of oral traditions tend to be tied strongly to the past. African oral poetry, claims Liz Gunner, is used "to formalize memory of the past, and to make the past comprehensible and accessible" (69). At the same time, however, "the set of cultural practices that the poetry embodied was not static. Rather, it was dynamic, changing in response to the historical pressures of the time" (68). Orature seeks to preserve past traditions, it "provide[s] a sense of the past in the present," but it also responds to change over time, often absorbing new ideas and abandoning those that no longer have clear utility (70).

The tendency to see orature primarily in relationship to past and present is consistent with conventional ideas about African time more generally. African time is often set in contrast to Western linear time, or what Benjamin famously described as "homogeneous, empty time" (261). Indeed, John S. Mbiti writes, "The linear concept of time in western thought, with an indefinite past, present and infinite future, is practically foreign to African thinking," which focuses more on the past and present, the "experience" of time, and the "rhythm of natural phenomena" (16–17). Because time in Africa is often assumed to be dictated by such rhythms, it is also characterized as cyclical: like the seasons, African time recurs and repeats, a past turning into the present and then returning again and again. This cyclicality suggests a lack of concern for what, in the West, we associate with the extreme ends of the linear timeline: the distant past and the far future. Okot p'Bitek himself writes, "The African of tradition is not much bothered about the distant past" or the beginning of time, "and he is not interested, in the least, about the end of time" (42, 44). It is not as though African thought has no sense of the future, but these characterizations suggest a much stronger orientation toward the present and a relatively recent past, particularly those aspects of the past retained in personal memory as well as the collective memory of oral tradition. Such generalizations have not stood undisputed, of course, and numerous scholars have challenged Mbiti's influential perspectives and, more broadly, the temptation to assert that there is a singular, identifiable thing as "*African* time." Instead, we must recognize that "each culture experiences time dynamically in its own way" (Adjaye 199). I strive to do this in my readings of the oral and literary works of postcolonial writers in East Africa, but despite the particularities of time among the Kikuyu or the Somali, for example, an intriguing theme emerges at the intersection of colonial law, time, and oral jurisprudence: futurity. Or, more properly, futur*ities*. Despite stereotypes of African time, not only are there diverse heterotemporalities grounded in everything from lived experience to myths of origins, but there are orientations toward and ideas about the future that have long been overlooked.[17]

These forms of futurity are important to recognize for several reasons, but two stand out as particularly critical for this project: first, the various models of futurity that we encounter in works that draw on oral traditions and deliberately critique colonial law and its legacies can be read in relationship to the colonial narrative of "not yet." The colonial response to violent rejections of their civilizing mission was to conclude that Indians, Africans, and others were *not yet* ready for modernity; this was the basis for indirect rule. The future was closed off, perpetually deferred until some undefined moment when native atavism would stop holding them back. This was not a promise of modernity,

17 In terms of futurity, an interesting indication of changing conceptions can be found in the recent growth of science-fiction (in both film and literature) in Africa, sometimes referred to as Afro-Futurism. See, for example, Hartmann (ed.), *AfroSF: Science Fiction by African Writers* (2012) and the many novels of Nnedi Okorafor. One might ask, however, whether such narratives of futurity have their basis in African thought or have only been made possible in the context of globalization. Given the forms of futurity we find in East African texts written long before the current science fiction trend, I would suggest the need seriously to consider the former, although the latter is no doubt playing a significant role as well.

of course, but a deterministic myth that Africa could never reach modernity. I argue that this myth had a dramatic impact not only during the colonial period, but also throughout the postcolonial period as nations struggled with the legacies of colonial ideology and the belief (deeply set in the mentality of the colonized subject, as Fanon, Ngũgĩ, and others have shown) that Africa needed but could never reach modernity. In contrast, then, the postcolonial futures we find in works by a range of writers in Kenya, Somalia, Uganda, and Tanzania[18] counter the colonial "not yet" through models of futurity that seek to disable colonial determinism and redefine, rather than reject, progress as such. Oral jurisprudence retains connections to the past and the power and immediacy of the present, but in the context of colonial temporalities and the normative visions of postcolonial writers, it also becomes a way of thinking about and by means of the future and what must be done both to undo the problems of colonial law and establish new foundations for systems of law suited to the needs of African nations in a globalized world.

The second reason these models of postcolonial futurity are important is that it is common to think of postcoloniality and anti-colonial movements as rejecting Western linear time and, therefore, to think of them as anti-modern or anti-progress, at least as modernity and progress were defined by colonialism. Renisa Mawani argues, "In postcolonial studies, scholars have long critiqued time as a Western and secular modernity and as an ontological and organizing

18 Of course, this is by no means geographically exhaustive—I recognize that in only including these countries in a book about "East Africa" I am omitting several other countries such as Rwanda, Burundi, Sudan, South Sudan, and Ethiopia that might fall under the broad regional designation. In doing so, I also overlook important authors from these countries. I have selected the countries and authors that I have, in part, because they stand out in terms of the particular narrative I am interested in telling (e.g., exhibiting a unique nexus of law, orature, and temporality), but my hope is that this project will promote interest in other writers in the region whose works are also in conversation with different areas of law. In terms of the scope of "East Africa," I include countries that were not part of "British East Africa" partly because ethnic boundaries do not align with those of national boundaries, and it is important to recognize the arbitrariness of the latter (the Somali people, for example, occupy an area that includes Ethiopia, Djibouti, Somaliland, Somalia, and the Northern Frontier District in Kenya). Additionally, it has become common practice to think of the region as broader than Kenya, Uganda, and Tanzania, as Simon Gikandi and Evan Mwangi have demonstrated in their book *The Columbia Guide to East African Literature since 1945* (2007). "One of the primary goals of this project," they write, "will be to define and redefine the area covered by East African literatures in English," and they discuss the need to include Ethiopia, Somalia, and Southern Sudan alongside Kenya, Uganda, and Tanzania (Preface). The UN geoscheme for Africa (which divides the continent into regions for statistical purposes) includes these countries and more in the subregion identified as "Eastern Africa." See "Composition of Macro Geographical (Continental) Regions, Geographical Sub-Regions, and Selected Economic and Other Groupings" (2016).

impetus of social and political life. As Anne McClintock observes, the field has, from its very inception, oriented itself against the 'imperial idea of linear time'" (74). However, this means neither an orientation against linearity as such, nor against modernization and development. The imperial idea of time, and the different forms it took, certainly had and continue to have negative implications, but postcolonial societies are still striving for and in need of progress, advancement, and development. But what does this mean? How can one insist on progress without falling prey to the temporally obstructionist ideology of *colonial* or even *neoliberal* forms of progress? There is no easy or simple answer, but I read the various forms of futurity we encounter in the works of postcolonial writers in East Africa as attempts to grapple with these questions. None of them gives definite or absolute answers (although, as we will see, Okot makes an explicit effort to redefine "progress"), but this is actually an important part of their experiments with oral jurisprudence and what we might call normative futurity, or narratives of future experience, progress, arrival, etc. that have implications for law and its foundations in the present. In other words, despite their cultural, contextual, and legal differences, *all* of the authors I examine encounter or deliberately deploy formal open-endedness in some way. This is a product, in part, of the authors' turn to oral culture: open-endedness is a characteristic of orality generally because it is unwritten and, therefore, fluid and always changing. It is at its core an open-ended system.

The formal open-endedness we encounter in the poetry of Okot p'Bitek, the plays of Ngũgĩ wa Thiong'o and his many co-authors, and the novels of Nuruddin Farah is a consequence of their formal incorporations of oral conventions, but it also creates and reinforces their respective orientations toward the future. In turn, this forms an essential part of their legal critique (generally, as noted, as a critique of the colonial "not yet," and specifically, as a critique of the particular aspects of colonial law to which they respond: e.g., labor law, emergency law, etc.), as well as their effort to imagine new temporal foundations for law in the postcolonial period. Robert Cover connects futurity and law in his claim that "Law is the projection of an imagined future upon reality" ("Violence" 1604), and this might provide some insight into the postcolonial futures we see in the works of so many writers in East Africa. I prefer, however, to see these works in terms of the proverb that opened the case *Mutua & others* v. *The Foreign & Commonwealth Office*: "*He who is defeated with unjust force will always come back, he who is dealt with justly will never come back*" (Letter to Gordon Brown). Each postcolonial author I examine addresses a historical injustice or the lingering consequences of the injustices of colonial rule, particularly as manifest in the law. All are engaged in a process of rectifying such injustices—they are, in other words, speaking for those who have been, and continue to be, dealt with unjustly, and the open-endedness of their texts is part of a process of coming back, of using the normative resources of oral culture to come back again and again until justice is done and new systems of justice and law are realized.

Thus, Chapters 2–4 examine the postcolonial legacies of colonial law and its underlying narratives of time; in all cases, we find authors turning to orature not solely as an alternative form of law, but as a jurisprudential imaginary that allows them to explore the conditions and cultural narratives needed to challenge the residues of colonial time and consider new models of futurity and whether or not they can sustain new normative regimes. On a basic level, I have organized the chapters chronologically, with Okot writing *Wer pa Lawino* (translated later as *Song of Lawino*) and *Song of Ocol*, in the 1950s, 1960s, and early 1970s, Ngũgĩ his plays in the mid-1970s and early 1980s, and Farah his dictatorship trilogy from 1979 to 1983. These periods, and the literary texts that represent them, correspond to key moments in the history of postcolonial East Africa, from that of independence to the emergence of neocolonialism, which manifest most destructively in dictatorships throughout the continent. However, there is another reason for placing Okot first: this entire project began many years ago when I first learned about Okot's experience studying law in Wales and his later observations about African poets as law-makers. Much of my thinking about the relationship between orature and law, and literature and law more generally, has been shaped by the work of Okot p'Bitek. After the first chapter on colonial law and non-fiction, therefore, I turn to Okot, who articulates more clearly than any other African author I know the deep and powerful relationship between the normative and aesthetic worlds in East Africa. Although Okot wrote about his own Acholi/Luo culture, the underlying principles of his particular form of oral jurisprudence establishes key terms and concepts that set up readings in subsequent chapters. Okot also powerfully illustrates how the legal affordances of African oral cultures have the potential to reorient our perspectives on matters of global concern.

Thus, Chapter 2, "A Song Whose Time Has Come: Northern Uganda, Apocalyptic Futures, and the Oral Jurisprudence of Okot p'Bitek," investigates the temporalities of international responses to authoritarian power, war crimes, and genocide, suggesting that there is often a gap between the rhetoric of immediacy in humanitarian interventions and the failure of such rhetoric to account for the deeper histories of the crises to which it presumes to respond. In movements such as "Save Darfur" and "Kony 2012," for example, international actors—typically humanitarians from the north—utilize narratives of immediacy and temporal urgency in attempting to provoke support for intervention in the south. Kony 2012 was particularly effective, launching a truly viral campaign by insisting that "the time is now" for decisive action against the Lord's Resistance Army (LRA) in Northern Uganda. Almost as quickly, however, critics pointed out the movement's failure to understand Northern Ugandan history and even the current state of the conflict. Despite the ostensibly good intentions of such interventions, I argue that they continue to operate according to the underlying logic of temporal difference which marks the global south as almost frozen in time: "not yet" modern (or, in the case of the humanitarian, not yet able to resolve the crises that limit modernization) and lacking a history worth noting. In contrast to the impulse toward immediacy in the rhetoric of humanitarian intervention, I suggest the need not only for historicizing a given conflict but for looking to past texts whose reception is altered by the conflict itself. In the case of Northern Uganda, I turn to the famously orature-infused poetry of Okot p'Bitek. *Song of Lawino* (1966) and *Song of Ocol* (1967) were written decades before the LRA conflict, and yet, given the texts' examination of post-independence domestic conflict and traditional approaches to reconciliation and community building, they have reemerged in the conversation about how to achieve reconciliation in the wake of LRA atrocities. I draw on Russell Samolsky's concept of "apocalyptic futures" in order to account for this reception, arguing that Okot's texts have "revealed [themselves] to be ahead of [their] time," anticipating and taking on a new force in the context of the LRA violence, particularly in their oral-literary enactment of Acholi legal principles that have proven essential to the post-conflict reconciliation process (Samolsky 7). Ironically, the failure of Kony 2012 was due, in part, to its belatedness, whereas texts like Okot's, seemingly anachronistic, are far more attuned to the realities of the present and what is needed to achieve the future ideal of reconciliation and a form of progress from the south defined not as forward-moving temporal linearity, but as democratic participation in the "productive activities of the society here and now" (*Artist, the Ruler* 49).

Chapter 3, "Between Formal and Infinite Time: Labor Law and Revolutionary Futures in Kenyan Popular Performance," examines the history of colonial labor law with a particular focus on how the recurring use of emergency laws in Kenya made labor regulations increasingly draconian. Recognizing that the state and the oral artist are "rivals" in articulating and disseminating the law, Ngũgĩ wa Thiong'o draws heavily on Kikuyu and other Kenyan oral traditions in addressing this history and the lasting effects of labor law in the postcolonial period. In particular, I argue that the temporal strategies (including formal open-endedness) of Ngũgĩ's collaboratively written plays of the 1970s and 1980s seek to destabilize the colonial myths of time and modernity embodied in the history of labor law. Particularly in *The Trial of Dedan Kimathi* (1976) and *Mother, Sing for Me* (1983), Ngũgĩ and his co-authors "[break] the barrier between formal and infinite time"[19] in order to make present a past myth of radically disruptive oral authority in Kikuyu law that allows them, first, to challenge colonial labor law explicitly as a mechanism of control rather than an avenue of progress; and, second, to work with the myths of orature to imagine the conditions necessary for the emergence of a future regime of moral and legal intelligibility based on collaborative, democratic work rather than colonial labor. Although Ngũgĩ's plays have not reemerged in an "apocalyptic" way similar to Okot's—not yet, at least—I nevertheless argue that they can contribute significantly to contemporary conversations

19 Ngũgĩ wa Thiong'o and Mĩcere Gĩthae Mugo, *The Trial of Dedan Kimathi* (1976), p. 2.

about poverty, labor, justice, and the ghosts of colonial history, particularly as they are manifest in the law. To that end, I offer some brief observations about how *Mother, Sing for Me* might speak to cases such as *Kenyan Tea Workers* v. *Unilever plc and Unilever Tea Kenya Ltd* [2015].

The wave of disillusionment with the post-independence state first reflected in Okot's poetry and then fully developed in Ngũgĩ's works gave way to fear and despair as political leaders began extending their rule indefinitely, and dictators, promising to succeed where the architects of independence failed, demonstrated how deeply the structures and underlying narratives of colonial rule had taken root. This is the starting point for Chapter 4, "Time Heals All Regimes: Temporality, Somali Oral Law, and the Illegality of African Dictatorships." In his *Variations* trilogy (1979–83), Nuruddin Farah provides a fictional account of the perpetual state of emergency that was Siyad Barre's dictatorship in Somalia and, in so doing, draws heavily on Western legal concepts, Somali orature, and Islamic law to enact *lex talionis*, or the law of retaliation, in sentencing the dictator as illegitimate. Somalia provides one of the more unique examples of an oral culture in which the legal and the aesthetic are truly inseparable, but it also illustrates how oral jurisprudence can serve both just and unjust purposes. As the dictator bans oral poets from speaking out against him, he employs other poets to sing his praises and reinforce his absolute control over time and space. The trilogy ends without closure—the narrative is open-ended; justice is not yet achieved; the dictator lives on. I argue that this apparently pessimistic gesture in Farah's texts punctuates a motif of futurity that comments on the tendency of dictators in Africa to hold on to power for as long as possible, sometimes decades. This suggests, ultimately, that the only true challenge to a dictator is time itself: one day, even if in "a future beyond the future of a future" (*Sardines* 45), the dictator will die. Given the persistence of totalitarian regimes throughout the global south, and the persistence of authoritarian power in both political and corporate regimes throughout the globe, I argue that Farah's novels provide a necessary understanding of the role of temporality in such power, as well as the resources that cultures of the global south have developed for resisting it.

In the conclusion, "Temp/orality and Law in the End Times," I acknowledge the fact that any book about normative worlds, temporality, and futurity must at some point address the problem of time's end. Taking a cue from Dipesh Chakrabarty's influential 2012 essay "Postcolonialism and the Challenge of Climate Change," in which he argues that all thinking about the present must be willing to address both globalization and global warming, I offer some preliminary thoughts on how my arguments might contribute to conversations about climate change—in particular, how climate change is dramatically altering how we perceive and experience time and what this means for law and the cultures of the global south. This may seem to be a departure from the rest of the book, and in some ways it is, but if East African authors are looking to the future with generous expectations and even hope, what happens to that hope when the future faces an unprecedented threat? Time, particularly for those in the global south who will be most affected by climate change, is effectively running out. I feel it is imperative that I respond, at least briefly, to this temporal crisis. I therefore offer some concluding thoughts about how the models of oral jurisprudence developed by East Africa's many writers who touch on, investigate, or otherwise sing about the legacies of colonial law and the crisis of modernity may ultimately offer new ways of thinking not only about modern law, generally, but the role of law and regions like East Africa in responding to the end times.

Why East Africa? Why Now?

To close this introduction, I want to say a few things about my choice of East Africa for this study, because the fact is that East Africa is not the only region of Africa, or even the world, where we can find important connections between orature and law, law and time, literature and all of the above, etc. This project could certainly have focused elsewhere or taken an even broader comparative approach. However, there are important reasons to pay particular attention to East Africa and to pay attention at this point in time. To explain why, I want to turn back briefly to 1907 when Winston Churchill, then a young Under-Secretary of State to the Colonies, made a semi-official visit to this newly acquired region of the African continent. Following in a well-established tradition of travel writing, he later published *My African Journey* (1908), an account of his time in Kenya, Uganda, and Tanganyika, during which he hunted, visited various administrative stations, and generally sought after the "[priceless] gifts of travel" (5). Known throughout the world at the time for its teeming animal life and "exotic" cultures, East Africa was a relatively recent addition to the empire and by writing of it to his readers at home, Churchill also hoped to "vivify and fortify the interest of the British people in [these] wonderful estates." Reading the text now, however, one also notices a degree of possible political grandstanding on Churchill's part. As a young promising politician and hero of the recent Boer war,[20] Churchill was on the rise and no doubt saw an opportunity to further demonstrate his political *savoir faire* by means of his already recognized literary talents. In the book, he does not merely describe the "wonderful estates" (a loaded phrase that divulges the clear purpose of the colonial presence in the region: to acquire land), but he frequently comments on the nature of colonial governance and the causes of and possible solutions to racial and political conflicts in the region. In a (perhaps deliberately) self-conscious moment following a long

20 As a war correspondent with the *Morning Post* in 1899, Churchill was captured and imprisoned, but he eventually escaped the prison camp, traveling nearly 300 miles to Delagoa Bay (now Maputo Bay in Mozambique), a feat that brought him fame back home. He later received a commission with the South African Light Horse and led battles in Ladysmith and Pretoria.

narration on the necessity of work and industry for African development, Churchill asks, "I wonder why my pen slips off into these labyrinths, when all I set out to do was to give some general idea of the politics at Nairobi?" (42). He then answers his own question: "But in truth the problems of East Africa are the problems of the world."

Of course, Churchill's metonymic turn in assessing the relevance of East Africa's problems was deeply imperial even if dressed up in a rhetoric of universalism. Churchill goes on to explain that the trials and tribulations of modern progress were playing out in East Africa in microcosm. He writes, "We see the social, racial, and economic stresses which rack modern society already at work here, but in miniature; and if we choose to study the model when the whole engine is at hand, it is because on the smaller scale we can see more clearly, and because in East Africa and Uganda the future is still uncompromised." Clearly, the temporal narrative is significant here—figuring the region in terms of temporal deferral and the logic of "not yet"—but the metonym is the operative device, not only identifying East Africa as a part of the world wherein the world's problems play out on a local scale, but also turning it into a sort of toy set, a "model" full of miniatures that replicates on the "smaller scale" the details of day to day life. (Indeed, Churchill's reference to the "whole engine" suggests a train set, which further suggests the Uganda Railway, which had been completed just six years before Churchill's visit and played a central role in the colonial project in East Africa.) On the one hand, Churchill's description of the challenges of modern society in East Africa invokes the central myth of the imperial project—namely, that imperialism promised to bring modernity to the pre-modern world—and seems to suggest that East Africa was capable of modernizing. On the other hand, the figurative device is highly paternalistic, belittling East Africa and casting it as a temporally arrested play area where the architects of empire experimented and played with different aspects of social, racial, and economic development for use on a more global scale.[21] In addition to being states of

21 The unintended implication here is not entirely flattering for Churchill and the Empire he represented—if East Africa is a toy set, then those who play with it, we must assume, are children or at least immature in some sense. Clearly this is not what Churchill meant—particularly given the tendency among colonialists in the nineteenth century to characterize Africa as child-like, which Churchill himself does later in the text (see p. 27)—but there is also a sense in which East Africa, as an exotic locale and safari destination, was (and perhaps still is, to some extent) treated as a play area for wealthy and adventurous Westerners. In terms of East Africa as a testing ground for imperial strategies and theories, a striking example can be seen in the State of Emergency declared in 1952 in Kenya. I discuss this in greater detail in Chapter 1, but, briefly, the lessons the British learned during the early emergency period were applied to similar emergency situations in other parts of the empire, including Malaya, Muscat and Oman, Cyprus, and Northern Ireland. The British General Frank Kitson, for example, developed counter-insurgency tactics in Kenya that were later used throughout

exception, as Nasser Hussain has argued, the colonies were also states of experimentation.[22]

And yet, in spite of the unsurprising imperial implications of Churchill's claim that the problems of East Africa are the problems of the world, there is also a sense in which Churchill was right: East Africa's problems or challenges in terms of economics, politics, security, the environment, etc. are similar to the problems nations the world over face every day, particularly in the age of globalization. More significantly, however, East Africa's problems are the problems of the world in the sense that their effect has a global reach, and much of the rest of the world is invested and *implicated* in many of those problems. What Churchill gets wrong—or, among the many things he gets wrong—is that East Africa was a mere play area for enterprising colonial modernizers; in reality, it was much, much more. As Jean Comaroff and John Comaroff write of the global south more generally, "modernity was, almost from the start, a north–south collaboration—indeed, a world-historical production—albeit a sharply asymmetrical one" (*Theory* 6). Modernity was not something that happened first in Europe and was then reenacted experimentally in the "miniature" of East Africa and the rest of the global south, although colonialists clearly maintained this influential if factually incorrect perspective. (Dipesh Chakrabarty has characterized this as the "'first in Europe, then elsewhere' structure of global historical time" [7].) Rather, the colonial "experiment" was a key phase in the development of modernity more generally, and, therefore, "To the degree that the making of modernity has been a world-historical process, it can as well be narrated from its undersides as it can from its self-proclaimed centers" (*Theory* 6–7).

East Africa can be seen as one of the many "undersides" of modernity, particularly as a region within the global south that the north has exploited and marked as temporally stagnant; however, it is also possible to see East Africa as much less hidden and more directly present in the formation of certain aspects of the modern world, most importantly (for my purposes) modern law. To use a different spatial metaphor, East Africa and the Western world are not (or at least not *only*) configurable as underside and topside, but instead as deeply intertwined, whether or not the latter recognizes it. As a result, in East Africa we find concrete examples of the "world historical process[es]" by which the global south collaborates, asymmetrically or otherwise, with the north in producing modernity. Of course, this is not the only region of the global south that has contributed to this process, and we must be careful not to assume that one region can necessarily speak for others (or even that one

---

the empire and, more recently, even entered the conversation about counter-terrorism during the Bush-era War on Terror. See Kitson, *Gangs and Counter Gangs* (1960); Kitson, *Low-Intensity Operations: Subversion, Insurgency and Peacekeeping* (1971); Kitson, *Bunch of Five* (1977); and Cavaleri, *The Law of War: Can 20th-Century Standards Apply to the Global War on Terrorism?* (2005).

22 See Hussain, *The Jurisprudence of Emergency: Colonialism and the Rule of Law* (2003).

country or culture can speak for a region), but the fact is that East Africa has had an unusual impact on the shape and direction of modern law in the last several decades. A series of crises have led to what Achille Mbembe would call new "regimes of intelligibility" in international law and foreign policy ("Figures of the Subject" 339). There are many examples of this, but some of the most important would include: the Kenyan State of Emergency (1952–59), which not only influenced British colonial responses to emergency in other parts of the global south in the final days of empire but also influenced discussions about counter-insurgencies in the recent wars in Iraq and Afghanistan;[23] the Meru Land Case, which went to the United Nations in 1951 and significantly strengthened the nationalist movement in Tanzania;[24] the Rwandan genocide, which, among other things, demonstrated the need for a permanent criminal court;[25] the 1998 US Embassy bombings in Kenya and Tanzania, which led to one of the first "terrorism trials" that has since been followed by those of the September 11 attacks;[26] the conflict with Joseph Kony and the LRA in Northern Uganda, which became the first case taken on by the International Criminal Court (ICC) after its creation;[27] the crisis in Darfur, which led, in part, to the ICC's indictment of Sudan's president, Omar al Bashir, for genocide and crimes against humanity;[28] Somali piracy, which prompted significant reevaluations of international maritime law;[29] Kenya's 2007 election violence, which led to

23 See Kitson, *Low-Intensity Operations* and *A Bunch of Five*; Cavaleri, *The Law of War*; and Branch, "Footprints in the Sand: British Colonial Counterinsurgency and the War in Iraq" (2010).

24 See Japhet and Seaton, *The Meru Land Case* (1967); Spear, *Mountain Farmers* (1997), pp. 209–35.

25 The ICC website explains that after the International Criminal Tribunals in Yugoslavia and Rwanda "there was general agreement that an independent, permanent criminal court was needed" ("About the Court" [n.d.]).

26 See *United States of America* v. *Usama bin Laden, et al.* (2001). In addition, the bombings prompted United Nations Security Council resolution 1189, which condemned the attacks and encouraged nations to adopt stricter anti-terrorism measures. Also see Hirsch, *In the Moment of Greatest Calamity: Terrorism, Grief, and a Victim's Quest for Justice* (2006).

27 See Finnström, *Living with Bad Surroundings: War, History, and Everyday Moments in Northern Uganda* (2008); Branch, *Displacing Human Rights: War and Intervention in Northern Uganda* (2011); and Chapter 2 of this book.

28 See International Criminal Court Press Release, "ICC Prosecutor Presents Case against Sudanese President, Hassan Ahmad Al Bashir, for Genocide, Crimes against Humanity and War Crimes in Darfur" (2008). In 2014, the ICC reluctantly ceased its investigation into war crimes in Darfur, citing the need to "shift resources to other urgent cases" but also criticizing the UN for not being more aggressive in pursuing Bashir's arrest ("Omar al-Bashir Celebrates ICC Decision to Halt Darfur Investigation").

29 See "Somali Piracy Exposes Weakness in UN Law of the Sea" (2009) and Treves, "Piracy, Law of the Sea, and Use of Force: Developments off the Coast of Somalia" (2009).

the creation of a new constitution that some have argued is one of the most progressive on the continent;[30] the 2007 violence also led to ICC indictments against several Kenyan politicians, including President Uhuru Kenyatta and Deputy President William Ruto;[31] the poaching crisis and illegal ivory trade, which of course are not specific to East Africa, but Kenya and Tanzania have been on the front lines of the battle with some recent success in prosecuting key players;[32] and, of course, there is the case of *Mutua & others* v. *The Foreign & Commonwealth Office* (2012) and the suit brought by 40,000 Kenyans against the British Government. This partial list does not necessarily suggest that East Africa is any more important than other parts of the global south in terms of its contribution to or place within the "world-historical production" of modernity, but the fact that the region has had an impact is undeniable, and although there have been a variety of studies of the individual events, more work remains to be done to make sense of this larger picture of dialectical exchange between East Africa and international law (Comaroff and Comaroff, *Theory* 6).[33] Is East Africa simply a "problem area" that requires the frequent

30 In his analysis of Kenya's constitutional "devolution of power," Ken Opalo writes, "On August 27, 2010 Kenyans promulgated one of the most progressive constitutions in the world. After more than two decades of false starts, the country finally agreed on a basic law for eastern Africa's biggest economy. The electoral violence in 2007–8, which left more than 1,300 dead and 300,000 displaced, served as a wake-up call. In the aftermath, constitutional scholars set to work on a governing framework intended to curb ethnic and political violence in future elections."

31 The ICC web page on *The Prosecutor* v. *Joseph Kony and Vincent Otti* (ICC-02/04-01/05) provides details about the case, including the fact that the charges against Kenyatta, like those against al-Bashir, were dropped in 2014. See also Mueller, "Kenya and the International Criminal Court (ICC): Politics, the Election and the Law" (2014).

32 In 2015, Tanzanian authorities arrested Yang Feng Glan, the so-called "Queen of Ivory," for her role in smuggling ivory to China for over ten years; see Kriel and Duggan, "'Queen of Ivory' arrested in Tanzania" (2016). And in 2016, a court in Mombasa sentenced Feisal Mohamed Ali to 20 years in prison for his role in an ivory-trafficking operation in Kenya; see Kahumbu, "Kenya Jails Ivory Kingpin for 20 Years" (2016).

33 This list also focuses solely on events of legal significance, but East Africa has a cultural centrality as well: at least since Isak Dinesen's widely read and highly influential *Out of Africa* (1937), East Africa has been a synecdoche for Africa as a whole. Many of the stereotypical images that the West associates with Africa generally (e.g., safaris [which is a Swahili word], wildlife, the savannah, "tribes" like the Maasai, etc.) often originate in East Africa, and popular representations of Africa in film and theater, including, among others, *Out of Africa* (1985), *The Air Up There* (1994), *The Lion King* (1994), *The Ghosts in the Darkness* (1996), *Hotel Rwanda* (2004), *The Constant Gardener* (2005), *The Last King of Scotland* (2006), and *The Book of Mormon* (the musical), are set in East Africa. Additionally, the region, and Kenya in particular, has been increasingly visible in the West since 2008 thanks to former President Barack Obama's family history.

attentions of international legal entities, or is the region's relationship to the recent history of modern law evidence of a deeper connection, of a more constitutive role in the development of normative regimes that shape and are shaped by the cultures of both north and south? This book assumes the latter and, further, asserts that orature's relationship to law and literature is a valuable part of the story, offering through authoritative idioms a range of cultural imaginaries wherein questions of time and legality are worked out, discussed, debated, critiqued, and, ultimately, left open because to stop speaking and debating would be to assume that justice has been done. As of now, that time—that *justice*—has not yet come.

CHAPTER ONE

Catching History by the Tail: Colonial Non-Fiction, Atavism, and the Crisis of Modernity in Kenya

> We Nations of Europe [...] who do not fear to floodlight our own inmost mechanisms, are here turning the blazing lights of civilization into dark eyes [...] essentially different from ours. If for a long enough time we continue in this way to dazzle and blind the Africans, we may in the end bring upon them a longing for darkness, which will drive them into the gorges of their own, unknown mountains and their own, unknown minds.
>
> Isak Dinesen, *Shadows on the Grass* (1960)

In 1962, just a year before Kenya received its independence, famed author of *Out of Africa*, Isak Dinesen, passed away.[1] Political freedom for the colony was something she had hoped for and looked forward to, having recognized more openly than most other white settlers that the problems of Kenya were in large part a product of colonialism. This was her take on the Mau Mau conflict as well, which she witnessed from a distance. In 1953, long after she had left her "farm at the foot of the Ngong hills" (*Out of Africa* 3) for Denmark, Dinesen began preparations to return to Kenya during the conflict as a newspaper correspondent, but at 68 years of age she was too frail to endure another journey to her beloved former home. Her age and distance did not, however, prevent her from commenting, at least indirectly, on the situation and attempting to explain the exceptional behavior of the Kikuyu people. In *Shadows on the Grass* (1960), her follow-up to *Out of Africa* which she was writing during the Mau Mau emergency, Dinesen reflected on the

1 Isak Dinesen, of course, is the pen name of Karen Blixen. For the purposes of consistency and because it was the name she used when she published *Out of Africa*, I will generally refer to her throughout as Isak Dinesen.

Europeans' denial that Africa had a history prior to colonialism, writing, "We white people [...] were wrong when in our intercourse with the people of the ancient continent we forgot or ignored their past or did indeed decline to acknowledge that they had ever existed before their meeting us" (428). This is a startling and remarkably liberal position for a white settler to take at the time but given Dinesen's attitude toward Africans throughout her years in Kenya, which was far more liberal than that of other settlers, it is perhaps not surprising. (At the same time, of course, it is important to recognize that Dinesen's apparent liberalism may be more an indication of her feudal-aristocratic perspective, which valued Africans for the role they played within the Lord/serf relationship that was the basis of the social microcosm on her farm. She did treat the Africans on her farm much more decently than many other settlers, but, as an aristocrat, her ultimate reason for doing so may have been less progressive than atavistic.)

Dinesen attempts further to critique the project of civilization in Africa but in doing so she not only reveals her continuing dependence upon the founding myth of civilization and modernity, but she repeats the myth of a crisis of modernity:

> We nations of Europe [...] who do not fear to floodlight our own inmost mechanisms, are here turning the blazing lights of our civilization into dark eyes [...] essentially different to ours. If for a long enough time we continue to dazzle and blind the Africans, we may in the end bring upon them a longing for darkness, which will drive them into the gorges of their own, unknown mountains, and their own, unknown minds. (429)

This is a familiar image. It repeats the concerns expressed by Henry Maine and others in the mid-nineteenth century when they witnessed violence similar to Mau Mau's in different parts of the empire and concluded that modernity could potentially have a harmful effect on the "primitive" mind. It was this realization that led to the formation of indirect rule, the purpose of which, in theory, was to prevent further crisis by protecting the "native" from modernity. In Africa, in particular, Karuna Mantena argues, indirect rule was primarily preventative, having been implemented on the foundation of lessons learned from other colonies and prior to full-scale colonization on the continent (173). If indirect rule in Africa was intended to prevent social disorder and the inevitable violence that follows the disintegration of traditional structures of authority, it should have rendered the crisis narrative obsolete. If this is the case, then why do we find Dinesen repeating that narrative nearly 100 years after Maine used it as an explanation for resistance to colonialism?

One answer is that the theory of indirect rule, as first articulated by Maine and Lugard, did not always map perfectly onto the day-to-day conditions and realities of colonial administration and, thus, Africans were not fully protected from modernity as intended. The process of implementing indirect rule was rarely a smooth one, largely because many of indirect rule's assumptions (e.g., about the nature of the "tribe" and the existence of "tribal chiefs") were generally mistaken. Kenya provides an interesting example. Certainly, we find many aspects of indirect rule used throughout the colony, including chiefs appointed to "administer native tribes" (Morris and Read 26 n. 61); Native Tribunals overseen by elders who administered customary law (272); and Local Native Councils designed to support the growth of an "administrative system based on the principles of Indirect Rule" (275). At the same time, however, there were challenges in Kenya that prevented indirect rule from being as fully realized as it was in places like Northern Nigeria and Uganda. Morris and Read offer two reasons for this inhibited growth: First, "The acephalous character of most of the African communities [in Kenya] made it difficult to identify the persons or institutions in whom authority traditionally reposed" (269). As a result, those identified as chiefs, headmen, or elders were very often colonial appointees rather than individuals with any pre-existing authority of significance in their local communities. Second, "the development of thorough-going principles of indirect rule was inhibited by the fact that Kenya was a land of European settlement." The settler demands for native labor conflicted with the imperatives of indirect rule as the "central state undertook to facilitate the labor requirements of local white employers" (Mamdani, *Citizen* 156). Ultimately, however, even if indirect rule did not function in Kenya as effectively as it functioned in other colonies, there were still fears that "without the preservation of the structure of chiefly authority, the fabric of tribal society would rapidly disintegrate and leave the handful of field officers to face an uncontrollable rabble" (Berman, *Control* 209). The perpetuation of these fears might explain why Dinesen repeated the crisis of modernity narrative to account for Mau Mau's "savage" behavior. In Kenya, that narrative never really became obsolete.

It is important to recognize, however, that Dinesen was not speaking alone and, in fact, that she was echoing what had become *the* dominant account of the origins of Mau Mau's violence. Indeed, her version of the crisis myth was decidedly tame in comparison to others. Not only did government officials and many throughout the West ignore Mau Mau's legitimate grievances and instead insist that their violence was simply evidence of their inability to cope with the demands of a rapidly advancing modernity,[2] but over time this belief became reified in the diagnostic accounts of the colonial-employed psychologist Dr. J.C. Carothers, who produced "scientific findings" to prove that Mau Mau was an actual mental disease. Mau Mau, he insisted, was a verifiable psychic disorder brought on by the crisis of modernity. And just as

2 As Bruce Berman explained in 1991 (*Control and Crisis in Colonial Kenya: The Dialectic of Domination*), "This characterization of Mau Mau, repeated almost daily for several years in press conferences, news briefs, and interviews from government information agencies in Nairobi and London, and widely disseminated in print and broadcasts by the press throughout the world, became and remains, especially in English-speaking countries, the image of the phenomenon in popular culture" (183)

the violence of colonial subjects in the nineteenth century prompted Maine and others to devise an exceptional form of law (which many considered to be temporary) in order to preserve social order, so too did the violence of Mau Mau lead colonial administrators in Kenya to devise an exceptional legal response that temporarily suspended the normal rule of law in order to preserve social order. The theory of Mau Mau as a disease therefore provided justification for the use of excessive military force, exceptional law in rushed emergency courts, and "rehabilitation" (i.e., imprisonment) for those suffering from the disease.[3] The uneven implementation of indirect rule and ongoing fears about the disruptive effects of modernity do not sufficiently explain why the crisis discourse took this particular form.

There are, no doubt, numerous factors that contributed to the discourse evolving into a (pseudo)scientific explanation for resistance to empire, and key scholarship in the last two decades has done much to enhance our understanding of the Mau Mau conflict and the various myths that fed into ideologies on both sides.[4] As a unique manifestation of the widely influential narratives of colonial time, however, the late-colonial crisis of modernity in Kenya deserves greater attention. I argue that although it can be traced, in a sense, back to Maine and others who explained resistance to empire as a crisis of native society, there is an important variation of that discourse that appears in Kenya between Maine and Mau Mau. The settlers who made indirect rule difficult to implement and who, like Dinesen, would later project the crisis onto Africans as a way of eliding the disruptive effects of colonial modernity, were themselves in a state of crisis. In other words, many European settlers, particularly those of the upper class, witnessed their status in Europe being threatened by modern progress and, unable to adapt to such rapid changes in the late nineteenth and early twentieth centuries, saw Africa's supposed temporal otherness as a promising refuge. Dinesen herself even uses the word "atavism"—such a morally and emotionally charged term when later applied to Mau Mau—in describing the anti-modern attitude of her "outcast" friends Berkeley Cole and Denys Finch-Hatton:

> It was not a society that had thrown them out, and not any place in the whole world either, but time had done it, they did not belong to their century. No other nation than the English could have produced them, but they were examples of atavism, and theirs was an earlier England, a world which no longer existed. In the present epoch they had no home. (206)

3 For the sake of clarity and consistency, and because "Mau Mau" was the term by which the Kenya Land and Freedom Army came to be known within colonial rhetoric and politics, I will use Mau Mau throughout this book, recognizing of course that the "Kenya Land and Freedom Army" was the organization's proper name.

4 Most important, of course, have been Caroline Elkins' *Imperial Reckoning: The Untold Story of Britain's Gulag in Kenya* (2005) and David Anderson's *Histories of the Hanged: The Dirty War in Kenya and the End of Empire* (2005).

These men did, however, strive to make a home in Kenya that reflected their lost values and reinstated status as the primary means of organizing relationships with the people around them. "Berkeley," she writes, "could have walked in and out of the Court of King Charles II" (207); and "Denys should be set in an earlier English landscape, in the days of Queen Elizabeth" (208). This nostalgia permeates Dinesen's *Out of Africa*, and one suspects that the atavism she ascribes to her friends is more an indication of her own search to regain the feudal past.[5]

This search, and the crisis that brought it to life, represents an important stage in the crisis of modernity discourse in colonial Kenya. Constructing this aspect of the narrative is best done, I argue, through an examination of key aspects of colonial law and the predominant literary form of the period, the colonial memoir, both of which sought to reinforce the pre-modern/modern divide that was essential to colonial justifications and alibis. Literature and law share common territory as symbols of European modernity (i.e., literature exemplified European literacy in contrast to African orality, and the rule of law was often held up as *the* distinguishing trait of European modernity),[6] and in colonial East Africa, literature and law were the primary vehicles through which Africa was produced for a European readership abroad and for European settlers on the continent: law produced and protected settlers' rights of contract and ownership (and denied such rights to Africans), and many settlers and visitors wrote works of "non-fiction" that reinforced the underlying myths of the law and produced a consumable version of Africa accepted as fact by distant readers in the West. The mutually reinforcing tendencies of colonial literature and law emerged in very stark ways during the Emergency period, as we will see in the latter section of this chapter, but their shared work of making meaning was an ongoing collaboration long before Mau Mau. In 1907, for example, Winston Churchill followed the conventions of colonial travel writing in *My African Journey* and took care to reinforce, through narrative, his belief about the need for "exact ... observance of the regular forms" of the law in the African colonies (28). Furthermore, many works of colonial non-fiction, including memoirs, ethnographies, and

5 Imagining Africa in this way, as a place where aristocrats could find a world that would welcome and support their values, was also reinforced through advertising. Winston Churchill writes in his brief travel memoir, *My African Journey* (1908), for example, that one of his intentions in describing his experiences is to "vivify and fortify the interest of the British people in the wonderful estates" of East Africa (v–vi). More directly, a famous advertisement in the early 1900s depicts a station of the Uganda Railway with the headline, "The Highlands of British East Africa as a Winter Home for Aristocrats." See MacKenzie, *The Empire of Nature: Hunting, Conservation and British Imperialism* (1988), p. 200.

6 As Mahmood Mamdani writes, "Colonialism claimed to bring civilization to a continent [i.e., Africa] where it saw life—to borrow a phrase from a context not entirely unrelated—as 'nasty, brutish, and short.' *Civilization here meant the rule of law*" (*Citizen and Subject* 109; emphasis added).

travel narratives, not only mythologized Africa as temporally other, thus normalizing the "denial of coevalness" (Fabian 31) that, in a broad sense, was the basis of the colonial legal system, but, like Churchill's text, they frequently represented legal circumstances and commented on the role and nature of law in colonial Africa. Legal thematics are important in such texts, but so too are their forms of address and narration, imagination and description, remembrance and critique: these literary forms were deeply implicated in and engaged with the forms of the law, whether by naturalizing the law's artificial claims to superiority via picaresque and pastoral or by exposing the deep contradictions at the law's heart through reportage and "letting the facts speak for themselves."

In what follows, I discuss colonial non-fiction and its relationship to the law in greater detail after an overview of the early, pre-Mau Mau instance of the crisis of modernity that, in effect, was foundational to the colony in Kenya. I then focus my analysis on two trials—one early, the other late—that appear in important works of colonial non-fiction. Both trials correspond to significant moments in the history of the crisis of modernity discourse in Kenya and, what's more, both also reveal the ways in which African orature responds to the temporalities of colonial law (specifically as manifest in contract law and the laws of evidence) in order to challenge assumptions, undermine authority, and reveal the actual crisis that underlying myths of time were meant to conceal. The first trial appears in Isak Dinesen's *Out of Africa* (1937) and the second in Montagu Slater's *The Trial of Jomo Kenyatta* (1955). Described by Thomas Knipp as "the paradigmatic white African memoir" (3), Dinesen's book describes a period from 1914 to 1931 and would, therefore, seem to have very little to do with a militant movement that began its campaign in the early 1950s, but the official accounts of Mau Mau's nature and origins have everything to do with Dinesen inasmuch as she exemplifies and allows us to trace the genesis and evolution of the crisis discourse. Dinesen's text, like most other memoirs of the time, also assumed a contrast between African pre-modernity and European modernity—indeed, according to Knipp, Dinesen "places the African at the beginning of a cultural time continuum—or even earlier in the inchoate world before culture" (7); however, she, like many other settlers, is attracted to Africa *precisely because* it is pre-modern. In Africa, she seeks to rediscover an age lost to modern Europe wherein aristocratic values, based on status relationships, might still thrive.[7] Yet, in the process

7 An important irony of this assumption is, of course, that Kenya was not the Edenic, pastoral land untouched by modern society that is described in her work. There were still pastoral and agrarian areas, of course, in which traditional culture thrived, but it is an indication of Dinesen's willingly myopic view that Kenya is largely reduced to this image in *Out of Africa*. During her time in Kenya, from 1914 to 1931, a vigorous labor movement led by Harry Thuku (who had connections to Marcus Garvey and Gandhi) had developed; many Kenyans, such as Jomo Kenyatta, had traveled to London for education and to advocate for

of attaining this movement backward in time, Dinesen experiences another crisis of modernity when an accident on the farm erupts into a trial, governed by the oral procedures of Kikuyu law, that threatens her status-based fantasy. Ultimately, she is only able to maintain that fantasy—temporarily—through the modern legal device of contract.

The trial, or "kyama," as it is called, on Dinesen's farm is comparatively minor, but it functions as a microcosm, I argue, of larger issues affecting the Kenyan colony. The second trial would seem to be of a different order altogether, but I argue that the similarities between the two are significant and, together, they are part of the larger story of law, crisis, and orality in colonial Kenya. Thus, in the latter part of the chapter, I provide a reading of Montagu Slater's *The Trial of Jomo Kenyatta* (1955), which chronicles the inaugural event of the Mau Mau emergency, the 1952 trial of Kenya's future president. In this trial and the wider conversations about Mau Mau of which it was a part, we encounter the most aggressive form of the crisis of modernity narrative.

Having seen the unusual form of this narrative in Dinesen, however, we can better identify the irony of its use against Mau Mau, a fact to which Slater is sensitive. And while the legacy of Mau Mau as a nationalist movement is certainly interesting, I focus more on the extent to which the *conflict with* Mau Mau (vs. just Mau Mau itself) perpetuated the legacy of the colonial discourse of modernity. So much has been written about Mau Mau, and I argue that the violence and sensationalism of Mau Mau and its representations tend to conceal a deeper and more lasting ambivalence in colonial culture. By reading the event through representative texts in which the literary, the legal, and the oral intersect, we can develop a better understanding of the discursive and ideological dimensions of the Mau Mau conflict, which, I argue, reveal a crisis within colonial modernity fundamental to the nature of colonialism's status-seeking objectives. This crisis did not begin with Mau Mau, but it also did not end with Britain's departure. As I demonstrate in subsequent chapters, contradictory temporal narratives that constitute the crisis have continued to be a fundamental part of crises in postcolonial African states (Mbembe 323).

Aristocratic Atavism and the Crisis of Modernity in Colonial Kenya

The Kenyan government's act of diagnosing Mau Mau membership or affiliation as a psychic disease brought on by a crisis of modernity betrays two great ironies: first, it was the British who brought so-called "modernity" into colonial Kenya, so they were, in effect, inadvertently accusing themselves of causing the outbreak—a culturally transmitted disease, perhaps—for

---

Kenyan rights; and various other events of national and international significance had taken place. See, for example, Thuku's *Harry Thuku: An Autobiography* (1970) and Simon Gikandi's "Pan-Africanism and Cosmopolitanism: The Case of Jomo Kenyatta" (2000).

which the Kikuyu people were being treated and punished; second, and more importantly, the colonial state was conceived in crisis. The conventional narrative of imperial expansion and colonial conquest focuses on the positive (for the colonizers, of course) motivations of acquiring resources and spreading the benefits of civilization. Europe's increased technological confidence and economic security following the Enlightenment allowed it to begin spreading its influence and expanding its power. As a justification for imperialism, this narrative has been critiqued, of course, but rarely has an alternative narrative been posited. Karuna Mantena, as we have seen, does argue that the justification model is displaced by the model of "culturalist alibis" in India in the mid-nineteenth century (9), but this only partly accounts for the contradictory nature of imperial ideology in colonial Kenya where the justification model continued to be used. Another aspect of the narrative of colonial conquest permits us to recognize that there were negative motivations in addition to the positive: for example, fear of the consequences of modernity for traditional aristocratic social structures, or, put differently, a crisis of modernity among the European upper-classes. From this perspective, it was not increased confidence and security, but *insecurity* on the part of a certain class of Europeans that, at least partly, motivated colonial expansion. According to David Cannadine, the "link between *nobilitas* and *imperium* has received remarkably little attention" (109), and yet that link played a formative role at a crucial stage in the history of colonialism, particularly in Africa. By recognizing this crisis as one of the core motivations of colonial practice and ideology that influenced both law and literature, we can develop a more complex and complete understanding of colonialism and the reasons for and the nature of its legacy of crisis in postcolonial Africa.

A few thoughts first on law: within the conventional narrative according to which Europe is motivated by the desire to civilize Africa, the law holds a central place. Gary Boire has argued that "law is colonialism's first language" (231) and, according to Mahmood Mamdani, "Civilization here [in colonial Africa] meant the rule of law" (*Citizen* 109). As discussed in the introduction above, James Fitzjames Stephen, the Victorian judge, legal theorist, and former legal member in India, described law as the "sum and substance" of what the empire offered its subjects; it was "the gospel of the English [...] which admits of no dissent and no disobedience" (168–69). Stephen is an interesting figure in the history of colonial law, in fact, not simply because of this legal evangelism, but because he and his immediate and arguably more influential predecessor in India, Henry Maine, planned, oversaw, and in some cases wrote a series of laws and codes that were used first in India but then exported to Africa. Maine made a name for himself with the 1861 publication of his treatise *Ancient Law*, and two years later he was appointed as a legal member of the Governor-General's Council in India. For eight years, he advised the government of India on legal matters and helped formulate a plan for the codification of Indian law; as historian George Smith once wrote, Maine embodied the principles of imperial policy "in legislative forms so that they became fruitful forever" (viii). These forms included the Indian Contract Act, which, along with the Indian Evidence Act, the Indian Penal Code, and others, some written by Stephen, was brought directly into Eastern Africa in the late nineteenth century.[8] And, of course, Maine was a key figure in the creation and promulgation of indirect rule.

Although Mantena draws attention to Maine's contributions to the formation of indirect rule, he is perhaps best known for his version of the narrative of colonial progress that posits a movement "*from Status to Contract*" (Maine 170; emphasis in original). In colonial Kenya, particularly among the settlers, both contributions are significant. In *Ancient Law*, Maine argues that traditional, pre-modern societies are hierarchically organized, relying upon status, rank, or position to determine the nature of human relationships and the role that each person plays within a given society. Such a society is structurally based on a principle of inequality and, according to Maine, *may* progress over time toward a more democratic principle of organization exemplified by contract. In his concluding thoughts on "Law in Primitive Society," Maine makes his famous statement that "the movement of the progressive societies has hitherto been a movement *from Status to Contract*" (170; emphasis in original). Modern, contract-based societies thus purport to displace status by leveling the playing field, so to speak, and by allowing individuals to enter freely into agreements without regard to status. In theory, at least, "Contract does not promise equality of conditions, but it does promise equality of opportunity" (Thomas, *American* 2).

Maine and others held this promise up as one of the many signs of modernity that both distinguished Europe as a "progressive" society and, at an early stage of imperial rule at least, constituted one of the doctrines of the "gospel" the English preached to colonized peoples. As Mantena demonstrates, however, Maine and his followers came to doubt the value of contracts for India in the nineteenth century, fearing, for example, that laissez-faire market relations for which contracts are indispensable would disrupt the social hierarchies of Indian society and lead, ultimately, to dissolution and revolt (163–64). Ironically, however, contract's disruptive power was being experienced less in India than it was in Europe, and it is my contention that the shift in the colonies toward preserving native institutions is part of what made

8 See Elias, *British Colonial Law* (1962), p. 15. To be precise, Maine did not actually write the Contract Act—it was drafted by the Third Law Commission of British India, which was formed in 1861 and chaired by Sir John Romilly. (See Lang, *Codification in the British Empire and America* [1924], pp. 83–86.) The Commission's report was submitted in 1866, when Maine was on the Governor's Council, and the Act was officially enacted in 1872. Maine's influence on the Contract Act and the larger codification of law in India was primarily administrative, although David J. Ibbetson, in *A Historical Introduction to the Law of Obligations* (2000), states that given resemblances between the Contract Act and statements in *Ancient Law* (on the topic of quasi-contracts, for example), "It is tempting to see in this [the Act] the hand of Sir Henry Maine" (284).

places like East Africa so appealing to some of its least-likely participants: namely, those Europeans who longed for the stage along the continuum from status to contract where hierarchies once preserved the privileges of the aristocracy. In their work on the relationship between class and colonialism during this period, both David Cannadine and Dane Kennedy describe the crisis of modernity among the British—and more widely European—upper classes. Kennedy explains that in Great Britain in the nineteenth century there was a "revulsion against [...] the allied forces of industrialism, urbanism, democracy, and egalitarianism that were transforming the whole of British life, reorganizing social relationships and remolding cultural values" (46). Contract, inasmuch as it promises egalitarianism and reorganizes social relationships, was no doubt central to these revolting allied forces.

Cannadine takes a wider view of these phenomena, noting how the "landed estates" became increasingly uncertain about their future and began looking to the empire for lasting security in terms of both investment and radical relocation. "[M]any of the greatest grandees," he writes, "sold off some of their properties and bought land in the colonies or shares in imperial companies" (109). Furthermore,

> Younger sons and more distant sprigs of nobility sought jobs in imperial administration, in the far-flung realm of the Anglican community, at the colonial bar, or on the colonial bench. More adventurous patricians—some with disreputable pasts to live down, others genuinely eager to make a new start overseas—became "gentlemen emigrants," and set out to establish new lives for themselves in Canada, South Africa, Australia, Kenya, and Rhodesia. Many a needy notable staved off his creditors by taking a comfortable, lucrative and honorific proconsular post in India or the great dominions: as A.J.P. Taylor once remarked, "going out and governing New South Wales" became the British aristocracy's "abiding consolation." (109)

In short, the residues of aristocratic life were threatened by modernity and, in a moment of crisis, many fled to the colonies. Speaking specifically of the consolations that Kenya provided, Kennedy observes, "Here was a rural, hierarchical society reminiscent of a past Britain more congenial to aristocratic sensibilities, sustained, so it must have seemed, by a semi-feudal relationship between European and African, with paternalism and deference the stable currency of interaction. [...] Kenya's appeal was its fresh environment, free from the pollution of modernity" (46–47). Many settlers came to Kenya in the haze of a reaction against modernization in Europe—they experienced the very crisis with which settlers and administrators would later diagnose Mau Mau: faced with the rapid changes of modernity, European settlers sought a retreat in the pre-modern forms of the past. One could even say that faced with the modernizing consequences of *contract*, including egalitarianism, industrialization, and democracy, Kenya's settlers sought a return to *status*.

We must recognize, of course, that the settler community was not simply a cohort of disgruntled, status-seeking lords and ladies, but, in fact, included people from all classes and multiple nationalities. However, as diverse as the settler community was, according to Kennedy, a "disproportionate element" included those with roots in or relevant connections to the middle and upper classes (44). In *Settlers of Kenya* (1948), Elspeth Huxley, daughter of early British settlers and author of the famed memoir *The Flame Trees of Thika* (1959), describes these people, telling us, "There were English aristocrats like [Lord] Delamere, who brought with them something of the grand manner of an age already dying, and tried, perhaps unconsciously, to create in this distant and beautiful land a replica of the feudal system of their fathers" (20). The feudal system is precisely the kind of status-oriented socio-economic system that Maine claimed progressive societies moved away from in favor of the modern promises of contract. As we will see, even aristocratic settlers like Delamere and Isak Dinesen could escape neither contracts nor modernity, but their efforts to do so tell us much about the origins and development of the crisis discourse in Kenya and what it means for our understanding of colonial culture and law.

To Status through Contract in Early Colonial Kenya: The Case of Isak Dinesen

Isak Dinesen was among some of the first Europeans to settle in Kenya, taking possession of her "farm at the foot of the Ngong hills" in 1914 (*Out of Africa* 3). Significantly, part of Dinesen's motive for settling in Kenya was to gain status through contract. Dinesen, who was born in 1885 in Denmark, traveled to Kenya after marrying her cousin, the Baron Bror von Blixen, for the sake of his title: according to their contract, in other words, she provided him with money and he provided her with an aristocratic designation, an official mark of status. In Dinesen's life and work, we witness not the movement of Maine's progressive society from status to contract, but instead the regressive, or atavistic, movement of a society *to* status *through* contract, a crucial version of the larger colonial movement-in-crisis away from modernity by means of modernity's forms. The years from 1914 to 1931 saw a period of intense change in Kenya, and although debates about *Out of Africa* have often centered on whether or not the text is, in fact, autobiography and thus can be read as a chronicle of her time,[9] the work's prodigious use of mythic, anti-modern discourse provides an exemplary case of literature's relationship to law in colonial Kenya and the extent to which imaginative representations of Africa and Africans both document *and* constitute the crisis of modernity. At the same time, given the wider function of non-fiction in this era, memoirs like Dinesen's also demonstrate the fundamental contradiction at the heart of

9 See, for example, Judith Lee's "The Mask of Form in *Out of Africa*" (1993), pp. 266–67; and Susan C. Brantley's *Understanding Isak Dinesen* (2002), pp. 74–75, 89–96.

the colonial project—which is to say, at the heart of colonial law—whereby law facilitates a modernizing project whose deeper intention is to help the modernizers escape modernity.

Although *Out of Africa* is the best-known and most influential colonial memoir not just of Eastern but perhaps all of Africa and beyond, it is important to point out that hers is one of many memoirs and works of non-fiction published in the colonial period. No other genre was as dominant at the time as the non-fiction narrative, and, I argue, its prevalence suggests the significant role it had to play in constructing myths of modernity and buttressing the colonial legal regime.[10] In memoirs about Africa, Western authors could claim first-hand experience with an "exotic" and generally unknown region. The subjective voice of the individual author, whether traveler or settler, became, because of the claim to direct experience, an authoritative voice of truth. In this way, non-fiction narratives supported the legal system by naturalizing the colonial perspective (us/them, modern/pre-modern, etc.) as objective. This has been true from the beginning of colonialism, and the early works of non-fiction indicate that the memoir's genealogy can be traced back to explorer narratives, such as those of Columbus or Vasco da Gama, who carefully documented each step of their journeys through "objective" and detailed descriptions and whose works had a crucial ideological function in the spread and justification of empire.[11]

10 An exhaustive list of the many works of non-fiction would be unnecessary and likely impossible here, but a few of the more important ones would include the following. The travel or safari genre is highly significant, of course, from early accounts such as John H. Speke's *Journal of the Discovery of the Source of the Nile* (1863) and Henry Morton Stanley's *Through the Dark Continent* (1879) to J.H. Patterson's widely popular *Man-Eaters of Tsavo* (1908) and Ernest Hemingway's *Green Hills of Africa* (1935), among many others. Memoirs by settlers were prevalent, including coming-of-age narratives such as *West with the Night* (1942) by Beryl Markham; *The Flame Trees of Thika* (1959) by Elspeth Huxley; and *White African* (1937) by Louis Leakey, who also wrote numerous other biographical and ethnographic works. During and following the Mau Mau war, when settler society was being challenged, there was an outpouring of non-fiction describing the history of white settlers in Kenya, as well as the "pre-history" of black Africans: *Before the Dawn in Kenya* (1953) and *Kenya's Warning* (1954) by Christopher Wilson; *White Africans* (1955) and *We Built a Country* (1956) by J.F. Lipscomb; *Out of Barbarism* (1955) by C.T. Stoneham; and *Cream Country* (1956) by M.F. Hill. There are also memoirs by military figures, such as Ian Henderson's *The Hunt for Kimathi* (1958) and Frank Kitson's *Gangs and Counter Gangs* (1960), and there began to be memoirs and autobiographies by Africans including Jomo Kenyatta's *Facing Mount Kenya* (1938), which critics acknowledge blurs the line between memoir and ethnography. A number of works by African writers also appeared following the Mau Mau rebellion when many detainees recorded their experiences of the emergency. See, for example, Josiah Mwangi Kariuki's *"Mau Mau" Detainee* (1976) and Gakaara wa Wanjau's *Mau Mau Author in Detention* (1988), among others.

11 Henry Morton Stanley's *Through the Dark Continent* (1878), for example, does not

Dinesen's memoir similarly objectifies and defines the world around her through an authoritatively subjective point of view (the great difference compared to most other settler memoirs being that Dinesen is a remarkably skilled writer), and early reviewers of *Out of Africa* accepted this authority, repeatedly observing that the book gave readers a glimpse of the "real" Africa. In her review for the *Times Literary Supplement* in 1937, for example, Brenda Colvin described the "direct unaffected style of the narrative and the strength and integrity of feeling in which it has its source," concluding that Dinesen "has understood Africa and been at one with it." More directly, Charles Poore, writing for the *New York Times* in 1938, maintained that Dinesen "knows that part of Africa" and that she captured "the essence of a continent"; through her descriptions of the African people, "she is able to make them remarkably real in this book." The same year in the *New York Times Book Review*, Katherine Woods noted the dramatic shift in Dinesen's writing from the fantasy of *Seven Gothic Tales* (1934) to the new memoir which is characterized by "the clearest reality, the utmost classic simplicity, the most direct—yet the most exquisitely restrained—truth." Like Poore, Woods made a repeated claim about the epistemological veracity of Dinesen's account: "the author knows how the hills look"; "She knows the practical details"; "It was not easy to get to know the natives ..." but, over time, "she came to know them." *Out of Africa* is filled with "clear objective details" and, though a "personal record," it contains "the sense of Africa's being." In a very broad sense, *Out of Africa* collaborated with the colonial legal system by providing a version of the cultural narrative upon which colonial law was based that readers accepted as factually and existentially true. Such readers, of course, already no doubt believed these narratives to be true, but Dinesen's memoir cast them in a powerfully and vividly influential form that, at the very least, reinforced such beliefs. For contemporary critics, however, Dinesen's point of view reflects not only a pretense to authority, but, more importantly, a "mythic consciousness" that produces a mixture of fact and fiction (JanMohamed 49).[12] Within this

---

normalize an existing claim to ownership, but systematically and scientifically describes the landscape in the mode of a surveyor checking the boundaries of a soon-to-be acquired property. In *King Leopold's Ghost* (1998), Adam Hochschild nicely describes this quality in Stanley's writing: "To read Stanley today is to see how much his traveling was an act of appropriation. He is forever measuring and tabulating things: temperature, miles traveled, lake depths, latitude, longitude, and altitude (which he calculated by measuring the temperature at which water boiled). Specially trusted porters carried fragile loads of thermometers, barometers, watches, compasses, and pedometers. *It is almost as if he were a surveyor, mapping the continent he crossed for its prospective owners*" (51; emphasis added). Even an "adventure tale" like Patterson's *The Man-Eaters of Tsavo* (1908) serves to normalize the legal and ideological establishment by portraying the efficient colonial civil servant as one who, almost single-handedly, brings order to the wilderness through modern technological means (i.e., rifles and the railway).

12 See also Lee, "The Mask of Form in *Out of Africa*" (1993).

mixture, I argue, we can find evidence of the deep crisis at the heart of colonial modernity and of the ability of oral culture to unsettle the dream of a return to pre-modern status.

Robert Langbaum, one of the earliest literary critics to examine Dinesen's work, initiated the discussion about the possible fictionality of *Out of Africa* by arguing that it is not simply a memoir, but is "perhaps the best prose pastoral of our time" (39). Like other works in the pastoral mode, *Out of Africa* constructs an idealized world that longs for and seeks to restore a lost golden age: in this case the aristocratic age of status. Langbaum writes that Dinesen's portrayal of Africa is one "of certain romantic expectations come true [...] expectations as to the possibility of recovering a kind of life that prevailed in Europe before the Industrial Revolution" (38–39). On her lush, 6,000-acre farm high in the hills above Nairobi, Dinesen, like many other aristocratic settlers, pursued a connection with the mythical past of Europe, in which everything had its place. As the abundantly generous "mistress of the manor," Dinesen portrays the Africans on her farm within the terms of this anti-modern myth as "the loyal, if often comical, feudal retainers to her white queen" (Simmons 99). One of the contradictions of Dinesen's fantasy of pre-modern status, however, and of the fantasy throughout Kenya, is that contract is used to construct and sustain status. We see this in her marriage wherein the status of an aristocratic title can only be attained through contract, but in order to purchase the farm, maintain it (which is to say, make it profitable), and populate it with feudal retainers, Dinesen had to use contracts, including contractual labor. Thus, the status/contract binary and the egalitarian promises of contract are both undermined as Dinesen and other settlers use the aura of contract as a modern instrument to dictatorially impose a "pre-modern" semi-feudal system.

Langbaum has analyzed the structure of *Out of Africa*'s five sections, arguing that there are "four acts of pure idyl, followed by a fall" (39). The memoir, in other words, is not only a pastoral, but is structurally based on the ultimate golden age, the myth of Adam and Eve. *Out of Africa* tells the story of Dinesen's loss of her very own "African Eden." The fall Langbaum refers to is the fact that the farm ultimately fails. The farm geographically is too high to grow coffee, their sole crop, successfully, and the venture falls into financial ruin. Furthermore, the fifth section, "Farewell to the Farm," deals not only with the loss of the farm but also the deaths of Kinanjui, the local (colonial-appointed) Kikuyu chief with whom Dinesen had a close relationship, and Denys Finch-Hatton, her close friend and lover. Reality does, indeed, seem to shatter Dinesen's Eden. However, what Langbaum misreads about the text is that not all of the first four chapters are pure idylls. Like Langbaum, Abdul JanMohamed observes that *Out of Africa* has a "tendency to exclude all painful or unseemly experiences" (53), but this is directly contradicted by a crisis in chapter 2, captured in the title "A Shooting Accident on the Farm." In chapter 2, a seven-year-old Kikuyu boy accidentally fires the careless farm-manager's shotgun at his friends, not knowing it was loaded. One child dies and another is severely injured. Dinesen rushes the injured child to the hospital where the doctors are able to save him and ultimately reconstruct his face. The majority of the chapter is then taken up with a trial, called a "kyama," in which a council of Kikuyu elders gathers to determine the compensations that need to be paid to the two victims' families. This chapter receives frequent critical attention primarily because of its portrayal of an illiterate Kenyan's encounter with literacy.[13] What scholars have yet to recognize as significant, however, is that this moment takes place in the context of, and indeed is a crucial step in the process of resolving, the legal dispute following the shooting accident. In my reading, this context is essential to understanding the full implications of Dinesen's representation of an orality/literacy binary and its relationship to the colonial narratives of modernity and crisis. The legal dimensions of oral culture present the real crisis for Dinesen, and within colonial culture more broadly, because they represent an alternative authority and system of signification that does not fit within the hierarchically organized world she has imagined into existence on her farm.

As elsewhere in the memoir, Dinesen is very much concerned in chapter 2 with comparing African and Western cultures. Although Dinesen admits that she knows nothing of traditional Kikuyu law and, therefore, feels extremely uncomfortable when the elders insist on her involvement in the Kyama, she does know enough to recognize (1) that such courts are "authorized by the Government" (92), and (2) that the "ideas of justice of Europe and Africa are not the same and those of the one are unbearable to the other" (96).[14] The accident on the farm and the subsequent court took place in 1923 and 1924,[15] and it is clear that the new mode of administration in which local "customary" law was allowed to operate within a limited jurisdiction was

13 See, for example, JanMohamed, *Manichean Aesthetics* (1988) p. 65; Aiken, *Isak Dinesen and the Engendering of Narrative* (1990), pp. 238–42; Ngũgĩ, *Globalectics: Theory and the Politics of Knowing* (2012), pp. 67–70.

14 This use of the word "unbearable" resembles or calls to mind colonial law's "repugnancy rule" (Elias 104).

15 The accident occurred on December 19, 1923. The incident was serious enough to receive at least a small amount of attention from the press. On December 22, 1923, a brief report appeared in the *East African Standard* under the headline, "Shooting Tragedy at Ngong. Native Children Play with Gun. One Killed, One Injured." The full text reads: "A fatal accident occurred on a shamba at Ngong on Wednesday resulting in the death of a native toto and serious injuries being inflicted upon another. The manager of the estate apparently entrusted a shot gun to his native cook for the purpose of scaring away birds etc. The cook left the gun in the kitchen. During the day in question five totos started to play with the gun. One seized hold of it and presented it at the others saying that he would shoot them. He pressed the first trigger and nothing happened, but on pressure of the second trigger a cartridge exploded causing the above mentioned serious consequences. The police have the matter in hand and are making enquiries. Meanwhile, it is understood, that the toto who was responsible for the occurrence has, in his fright disappeared."

in the process of being instituted. The Kyama, as Dinesen describes it, thus operates according to fluid rather than fixed principles and this is something that she, with her European ideas of justice, finds "unbearable." She writes, "To the African there is but one way of counterbalancing the catastrophes of existence, and it shall be done by replacement; he does not look for the motive of an action" (96). This focus on restitution, on righting wrongs through the payment of compensation, is, in fact, characteristic of many legal systems in East Africa, as we will see of the Acholi in Uganda in Chapter 2, but also of Anglo-American and other approaches to civil wrongs worldwide. Nevertheless, Dinesen considers this method reprehensible and claims that the native, by engaging in "endless speculations" about how many sheep or goats are needed to make up for a crime committed, "leads you solemnly into a sacred maze of sophistry" (96).[16] Here Dinesen begins to demonstrate her bias against the oral qualities of Kikuyu legal culture and its approach to crisis, dismissing as a "maze of sophistry" the procedure of discussing, debating, and engaging in oral dialectic to achieve legal resolution. The legal procedure, to her, lacks coherence and would seem to be improved through the imposition of procedural order and the written word. In fact, she goes on to demonstrate this preference for written, codified law in two ways: first, by transcribing the oral testimony of one claimant so he can legally prove his rights to compensation to the District Commissioner, and, second, by forcing the Kyama to end their deliberations over the rights of the other claimant by signing a written contract.[17] I will discuss these events in turn.

In the case that comes before the Kyama, there are two claims: that of Jogona Kanyagga, the father of the dead child, and that of Wainaina, father of the child who was injured. Kanyagga's claim is complicated by the fact that he adopted his son years earlier, and the child's extended relatives submit a

16 In a letter to Ingeborg Dinesen in 1924, Dinesen expresses her feelings about African legal customs even more strongly: "I think all the Kikuyu customs in this kind of case are quite atrocious, all they want is to squeeze sheep and cattle out of the family of the killer, and in fact there is not the least justification for that ... I must say that *I hate their 'kiamas'*; they consist only of the old Kikuyu who just want to sit chattering, drinking and eating endlessly, their judgments are completely worthless, I think they are absolutely fortuitous or dependent on bribery" (*Letters* 221–22; emphasis added).

17 One must be fair in reading Dinesen's text by recognizing the "more accurate" versions of some of these stories as revealed through her letters. Describing how Dinesen was unusually concerned for the welfare and advancement of the natives on her farm (which is true), Brantley notes that from her letters we learn that she approached the government to request approval for a Kyama to be held on her farm that would not be under the jurisdiction of the government-appointed chief, Kinanjui. Brantley observes that these "efforts seem to be an attempt to gain the natives more local autonomy" (79). Be that as it may, Dinesen eventually comes to regret this attempt, not only bringing Kinanjui in to control the Kyama's excessive autonomy but, as noted above, describing in unequivocal terms how much she hates the Kyama and considers it to be a waste of time.

competing claim to compensation. Kanyagga is distressed by the situation and one evening approaches Dinesen, who has been working at her typewriter, and asks if she would oblige him by recording his life story so he will have something to show the local District Commissioner in making his case against the competing claims. Dinesen agrees to the simple favor, and in recalling and narrating years later, she takes the opportunity to interpret the significance of the event in ideologically charged and mythical terms. Dinesen listens patiently to Kanyagga and records his testimony, which she characterizes as "difficult to follow" and filled with "complicated circumstances and irrelevant details" (115). She then rereads the testimony to verify its accuracy, and in watching Kanyagga's response, she witnesses, experiences, and *brings about* what she sees as a rebirth in this man from the dark womb of illiteracy to the new life of the word. This is one of the most fascinating passages in Dinesen's text in the way it illustrates multiple facets of the myths of colonial modernity, combining an extended (and distinctly self-serving) religious metaphor of creation and rebirth with the myth of literacy's effect on the "savage" mind.

When Dinesen reads Kanyagga's name, she describes his intense reaction as he turns to her, giving her "a great flaming glance, so exuberant with laughter that it changed the old man into a boy, into the very symbol of youth" (115). The language of transformation continues as she reads further, reaching the end of the document and once again reading Kanyagga's name out loud. Kanyagga changes now from symbol of youth to one filled "with a new dignity." This expression could be read simply as pride in having successfully accomplished his objective of recording his testimony, or, yes, even joy at hearing his name read aloud, but Dinesen interprets the event as something far more significant. Putting words to his silent expression of "new dignity," Dinesen writes:

> Such a glance did Adam give the Lord when he formed him out of the dust, and breathed into his nostrils the breath of life, and man became a living soul. I had created him and shown him himself: Jogona Kanyagga of life everlasting. When I handed him the paper, he took it reverently and greedily, folded it up in a corner of his cloak and kept his hand upon it. He could not afford to lose it, for his soul was in it, and it was the proof of his existence. Here was something which Jogona Kanyagga had performed, and which would preserve his name forever: the flesh was made word and dwelt among us full of grace and truth. (115)

What, again, is a simple act of recitation—i.e., reading Kanyagga's testimony to ensure accuracy—becomes comparable for Dinesen to the myth of myths, the biblical moment of creation itself. Ironically, her attribution of divinely creative power to the written form of Kanyagga's name resembles the stereotypical view of so-called "pre-modern" cultures for whom "writing is often regarded at first as an instrument of secret and magic power" (Ong 93). Such hyperbole might, in a different context, be ironic, but here it is not. Dinesen is deeply impressed by this experience, and, with a tone of high seriousness, actually compares herself to the Judeo-Christian God who gives form and life to Adam, the first man. Kanyagga, entering so suddenly into the realm of the word, is, in Dinesen's estimation, an Adam, a man newly created by an ultimate power—that of the *written* word. She has *created* him and given him "proof of his existence."

For Dinesen, this moment exemplifies the defining transition of the illiterate African from the traditional world of orality—a sort of death, or pre-life in Dinesen's representation—to the living world of literacy. Never mind the fact that she does not actually teach Kanyagga how to write or read and that he regularly returns to have her read the text to him aloud (it is an *aural* artifact for him, in other words, as much as or more than a written one), Dinesen provides us with a glimpse of one of the crucial steps in the colonial myth of progress from pre-modernity to modernity. Not only is it significant that she describes this in terms of a transition from orality to literacy—as a central component of modern progress—but she does so in the context of law.

Dinesen's description of Kanyagga's testimony as it is *orally* performed marks it as consistent with the sophistic procedures of the Kyama: his story is "difficult to follow" and full of "irrelevant details" just as the Kyama's discussions are maze-like and full of "endless speculations." Both from her perspective represent traditional procedure and justice as expressed through oral culture: they are disordered, inconsistent, irregular. However, once Kanyagga's testimony is written down, it has legal force in the modern establishment *because* it is written and, therefore, can be regularly (re)produced.[18] This is illustrated by the fact that Kanyagga takes the text

18 In fact, Dinesen claims to have made a copy for herself. Specifically, she writes, "I took a duplicate of the report. I have still got it" (113). Intrigued by the possibility of getting closer to what Jogona actually said, I searched the Karen Blixen Archive at the Royal Library of Denmark for his report in 2013. It was conspicuously and disappointingly absent. The Archive directors could only speculate that it must have been lost at some point if it ever existed at all. The 2007 critical edition of the Danish translation of *Out of Africa* includes a footnote on this passage that states simply, "kopien er ikke overleveret" (356): essentially, the document has not been found. Interestingly, there is another document within the text to which Dinesen refers in *Shadows on the Grass* (1960) that also represents her approach to the orality/literacy issue and that she also claimed still to have in her possession. Dinesen sent a lion pelt to the King of Denmark, Christian X, and received a brief letter in reply thanking her for the gift. She had the letter with her at one point in Kenya when one of her workers broke his leg and she had no pain medication for him. In desperation, she tells the injured man that her *Barua a Soldani*, or letter from a King, would do more to cure pain than anything else, and she then places the letter on the man's chest. "It was a very strange thing," she writes, "that almost at once the words and the gesture seemed to send an effect through him" (414). Word of the remarkable power of the letter spreads through the community, and many other patients request its treatment. Like Jogona's document, the letter is placed in a "leather bag with a string to it" (416) and Dinesen writes (presumably in the 1950s) that even though it is "undeciperhable,

to the District Commissioner who, after reading it, promptly dismisses the (unwritten) claims of his deceased son's Nyeri relatives (118). The written word for the colonial legal establishment is stronger evidence than the spoken. The text has become Kanyagga's own personal constitution—or even, perhaps, a memoir—outlining and providing evidence of his legal rights with respect to his son and the compensations that were to be paid for his loss.

Dinesen implicitly contrasts Kanyagga's success with the sophistic wanderings of the Kyama as they try to resolve Wainaina's claim to compensation. The oral dimensions of their procedure produce a crisis for her, I argue, because of the inherent, autonomous authority that oral culture represents, within which her word is no more authoritative than anyone else's. She cannot dictate order within the terms of the Kyama's oral culture in the way she was able to do with Kanyagga by committing orality to written form. Dinesen attempts to steer the Kyama out of the maze of sophistry, commanding them to resolve the problem quickly and turning attention to the motive of the accident: it is not a murder case, she insists, "but a bad accident" (109). Their concern, however, is not with the motive, but the consequences. Dinesen describes their reaction to her suggestion: "The Kyama honored my speech with their attention, but as soon as it was finished they opposed it." Dinesen refers repeatedly to her "greatness as a judge" for the Kikuyu on her farm and seems to revel in the authority of the position, offering judgments based almost entirely on her status as head of the farm rather than on actual legal principles. Here, however, Dinesen's status has no effect. The elders listen to her contribution as they would any other, and then decide that she is wrong: "Msabu," they tell her, "we know nothing. But here we see that you do not know enough either" (109). She seems quite put out by this obvious disregard for her status, but in the Kyama's terms this give-and-take is merely part of the process of discussing alternative proposals. Ultimately, however, this becomes too "unbearable" for Dinesen. The Kyama's deliberations go on for months, and because this indigenous institution does not fit within the hierarchical order of the farm, she cannot let it continue.

Much later, after she clearly cannot resolve the crisis alone, Dinesen invites the Kikuyu chief Kinanjui, believing that his authority will back her

brown and stiff with blood and matter of long ago," "I have still got the King's letter" (419). Furthermore, comparing the soiled letter to the handkerchief of King Christian IV, which was bloodied in a battle and is on display at the Rosenborg Castle, Dinesen sees the letter as a kind of contract: "No ode will be written about my letter; still, today it is, I believe, history as much as the relic of Rosenborg. Within it, in paper and blood, a *covenant* has been signed between the Europeans and Africans—no similar document of this same relationship is likely to be drawn up again" (emphasis added). Dinesen was perhaps unaware at the time that the King's letter would one day be available for viewing by a wider public. Unlike Jogona's document, the King's letter actually is in the Karen Blixen Archives, and it is well-preserved, white and pristine, suggesting at the very least that the covenant was imaginary and one-sided.

own. She knows enough of Kenyan legal history to recognize that he is not a real chief, according to any kind of Kikuyu custom, but that he "had been made so, many years ago, by the English, when they could no longer get on with the legitimate ruler of the Kikuyus of the district" (136).[19] He is a product of the system of indirect rule, in other words, and, just as Kinanjui's very existence as chief was part of a larger colonial effort to prevent social unrest, Dinesen's eventual decision to involve him has the same objective. Although she has resisted involving the colonial authorities, she is desperate and makes an exception: she brings the colonial appointee to the farm to oversee and provide his authoritative approval of a written agreement designed to settle the Kyama for good, "since," she writes, "nobody could stand it any longer" (146). What she introduces, in other words, prompted by a crisis that has threatened her status-based paradise, is a contract. This is an act of emergency, in effect, as Dinesen has to suspend her normal methods of administering justice to introduce an exceptional instrument backed by colonial authority that, she hopes, will bring the crisis to an end. Furthermore, the contract is an agreement that has binding power precisely *because* it is written and bears the written signatures (or signatory marks) of the concerned parties. Dinesen concludes the entire second chapter with the whole text of the agreement, brilliantly closing off the chapter in the very act of closing off the actual dispute. The contract is written into the form of the text, providing closure to the narrative and the event about which she narrates.

However, her use of this mechanism reveals a number of complications and contradictions. Dinesen sharply criticizes the freewheeling, formless, irregular oral procedures of the Kyama. They are not rule-bound in the same way Western law typically is, or purports to be, and, in the end, she forces a written ruling upon them. At the same time, however, Dinesen is highly critical of the Victorian English character, which demonstrates "a predilection for memoranda" and for "<u>laying down rules</u>" (*Letters* 234; emphasis in original). For her, the "true" (pre-Victorian) English character "is particularly bound up with the need and demand for human freedom." Throughout *Out of Africa*, in fact, she reiterates this romantic belief in "unlimited freedom," in that which defiantly stands outside the law, in the unrestricted character of dreams and dreamers. This freedom is central, in fact, to her myth of a feudal lifestyle free from the constraints of modern egalitarianism and industrialization. This places her definition of freedom firmly within the framework of status. She criticizes the freedom of the Kyama's procedures because it is part of a process that threatens her own myth of status *and* because she associates

19 Despite recognizing that he is a colonial appointee, Dinesen observes him arrive on the farm and strangely claims that as he pulls his cloak around him, "in that one movement he stepped back two thousand years, into Kikuyu justice" (140). Dinesen, apparently, cannot pass up an opportunity to romanticize, historical fact notwithstanding.

most of the Kikuyu with the lower-classes of Europe.[20] They do not deserve, or are incapable of experiencing in their current state, freedom in the same way as the upper-classes. And when the Kyama exhibits the freedom characteristic of oral traditions, she has to come down out of the clouds and employ a non-feudal instrument to restore paradise. Contract, an instrument and symbol of modernity, is used to reinforce and reinstate status. The matter *did* need to be resolved, of course, but Dinesen does it in a way that asserts her judgment over all others.

Earlier, she muses on the freedom of dreamers, which, she is quick to note, "is not the freedom of the dictator, who enforces his own will on the world, but the freedom of the artist who has no will, who is free of will" (83). Dinesen cannot sustain a romantic will-lessness because she is faced with the real, nightmarish accident and subsequent Kyama, so she enforces her own will on the world. Not only does this expose her world of status as myth, but it similarly reveals the myths of contract. Although Maine says that contract undermines hierarchies by allowing the free and dynamic creation of agreements among equals, here contract is used by someone from a presumably "progressive" society to reinforce hierarchies. While invoking the liberal–egalitarian aura of contract to solidify the image of European modernity in discourses of justification, colonialists used contract to sustain semi-feudal hierarchies.

Interestingly, however, according to the Indian Contract Act of 1872, which was in force in Kenya at the time (again, thanks distantly to Maine and Stephen), Dinesen's contract would, strictly speaking, very likely have been void. According to the Act, "undue influence" is one of the factors that would invalidate a contract and occurs when someone uses their "real or apparent" authority to force another into an agreement against his or her free will. Dinesen actually describes how one of the disputing parties who is forced to accept the agreement places his thumbprint very reluctantly, whimpering as he does so, she says, "as if it was burning him" (148). Additionally, the notes to the "undue influence" section of the Act cite a case in which the judge argues that "*moral command asserted and yielded to for the sake of peace and quiet, or of escaping from distress of mind or social discomfort* […] will constitute undue influence" (73; emphasis added). By imposing the contract on the Kyama, Dinesen is asserting moral command very specifically for the sake of peace and quiet and to escape distress of mind and social discomfort. I should note, however, that she was a third party in the contract: she signs her name as a witness, not as either the promisor or promisee. However, her involvement would likely still constitute undue influence because she asserts a command to force an agreement. Thus, there is an implicit contract between her and the two other parties in which they agree with her to agree between themselves. Dinesen probably did not know the details of the Contract Act, so

20 See, for example, *Out of Africa*, pp. 115 and 123.

the conclusions we can make in comparing her text with the Act are limited; but, as Dinesen was part of what JanMohamed has described as a "capital-centered mode of agricultural production" (she is, after all, running a farm for profit), contract is one area of law with which, in practice at least, she would have been familiar (55).[21]

In addition to closing off the dispute and the narrative, the agreement also constitutes a final denial of orality. After stating the terms of the agreement, the contract reads, "With the payment of this cow and her heifer calf the Shaurie shall be finally settled. Nobody, after this must *speak* of it or *mention* it at all" (148; emphasis added). The written agreement attempts specifically to ban any *oral* continuation of the dispute. The written word not only concludes the material aspects of the dispute, but it also concludes the oral aspects of the dispute that have characterized the Kyama's procedures. By denying the spoken word Dinesen denies the "unbearable" traditions of Kikuyu law. Although Dinesen stands as witness, signing her name and title ("Baroness Blixen") at the end of the document, and is presumably also bound never to speak of the matter again, she leaves herself a loophole: the agreement says that no one must *speak* of it again, but it says nothing about *writing* of the matter. It is enough to say that no one may speak of it again because most of the Kikuyu involved (like Jogona) are illiterate; all they can do *is* speak of it. She, however, does "mention" the matter again without violating the agreement because she can write (and, perhaps, because she writes under her pen name "Isak Dinesen" rather than the name she used on the contract).

The tendency among critics to refer to *Out of Africa* as a novel has emerged, in part, because research and the publication of her letters (1978 in Denmark and 1981 in the USA) have revealed discrepancies between what Dinesen describes in the memoir (which early reviewers accepted as fact) and what actually happened. Hence, Susan Brantley demonstrates that we must make better use of Dinesen's letters, which often tell a somewhat different story than the memoir (75). Similarly, papers in the Karen Blixen Archive in Copenhagen reveal important moments of fantasy, fabrication, or at least embellishment in the text of *Out of Africa*, and this is true in the case of the contract. The draft manuscript of the memoir found in the Archives[22] contains

21 In addition to likely having had experience with contracts in administering transactions with coffee buyers, Dinesen was technically the employer of the squatters on her farm and, thus, had "rights of contract." As David Anderson writes, "The Resident Native (Squatters) Ordinance (1918) sought to regulate these practices [of employing squatters] by formally defining squatters as 'labour tenants' rather than as tenants paying a cash rent, thereby bringing them under closer legal control and giving employers rights of contract" ("Kenya" 507).

22 I examined the different drafts in person, but the Archive has also digitized and made the English version available online. See "The Manuscript for 'Out of Africa.'"

the same contract that appears in the published version of the text, but in other parts of the Archive there are two additional copies of the contract: one undated that appears to be a copy of an early or original draft of the agreement and the other dated March 1931, just months before Dinesen returned permanently to Denmark (she arrived at Rungstedlund on August 31, 1931—see *Letters from Africa* 432). There are no accompanying or explanatory materials for either document, so we can only deduce and speculate based on the texts themselves. The first copy of the contract, for example, appears to be a reproduction of the original contract. Just as Dinesen says, she typed herself a copy of Jogona's story, so she could have typed a copy of the contract given its importance in bringing the crisis to a conclusion. This copy does not bear any handwritten signatures (or thumbprints), just typed names with "X"s next to them, and we must assume the original contract was submitted to the District Commissioner to confirm that the Kyama had reached resolution. Whatever the context of its production, the copy contains language that differs in important ways from the published version—specifically, the tone is more routine and there is less emphasis on orality. The relevant portions of the contract state:

> The following agreement has been made at Ngong on the 26th of September 1924, in the presence of the Chief Kinanjui, between Kanyerra wa Bimu and Kaninu wa Nyagga.
>
> That Kaninu pays to Kanyerri a cow and heifer calf, which have to be given to Kanyerri's Toto Wyanyangerri, who was on the 19th of December 1923, wounded by a shot gun fired by accident by Kaninu's Toto Kabir, and that by payment of this cow and heifer calf the whole Shaurie shall finally be settled and never brought up again.[23]

The wording here is somewhat simpler and more direct than in the version that Dinesen published, and some of the names are slightly different. There is also a distinct lack of emphasis on orality—nowhere does it bar anyone from speaking of the case any longer; rather, it simply says that the case shall "never be brought up again." Without more information, it is difficult to know exactly why Dinesen changed the wording in the version of the contract that appeared in the memoir. However, the second copy of the contract in the Archive offers an intriguing possible explanation.

The second copy is particularly strange given the fact that it is dated six and a half years after the conclusion of the Kyama. Additionally, the contract is not a word-for-word reproduction of the other contract in the Archives and, in fact, would likely not be considered a contract in the same sense as the earlier version since it includes several paragraphs explaining the circumstances of the case and the need for the contract. It begins simply enough, certifying that "the following Shaurie has been settled and finished for good, and is never to be brought up again." Eleven short paragraphs then

23 The Karen Blixen Archive III.2.

follow that detail the injuries committed in the case and the compensations paid. The final paragraph states: "Nobody can claim any more damages from Kaninu in this matter, or has got any right to make him any sort of trouble about it. Full damages have been paid to both Jogona and Kanyeri, and they have themselves declared that they were fully satisfied."[24] Why would Dinesen reproduce a more detailed version of the agreement so long after the event it was meant to resolve? My hypothesis is that the event was not yet resolved. One reading of the 1931 contract, in other words, is that despite the original contract's purpose of bringing an end to the Kyama's deliberations, the community continued to mention, speak of, and discuss the matter even six years after the contract was signed. In short, the contract failed, and the case remained open-ended. This scenario may help explain why Dinesen changes the language of the contract in the version that appears in the memoir. If, in fact, the 1931 version is evidence of the failure of the contract, one can imagine her rethinking its terms. One can imagine her thinking, "If only the contract had banned them from *speaking* of the matter, then it would have been resolved." Thus, in her imaginative recreation of the events for *Out of Africa*, she rewords the contract, subtly changing the terms to reflect both her wish that things had been otherwise and an increased emphasis on the power of the written word over the oral, reinforcing an important theme that dominates that section of the memoir. In other respects, Dinesen's memoir employs oral allusions and myths, but often these are congruent with her aristocratic, status-based mythology, such as her repeated references to *One-Thousand and One Arabian Nights*, in which she is the tireless Scheherazade.[25] When reality disrupts this myth and she is forced to avert a crisis, she relies upon written over oral forms, and her increased emphasis on this in the published contract reveals more broadly the colonialist fear of the disruptive, unrestricted nature of orality with its potential to function in spite of and thereby unsettle colonial law by laying bare its contradictory nature borne of the crisis of modernity. Although Kenya's settlers, including Dinesen, would later project the crisis onto Africans during and as a way of explaining the Mau Mau conflict, the emergence of orality in the context of a second trial further reveals its history of resisting colonial narratives of time and modernity and exposing the deep crisis within colonial culture itself.

24 The Karen Blixen Archive IV.B.2.C.

25 Writing of the "art of listening," for example, Dinesen describes how in the evenings when Denys Finch-Hatton visited her farm, she would sit on the floor, "cross-legged like Scheherazade herself," telling tales to her lover as he listened attentively, preferring to hear a story rather than read one (218).

To Nationhood through Crisis in Late Colonial Kenya: The Trial of Jomo Kenyatta

In 1952, Jomo Kenyatta, the Kenyan nationalist leader who became Kenya's first president following independence in 1963, was put on trial by the British colonial government for allegedly managing Mau Mau.[26] The trial, *Regina v. Kenyatta & others* (1952), has been described as "one of the most important and dramatic of [the twentieth] century,"[27] marking in many ways a crucial confrontation between "tradition" and "modernity" in the late colonial period. In 1955, after Kenyatta had been convicted and sentenced to seven years' hard labor, the British novelist, poet, playwright, and librettist Montagu Slater wrote a work of non-fiction titled *The Trial of Jomo Kenyatta*.[28] The book, which has been largely neglected by both literary and legal scholarship of East Africa,[29] purports to be a "comprehensive" account of the trial, but at 252 pages, compared to the 2,064 pages of the trial transcript, is necessarily selective. My reading will draw on both texts, particularly when

26 Kenyatta was born in the 1890s (the exact date is unknown) in Gatundu, Kenya. His early education was in Scottish Mission schools, and in the 1920s he joined the Kikuyu Central Association (KCA), a political organization that petitioned the British Government to recognize the rights of the Kikuyu people, particularly with respect to land issues. In 1929, the KCA sent Kenyatta to London to negotiate directly with the British Government, and he remained there, except for brief visits to Kenya, until 1946. While there, he studied anthropology with Bronislaw Malinowski at the London School of Economics. At the outset of World War II, the Kenyan government banned the KCA, and it was replaced by a new nationalist organization, the Kenya African Union (KAU). KAU embraced Kenyatta as its leader upon his return to Kenya after the war, and it was during his tenure as KAU's leader that Kenyatta was arrested and tried for managing Mau Mau.

27 From the dust jacket synopsis of Montagu Slater, *The Trial of Jomo Kenyatta* (1957).

28 Slater is best known as a co-founder of *The Left Review* and its original editor. Additionally, he famously wrote the libretto for Benjamin Britten's opera *Peter Grimes* (1945), which opens with a court inquest over the death of Grimes' apprentice and is set in a seaside village. Interestingly, Britten's other opera dealing with law and set at sea is an adaptation of *Billy Budd* (1951). This time, however, the libretto was written by Eric Crozier and E.M. Forster, whose novel *A Passage to India* (1924) is another colonial narrative concerned with the forms of the law.

29 There were, of course, contemporary accounts of the trial, including reports in the international media, and accounts in various memoirs and histories of the time period. See, for example, Leigh, *In the Shadow of Mau Mau* (1954); Rama Rau, "The Trial of Jomo Kenyatta" (1954); Rawcliffe, *The Struggle for Kenya* (1954); and Pritt, *The Autobiography of D.N. Pritt*, Part Three, *The Defence Accuses* (1965–66). In terms of scholarship, the trial is discussed briefly in histories such as Anderson's *Histories of the Hanged* (2005) and Elkins' *Imperial Reckoning* (2005), but one of the only extended analyses of the trial is John Lonsdale's "Kenyatta's Trials: Breaking and Making an African Nationalist" (2000).

the transcript provides additional context or complexity that Slater overlooks (or deliberately leaves out),[30] but my ultimate focus is on Slater's representation of the trial and his choice of a narrative form that situates his work within the larger discourse of colonial non-fiction but ultimately achieves a very different end. More specifically, Slater crafts a coherent and compelling non-fiction narrative (somewhere between memoir and reportage) out of the raw material of the lengthy trial, paradoxically achieving amplification through selection. In other words, by making the trial transcript smaller and more accessible, Slater draws attention to and amplifies certain aspects of the trial, providing subtle commentary on colonial law under the ironic guise of an objective report.

I do not use the metaphor "amplify" arbitrarily here—indeed, Slater focuses on issues that highlight the trial as a contact zone between African oral culture and colonial literate culture, including an incident involving *literal* electronic amplification. At a crucial point in the trial, when the Prosecution insists that Kenyatta's public speeches as recorded in the newspapers do not include denunciations of recent acts of political violence by Mau Mau, Kenyatta points out that newspaper reports are selective and that there are audio and video recordings of one of his speeches in which he explicitly denounces Mau Mau. In Slater's telling, this moment threatens to disrupt the Prosecution's case and leaves the judge, who is understood now as having been severely biased against Kenyatta, in a quandary. In this moment, a key question poses itself: what, according to the law, is a "document," particularly when the culture in question is an oral culture? While some might dismiss this incident as a mere technicality, I argue that Slater's amplification of this event in the trial, referring to it at five different points in the text, as well as his attention to the law's treatment of other forms of orality, exposes the anxiety and instability that African orality created in its contact with colonial culture, an anxiety that we have already seen expressed in Dinesen's text. In Kenyatta's trial we see the colonial powers attempt, like Dinesen, to control and suppress oral culture, now as it has adapted to electronic culture; in doing so, however, the law contradicts itself, rejecting a product of the very modernity upon which colonial rule was supposedly built. This reveals, I argue, the persistence of the deeper contradiction or crisis at the heart of colonial modernity that can be traced both to the mid-nineteenth-century colonial responses to violence and to the early twentieth-century crisis among settlers in Kenya.

30 The original trial transcript is held at the Kenya National Archives (KNA), but D.N. Pritt, head of Kenyatta's defense team, also kept a copy, which is at the London School of Economics and is the version Slater consulted. See Lonsdsale, "Kenyatta's Trials," p. 215 n. 50. John Lonsdale, at Cambridge University, acquired a copy of the original from the Archives in Nairobi, and he generously allowed me to consult—and, ultimately, digitize—his copy, which I hope the KNA will allow us to make available online in the near future. When citing the trial, then, I refer to this version, using the volume numbers and pagination specified by the KNA.

The imposition of literacy in Kenya at the expense of oral culture had significant legal implications, as colonial literate culture interfered with the deep-seated normative values along which Kenyan societies were organized. The colonial imposition of literacy is an example of what Jacques Derrida calls the "founding violence" of the law, or an act of performative violence that inaugurates a legal regime (21). One example of such an act, Derrida says, is the imposition of "a language on national or ethnic minorities regrouped by the state," something that has occurred in various countries and throughout time. This kind of violence took place in Africa with the imposition of English, French, and other European languages, but also with the imposition of writing, an entirely new technology of communication. Again, this was not a politically innocuous educational venture, but an act of repression, of controlling and destroying the Other's law. Derrida writes further that what the State fears most is not crime or "brigandage," but "fundamental, founding violence, that is, violence able to justify, to legitimate, or to transform the relations of law, and so to present itself as having a right to law" (34). One of the reasons, I argue, that Mau Mau and Kenyatta—like Dinesen's Kyama—were such threats to the colonial state was that they demonstrated this very violence—that is, violence (both physical and political) able to "transform the relations of law" and "present itself as having a right to law"; indeed, as having access to an alternative law through oral culture, which the state had tried so desperately to restrict through its own acts of inaugural violence. Mau Mau and Kenyatta both proved that they could employ oral traditions in a way that bound their listeners, bound them as a community and bound them to obligations: Mau Mau used the infamous oath and Kenyatta was a skilled orator whose speeches and traditional curses influenced massive crowds of Kikuyu listeners. And while history has shown us that the colonial government was incorrect in assuming that Kenyatta was Mau Mau's mastermind, the government's anxious response to both the oath and Kenyatta's oratory tells us something about what the state feared most: that is, a founding violence capable of legitimating itself as law and thus rendering the state as criminal. We see all of these issues converge in Kenyatta's trial under the State of Emergency, which was declared on October 20, 1952.

The trial began in 1952, approximately a month after the Emergency was declared, but it is important to note that Slater's account of the trial was published three years later, in 1955. By this time, Kenyatta had submitted appeals to the Supreme Court in Kenya and the Privy Council in England, both of which upheld the original ruling of Judge Ransley Thacker that Kenyatta and four of his co-defendants[31] were guilty of the charge of managing Mau Mau. They were sentenced to seven years' detention with hard labor, and indefinite restriction within the colony. In 1955, they were serving their

31 There were six defendants convicted in the original trial, but one of them was acquitted on appeal.

time in massive prisons overflowing with suspected Mau Mau members and sympathizers, most of whom had not been given the luxury of an extended trial like Kenyatta. Most were rushed through Emergency courts and into the prisons, others directly to the noose. The prison system grew in tandem with the developing theory of the origins of Mau Mau, a theory that relates directly to Slater's text and the ways in which it makes intelligible a powerful crisis afflicting colonial rule in the 1950s.

Though it had deep roots in the disaffection of colonized subjects going back to the beginnings of colonial rule, the Mau Mau movement essentially began its campaign against loyalist Africans and white settlers in the late 1940s. By the end of the State of Emergency in 1959, they had carried out a number of attacks in central Kenya, killing 1,880 people. Although the colonial government killed 12,590 Mau Mau members and suspects in action, by hanging following rushed emergency trials, or through horrific acts of torture in the infamous "rehabilitation camps," the movement was popularly characterized as a nightmarishly violent organization that challenged the colonialists' belief in the ability of Africans to become "civilized." Prior to Mau Mau, and despite the theoretical aims of indirect rule, many colonialists in Kenya—including administrators, settlers, and missionaries—believed the process of civilizing the uncivilized to be fairly straightforward, a "linear, compensating, process of loss and gain in which small, tribal identities were diluted into a larger, civilised one" (Lonsdale, "Mau Maus" 404). This had been particularly successful among the Kikuyu, whom the Europeans saw as "industrious and progressive, the kind of Africans who seized upon the benefits of European civilization and made the best of it" (Anderson, *Histories* 279). In other words, the kind of Africans who did not necessarily need to be protected from modernity. But then, John Lonsdale observes, "Mau Mau smashed that innocent picture":

> Transition now looked like trauma. Loss of identity seemed to stir somnolent savagery. Education did not lead modern men out of the past; it made amoral men who manipulated its darkest fears. With a linear, if always subversive, model of progress now challenged by a movement which suggested that modernity could recreate savagery, whites had to rethink their ideas of social explanation. (404)

The liberal efforts to rethink the narrative of progress led to what Lonsdale and others identified as the "myth of crisis," or the belief that Mau Mau was the product of a crisis experienced by Africans who had tried to modernize too quickly. Of course, given the above analysis, we know that this myth did not originate at this time, but was a resurgence or rekindling of an older myth tied both to settler society and the origins of indirect rule. In 1950s Kenya, however, the crisis myth was one among several myths of Mau Mau, as Carl Rosberg and John Nottingham called them, that were influential in the 1950s.[32] Lonsdale, who has contributed significantly to historical

32 See Rosberg and Nottingham, *The Myth of Mau Mau: Nationalism in Kenya* (1966).

scholarship on Mau Mau and colonial Kenya, explains that the crisis myth was offered primarily by liberal administrators who tended to avoid the harsher conservative perspectives of many of Kenya's white settlers.[33] Liberals instead hoped that by understanding Mau Mau as a manifestation of psychic disorder caused by the "trauma of transition" they might restore order by completing the transition. "Liberals saw border unrest within the African soul," Lonsdale writes, "on its psychic frontier between tradition and modernity, community and society, past tribe and future nation. [...] But while diehards fought to keep the Kikuyu on the far bank of the river of transition [...] white liberals knew it had to be crossed. Peace would come only when Kikuyu society was on the modern side" (405).

This discourse culminated in the "scientific" account of African psychic distress offered by Dr. J.C. Carothers in his books *The African Mind in Health and Disease* (1953), and *The Psychology of Mau Mau* (1955), and in reports produced for the colonial government. Carothers "diagnosed Mau Mau as a disease"—a not uncommon tactic in the history of racist regimes[34]—and provided a "scientific" rationale for the detention camps where former Mau Mau were rehabilitated and "cleansed by public confession as performed in Kikuyu law, paid manual labour, literacy classes, instruction in the beneficent colonial history of Kenya and, if they chose, by Christian witness" (Lonsdale, "Mau Maus" 410). They were guided, in other words, through the crisis in order to complete the transition to modernity.[35] In time, this myth, says Anderson, "very quickly came to dominate the official government analysis of Kenya's dreadful troubles" (*Histories* 280). Bruce Berman adds, "This characterization of Mau Mau, repeated almost daily for several years in press conferences, news briefs, and interviews from government information agencies in Nairobi and London, and widely disseminated in print and broadcasts by the press

33 The conservative position maintained that Africans were inherently primitive and that Mau Mau's violent acts and evil rituals—the famous initiation "oath" that was widely and luridly described by the press during the Emergency—were simply evidence of their irredeemably barbaric natures, the only solution to which was, as Lonsdale reports, a "[hardened] polemical frontier between white civilization and black savagery" ("Mau Maus" 404).

34 In the USA in 1851, for example, Dr. Samuel A. Cartwright, a physician from the South, diagnosed slaves who tried to run away with "drapetomania," the disease of wanting to be free. See Cartwright, "Report on the Diseases and Peculiarities of the Negro Race" (2004), p. 33.

35 The horrific irony of this is that, whereas the detention camps were supposedly based on this altruistic theory of "guided transition," the reality proved that the war brought out the worst in many of the colonialists and loyalist Africans (Lonsdale, "Mau Maus of the Mind" 410). The conditions of the camps and the atrocities committed against prisoners were so severe that their discovery by the outside world toward the end of the Emergency is thought to have rapidly accelerated Britain's withdrawal from East Africa. See Anderson, *Histories of the Hanged* (2005), pp. 313–27 and Elkins, *Imperial Reckoning* (2005).

throughout the world, became and remains, especially in English-speaking countries, the image of the phenomenon in popular culture" ("Nationalism" 183).

We understand now that this theory or myth served to conceal legitimate grievances on the part of Kikuyu, primarily having to do with the land question. Most of the land that, traditionally, had belonged to Kikuyu in the highlands surrounding Nairobi now belonged to white farmers, and the indigenous people were forced to become squatters in order to survive.[36] Kenyatta's KAU sought to correct this injustice "in a constitutional way," but many, particularly of the younger generation, were dissatisfied with his moderate politics, preferring instead direct, militant action (Slater 160). Mau Mau galvanized around those willing to express these views and, in time, broke with KAU. However, the colonists' perspective ignored these "critical internal dynamics of Kikuyu politics," and, when looking at the resistance, simply saw a singular "tribe" that had failed to cope with modernity and, consequently, fallen into atavistic crisis (Anderson, *Histories* 68). As this discourse reached its height in the mid-1950s, Slater published *The Trial of Jomo Kenyatta*.

Before Kenyatta's trial, a few people worldwide had perhaps heard of the troubles in Kenya, but the trial caught the world's attention and brought public scrutiny to the colony in ways not previously experienced. It is clear now that the colonial government wanted to make an example of Kenyatta, believing that if they convicted him it would quickly bring an end to Mau Mau. Because he was *not* Mau Mau's leader, however, the show trial not only failed to achieve its stated purpose, but it provided a forum for Kenyatta to make his people's grievances public. Despite the political leanings of the different newspapers that reported on the events, the justness of Kenyatta's cause as he outlines it in the trial and as it was reported in newspapers is difficult to deny. Slater's book similarly lets Kenyatta speak for himself; but in order to be fair he also lets the Crown speak for itself—or so he claims. As mentioned, the trial transcript is over 2,000 pages long. Slater admits in his introduction to *The Trial* that it is difficult to give a "true" account of the proceedings in a mere 252 pages and, further, that his own socialist politics lead him to sympathize with Kenyatta's nationalist organization, but not Mau Mau (26–27). To make his account more objective, therefore, he decides to give more direct quotation to the Prosecution and to summarize more of the Defense. Some 100 pages of the book, he says, "are devoted to evidence for the Crown," and only 60 are given to the Defense (27). "I am now convinced in my own mind," he concludes, "that the summary is not only as fair as I can make it but is in fact a true account of the trial." How are we to take the word "true" here? Is the summary true in the sense of "objective," i.e., that a true

36 On the land question as it affected the Kikuyu, see Kanogo, *Squatters and the Roots of Mau Mau, 1905–1963* (1987) and Elkins, *Imperial Reckoning* (2005), pp. 9–18.

account is one which just gives the facts? Or is it true in the sense of revealing the deeper meaning beneath the trial's procedural and "factual" surface? I maintain that Slater, ultimately, strives for a truth of the latter kind, offering an intervention not only in the context of the "crisis of modernity" myth, but also in the context of the history of colonial non-fiction that claimed to provide "true" accounts of Africa in the former sense.

Dinesen's text is a part of this literary history to which Slater responds by publishing his summary of Kenyatta's trial and claiming it is a true account but not necessarily an objective one. He performs a critique of the conventions of colonial representation, claiming truthfulness but openly staging his process of selectivity—no account can be comprehensive, he seems to say, and the choice of what to include and exclude in relating historical fact says as much about the author's perspective on the issues described as can openly biased statements. And, of course, this issue of inclusion and exclusion is at the heart of the very episodes from the trial that Slater chooses to represent, which ask: can Kenyatta be *included* as a Mau Mau leader who administered oaths? And what can or cannot be *included* within the definition of "document" according to the rules of evidence?

The key piece of evidence that a person was infected with the disease of Mau Mau was the oral oath, and Slater's text demonstrates how the oath became a key issue within Kenyatta's trial as well. The oath was, in its simplest form, a ritual administered by a person of authority to initiate another into Mau Mau membership, committing that person to certain obligations. The oath involved animal sacrifice, ritual recitations, and other symbolic implements drawn from Kikuyu traditions. In *Facing Mount Kenya* (1938), Kenyatta describes a legitimate form of this oath, used in traditional court procedures both to commit adjudicators to the performance of justice and to determine the guilt or innocence of accused persons (214). Thus, the oath was an oral performance with legal significance—it had binding force and, according to Kenyatta, was "terribly feared, morally and religiously" because of its power to harm those who violated it.

Kenyatta and the colonial government saw the Mau Mau version of the oath as a perversion of the traditional Kikuyu procedure, but Kenyatta viewed the problem primarily, but not exclusively, in generational terms—i.e., only elders had the right to administer the oath and those, mostly young men, administering it in the name of Mau Mau did not have the proper authority[37]—whereas the government and settlers viewed it in terms of its absolute distance from "civilization." For example, in his book *Defeating Mau Mau* (1954), the famed "white African" archaeologist Louis Leakey discusses how the Mau Mau oath increasingly became perverted by "elaborate and bestial accompaniments" that were so "debased" and "unclean" that he refuses to describe the "horrible, filthy, and degrading acts which are used in the more

37 See Anderson, *Histories*, pp. 67–68 and Lonsdale "Kenyatta's Trials," pp. 206, 208.

advanced Mau Mau oaths" (77, 84, 85).[38] He did not have to describe them because the government was in the habit of disseminating sensational press releases claiming that Mau Mau oaths involved "bestiality, orgiastic group sexual melees, drinking the menstrual blood of prostitutes, and cannibalistic frenzies that involved killing traitors, drinking their blood, and eating their brains" (Edgerton 135).[39] The extensive rumors surrounding accounts of the oath have made it difficult to verify whether or not such practices were ever used, and we now know that the government press releases "were intended to discredit Mau Mau in the eyes of the security forces and the world"; as such, they "were often exaggerated and sometimes entirely false" (135). The obsessive and sensational amplification of the oath's ritualistic elements in colonial discourse directed focus away from the more fundamental fear that the oath generated in the colonial mind: colonialists constructed their representations of the oath as a return to savagery when in reality it represented a form of inaugural violence capable of presenting itself as having a right to law.

From the perspective of Mau Mau, colonialism was organized crime, not the standard of civilized law and order. This view was a threat to the very foundations of colonialism and, for some, Western civilization itself. The oath symbolized the continuing power of African oral traditions to bind people together as a community and to elude the regulating efforts of colonial

38 Leakey is a fascinating figure, born in 1903 in Kenya to British settlers and raised in Kikuyu country where he was actually initiated as a Kikuyu elder. Considered a pioneer in the study of human origins, along with his wife, Mary, Leakey trained in archaeology, paleo-anthropology, and social anthropology at Cambridge University and was extremely prolific, publishing 216 books, monographs, articles, book reviews, and letters over his lifetime. Described by Lonsdale and Berman as Kenyatta's intellectual rival (on the rivalry, see their forthcoming book *House of Custom: Jomo Kenyatta, Louis Leakey and the Making of the Modern Kikuyu*), Leakey was initially appointed as the court translator in Kenyatta's trial but stormed out in a rage after the defense accused him of, first, deliberately mistranslating witness testimony to the prosecution's favor and, second, committing criminal libel against his clients by publishing a book that, without naming Kenyatta, essentially blamed him for Mau Mau (the book, *Mau Mau and the Kikuyu* [1952], was published shortly after the trial began). See Lonsdale and Berman, "Louis Leakey's Mau Mau: A Study in the Politics of Knowledge" (1991); Slater 116–17; and KTT, vol. 2, pp. 509–11 (January 7, 1953). Although sympathetic to the Kikuyu, Leakey was vehemently opposed to Mau Mau and replicates—though not in full detail—some of the more lurid and sensational descriptions of the oath in his second book about the war, *Defeating Mau Mau* (1954).

39 From Edgerton's *Mau Mau: An African Crucible* (1989), this is actually a relatively tame description of the alleged Mau Mau depravities. Edgerton goes on to describe how other government-produced reports went into even more detail about shockingly bizarre sexual and bestial practices used in Mau Mau oathing, which I will not reproduce here. The irony of such allegations is that because they were typically exaggerations or pure fabrications, the horrifying narratives actually originated in British, not African, minds.

law. Because the oath was an oral performance administered in secret, the government had difficulty proving a given individual had taken it. This did not stop them from trying, of course, and Kenyatta's trial demonstrates the government's reliance upon (ironically) the *unreliable* oral testimony of police informants to prove that someone had administered or taken the Mau Mau oath.

In *The Trial*, Slater includes lengthy examinations of police informers whom the Prosecution, led by Deputy Public Prosecutor Anthony Somerhough, used to prove Kenyatta's alleged role as an oath administrator. The descriptions of the oath lack the sensation of Leakey's and others' accounts, but, to the colonial court, the implication was the same: the presence of the oath was evidence of the disease of Mau Mau. One of the witnesses examined by the Prosecution claims to have been present when Kenyatta administered a Mau Mau oath to several men. According to the informer, Kenyatta urged, "When we agree to drive Europeans away you must take an active part in driving them away or killing them" (Slater 42). The objective of the Prosecution was, of course, to prove that Kenyatta was Mau Mau's leader and had thus, in the beginnings of the movement, been the primary oath administrator. The evidence is inconclusive, circumstantial, and, ultimately, contradictory, as cross-examination by defense counsel D.N. Pritt proves.[40] The significance of Slater's representation of this evidence is threefold: one, by letting the Prosecution's evidence "speak for itself," Slater shows how weak the case is against Kenyatta; as Anderson says, "None of the evidence was strong, and little of it was coherent" (66). Two, the oath evidence emphasizes the threat that orality presented to the colonial legal establishment—even with scant and unreliable evidence, the Prosecution knew that the oath represented the ultimate threat and that if they could just connect Kenyatta to it, they would be able to bring him down. And, three, in a selective text that is concerned with the narrative positing a clash between "tradition" and "modernity" and the various crises that undermine the hierarchy between the two, Slater includes the oath with a recognition of its centrality in the colonial imagination as a symbol of African atavism. In connection with his later discussion of Kenyatta's actual, demonstrable oral performances and the debate over what constitutes a document, the presence of the oath helps to underscore the extent to which African orality unsettled colonial culture and exposed its fatal contradictions. This brings us then to the crucial moment in the trial that further amplifies the orality/literacy conflict.

Before his arrest, Kenyatta went on a "stump campaign" in 1951–52, speaking to audiences of thousands throughout central Kenya about the aims

40 Denis Nowell Pritt was an English barrister and a politician with the Labour Party, well-known for his pro-Soviet sympathies. He was an MP from 1935 to 1940 and 1945 to 1950. In addition to defending Kenyatta, Pritt in a later trial represented Julius Nyerere, the future president of Tanzania. See *The Autobiography of D.N. Pritt*, Part Three, *The Defence Accuses* (1965–66).

of KAU and the need to struggle by constitutional means for their rights. This became a period of scrutiny in the trial as the Prosecution sought to prove either that Kenyatta did not condemn Mau Mau in his speeches or that his condemnations were veiled instructions for Mau Mau to go underground. On the third day of Somerhough's cross-examination, some two months into the trial, the newspaper reports of these speeches became a matter of intense debate. As Slater writes, "Crown put to witness the first of what became a very long series of newspaper reports of [Kenyatta's] meeting, the point being that the reports contained no mention of any denunciation of Mau Mau" (165). Kenyatta's reply: "Using common sense you will understand that I could not speak for half an hour and be reported accurately in just ten lines." Somerhough is not satisfied, however, and continues to produce reports, showing 16 different accounts of his speeches as recorded in the newspapers. "Most of them Kenyatta found inadequate or inaccurate," Slater comments. "He was asked had he complained of the inaccuracies. [...] He replied, 'No. I rely more on meetings than the press because the majority of my audience cannot read or write'" (165).

The next day, Somerhough puts forward additional newspaper reports, asking repeatedly if they mention anything about his alleged denunciations, and Kenyatta patiently insists that the reports are incomplete. Slater observes that a newspaper article is not, on its own, admissible evidence, and in the full trial transcript it becomes clearer that this is a point of contention between the prosecution and defense: when Somerhough tries to have a particular article admitted as evidence, Pritt observes that he will agree to it "If and in so far as the witness adopts it and says it is correct"; and they go back and forth on the issue a number of times. In other words, the reports are only admissible if authenticated orally by the witness.[41] Somerhough's point, of course, is that there is a discrepancy between what the newspapers report and what Kenyatta claims to have said, so, despite the problem of inadmissibility (and no doubt because of the weakness of his evidence generally), he continues presenting articles in an effort to undermine Kenyatta's claims about his denunciation.[42] The fact that Thacker

41 KTT, vol. 5, pp. 1195–99 (February 5, 1953).

42 Section 81 of the Indian Evidence Act, 1872, which was in force in Kenya at the time of the trial, outlines "Presumptions as to Documents," including the following about newspapers: "The Court shall presume the genuineness of every document purporting to be the *London Gazette*, or the *Gazette of India*, or the Government Gazette of any Local Government, or of any colony, dependency, or possession of the British Crown, or to be a newspaper or a journal, or to be copy of a private Act of Parliament printed by the Queen's Printer, and of every document purporting to be a document directed by any law to be kept by any person, if such document is kept substantially in the form required by law and is produced from proper custody" (186). The question Somerhough is attempting to raise is not necessarily one of genuineness but, given the fact that all government newspapers are presumed to be genuine, it is interesting that the newspapers

does not object to this strategy is itself evidence, no doubt, of the fact that "there was a universal presumption of [Kenyatta's] guilt" (Lonsdale, "Kenyatta's Trials" 214), particularly among the settlers of whom Thacker was one, and also that Thacker, who came out of retirement to judge the case as Magistrate, was out of his depth: as Lonsdale writes, "Thacker's judicial control was not up to the task" and he often struggled to keep up with the speed and complexity of the various arguments (222).

One of the more significant moments illustrating Thacker's lack of control appears on the sixth day of cross-examination when there is discussion of an important speech Kenyatta gave in which he claimed to have used a traditional Kikuyu curse in condemning Mau Mau. The problem of the curse first arose when Kenyatta was questioned during evidence-in-chief on January 28, 1953, and Slater does not cover this earlier discussion in as much detail. In the Kapenguria Trial Transcript (KTT), the Kikuyu curse is transcribed as, "Ugai Mau Mau irothie na miri ya mikongoe,"[43] which means, literally, "Let Mau Mau go to the roots of the *mikongoe* tree" (Lonsdale, "Kenyatta's Trials" 230). Kenyatta insisted that this was a denunciation of Mau Mau in the strongest possible terms within Kikuyu culture, but Thacker, in particular, struggled to understand the significance of the word "*mikongoe*," which Kenyatta confusingly said both was and was not an actual tree. What Kenyatta failed to convey, and Thacker failed to understand, was that "*mikongoe*" was a tree of myth and symbol, or, as Lonsdale puts it, "an underworld tree" (231). To curse Mau Mau to the roots of such a tree is to banish it forever to the underworld. During Somerhough's later cross-examination, he returns to the curse but uses a Swahili newspaper's translation rather than the ambiguity of "*mikongoe*" to claim that Kenyatta was actually ordering Mau Mau to go into hiding. The court translator renders the relevant passage as: "Kenyatta told Mau Mau to go and be hanged." Somerhough tries to insist that the phrase could have been an order telling Mau Mau to hide and "go underground." Slater writes, "Kenyatta who had been speaking in Kikuyu called the question 'absurd.' In any case the speech was recorded on magnetic tape, 'so do not beat about the bush, bring the record and you can hear what I did say'" (167). The judge replies, "Of course it would be the best evidence of what he did say."

Somerhough presents to Kenyatta are the African-language newspapers *Sauti ya Mwafrika* and *Mumenyereri*, the official newspaper of Kenyatta's Kenya African Union (KAU). However, Somerhough's point is that if Kenyatta's own newspapers did not accurately report his speeches and, in particular, did not report the denunciation, then he must not have said it; Somerhough, in other words, *presumes* the non-government papers to be genuine and accurate as well. When Kenyatta observes that the *East African Standard* (*EAS*), which was not a government paper but did report in English and tended to be pro-colonial, carried a fuller report of the speech, Somerhough does not reply. Pritt even—we must imagine somewhat cheekily—offers to share his copy of the *EAS*, but Somerhough still remains silent. See KTT, vol. 5, pp. 1200–01 (February 5, 1953).

43 KTT, vol. 4, p. 976 (January 28, 1953).

This is the first mention of this recording in Slater's account of the trial (Pritt actually mentions it a few days earlier with little fanfare as part of a request for several subpoenas)[44] and he returns to it several times. In this exchange, particularly in the form Slater gives it, we see a dramatic conflict between African orality and an obsessive colonial literacy. Kenyatta was a skilled orator and, as he insists, he was not particularly concerned with what the newspapers printed because most of his audience was illiterate. He spoke to them directly in the Kikuyu language, utilizing a traditional performative utterance—the curse—which has binding force for its hearers. The curse, like the oath, was a powerful oral mechanism in Kikuyu society that was essential to the maintenance of law and order. In fact, in *Facing Mount Kenya*, Kenyatta claims that the curse fills the function of a "police force": "The fear of public opinion, expressed in the way of curses was the chief preventative of mischief and crimes, because there was no police organisation in the Gikuyu society" (214). Thus, by using a curse in his speech to thousands of illiterate Kikuyu, Kenyatta, who as an elder possessed the recognized authority to utter curses, simultaneously bound his listeners together as a community within a mutual obligation and demonstrated the continuing legitimacy and power of Kikuyu oral law. The Prosecution's effort to prove either that this did not happen or, as Somerhough himself says, "that it was not a strong curse [...] and that it had a double meaning,"[45] could thus be seen as, again, a fear of that which can present itself as having a right to law. Furthermore, the obstinate presentation of texts to Kenyatta, and Slater's representation of this moment, exaggerates this as a conflict between orality and literacy, and asks: which constitutes evidence under the law, the written version or Kenyatta's spoken word? The Crown confronts Kenyatta with the authority of the written word, pitting text against speech as has been done in the colony for decades: like Jogona Kanyagga's District Commissioner in *Out of Africa*, Kenyatta's prosecutor maintains that if it is not written down then it must not be true.[46]

44 KTT, vol. 5, p. 1231 (February 5, 1953).
45 KTT, vol. 5, p. 1208 (February 5, 1953).
46 Another dimension of this conflict comes through as Somerhough uses the Swahili translation of one of Kenyatta's denunciations to argue for its ambiguity. See KTT, vol. 5, pp. 1187–91 (February 3, 1953). In particular, he turns to *Madan's Standard Swahili–English Dictionary* by Sir Frederick Johnson in trying to prove that Kenyatta's translation of the Swahili word "itoweka" as "perish" (as in, his call for Mau Mau to "perish") was actually a call for Mau Mau to "vanish," or hide. Somerhough presses Kenyatta, almost daring him to disagree with the authoritative text on the Swahili language, which defines "itoweka" as to "be lacking, missing and hence vanish, disappear, or pass out of sight" (1188). The authority of the dictionary is meaningless to Kenyatta who says that in translating the word, "I was not going by the dictionary – I was going by the usage" (1189). Somerhough does not accept this and pushes harder, turning to another phrase: "Again I am going to put the Standard Swahili dictionary to you at the passage where it says

But then Kenyatta introduces the recording. In Walter Ong's lexicon, this is "secondary orality," or the adaptation of "primary" oral culture to electronic culture (136). The judge admits that this would be the best evidence of what Kenyatta actually said, and Pritt requests a subpoena to obtain the recording. When the opportunity to introduce the recording within the trial arrives, the judge hesitates: "I am afraid of short cuts and departing from the rules of evidence" (181). Discussion then arises about whether or not a magnetic recording could be considered a document. Slater writes:

> Now it emerged there were two recordings, one on film, another on tape. The Magistrate hesitated about the film. A document is something with recognizable marks on it, and perhaps one might stretch the definition to include a film sound track. But he felt that a piece of magnetic tape on which there are no marks that any microscope can make visible, could hardly be squeezed in. (181–82)

Pritt provides a thorough and accurate description of the recording process (omitted in Slater's text; see KTT, vol. 6, p. 1463 [February 13, 1953]) and Thacker ultimately observes, "From Mr. Pritt's description of this scientific invention, there seems to be considerable doubt whether these two things or either of them does come within the meaning of the word document" (182). The Indian Evidence Act of 1872 applied in Kenya at the time, and Slater recognizes that the laws from Queen Victoria's day have much to say about documents but nothing about tape recordings. Thacker takes the weekend to think the matter over and returns on Tuesday to announce with "a *written* ruling that the sound recordings of Kenyatta's speech were not admissible as evidence" (183; emphasis added).[47]

'potelea mbali'. It says there that the words are a common imprecation of 'go and be hanged'. Do you agree that that is what the Standard Swahili dictionary says?" (1190). Kenyatta cannot disagree, of course, since that is in fact what the dictionary says, and he replies, "Yes." "But," he adds, "when we were translating, we were not using the Swahili dictionary. We were translating what the ordinary man and woman understand as the language." There is, in other words, the "standard" Swahili that Somerhough relies upon, embodied in an authoritative written text that the law recognizes, and then there is the Swahili of the common person, the Swahili of orality which derives its meaning from common use. Kenyatta's position recalls Ludwig Wittgenstein's famous assertion in *Philosophical Investigations* (1953) that "For a *large* class of cases—though not for all—in which we employ the word 'meaning' it can be defined thus: the meaning of a word is its use in the language" (20; emphasis in original).

47 The Indian Evidence Act, 1872 defines a document as follows: "'Document' means any matter expressed or described upon any substance by means of letter, figures, or marks, or by more than one of those means, intended to be used, or which may be used, for the purpose of recording that matter." It then lists several illustrations of documents: "A writing is a document. Words printed, lithographed or photographed are documents. A map or plan is a document. An inscription on a metal plate or stone is a document. A caricature is a document" (149).

Slater's presentation of this issue is compelling and stands out for its drama, for the absurdity of the dismissal, and, again, because he emphasizes it through repetition (he returns to the recording later, as we will see). Before continuing, however, it is worth pointing out that as dramatic as Slater's narrative is, it is also incomplete. There are actually two issues that overlap throughout the discussion of the recording, the second of which is not as clear in Slater's version: the first is whether or not the recording can be admitted as documentary evidence; and the second, whether or not the man who possesses the recordings, John Reiss, Director of the African Information Services, should be sworn in as a witness if he delivers the tapes to the court. Slater does mention this fact, but he does not convey the extent and nature of the debate. Pritt asks the court to grant a *subpoena decus tecum*, which would permit Reiss to deliver the recordings without being sworn in as a witness, but Somerhough wonders whether Reiss will need to explain, in order to authenticate, what he has delivered; if so, he should be sworn in.

Thacker says he has never come across anything like this (i.e., the issue of the witness, but also, presumably, the recording) and Pritt replies that he has seen it in four different cases.[48] Pritt is hesitant to treat Reiss like an actual witness because he does not want him open to cross-examination and, therefore, vulnerable to manipulation by the prosecution, and Somerhough thinks it "irregular" that the documents would be produced without a sworn witness to authenticate them.[49]

It is, perhaps, understandable that Slater would omit this discussion, focused as it is on a procedural question with little readerly interest compared to the related question of whether or not the recording constitutes a document. However, Reiss is an important part of the deeper narrative of which Slater's is an abbreviation; put differently, if Slater amplifies the issue of the recording to emphasize and draw out the underlying ideology of colonialism that sits uneasily with forms of African authority, Reiss is part of the background noise that is filtered out. But some of that noise can do much to help us understand the context and significance of what is amplified. For instance, according to John Lonsdale, Reiss is the real reason the recordings were never admitted ("Kenyatta's Trials" 231). It is not mentioned in either Slater's version or the KTT, but Reiss allegedly recalled years later to Bodil Fredricksen (in 1993) that he had a private meeting with Thacker and the two leading counsels in which he informed them that "the tapes had been doctored, to delete any equivocation by Kenyatta before being broadcast; but nor was there

48 In attempting to determine whether or not Reiss must be sworn in, Thacker and others reference section 139 of The Indian Evidence Act, which states, "A person summoned to produce a document does not become a witness by the mere fact that he produced it, and cannot be cross-examined unless and until he is called as a witness" (205).

49 KTT, vol. 6, p. 1460 (February 13, 1953).

any audible curse."[50] This might explain why Pritt does not fight harder to subpoena the recordings even though, as he passionately argues in the midst of Somerhough's stonewalling, the meeting is of "the greatest importance to the case."[51]

At the same time, as important as Pritt claimed the meeting to be, it is unclear whether or not the recordings would have made a significant difference in the trial. Even if they had been admitted (with or without Reiss as an official witness), the recordings would simply have verified that Kenyatta gave a speech, and uttered a curse, in Kikuyu: like the Swahili version, it would still need to be translated, and Somerhough would, no doubt, have found a way to cast doubt on the seriousness of Kenyatta's denunciation. Somerhough's determination to interfere with Pritt's subpoena is telling, however, and perhaps just as Pritt feared a witness (Reiss) over whom he had little control, Somerhough feared the recordings for the same reason. It is important, of course, to be aware of Reiss's claim that the recordings were doctored, but the focus of the discussion in the trial, and Slater's presentation of that discussion in his book, reveal anxieties that lead to important strategies on Somerhough's part that say a great deal about tensions between African orality and colonial literacy in the law and, further, about African orality's ability to unsettle colonial legal hegemony and expose an underlying crisis within colonial modernity itself. Whether or not we trust Reiss's memory (and it does seem strange that were the recordings "doctored" it is never mentioned in the trial),[52] the debates surrounding the recordings reveal much about colonial legal ideology. Strangely, Somerhough at first seems open to having the recordings brought in. Not only does he agree that they would be the best evidence of Kenyatta's speech, but he admits that he actually has some experience in the area:

> COURT: Are such things accepted as evidence in English courts?
> MR. SOMERHOUGH: I believe it is. I should raise no objection, you could not really have anything better if it is a question of what is merely said.
> MR. PRITT: I know some things have been accepted after anxious thought by the judge.
> COURT: I would not like to reject that, it would be better than any newspaper reporting, because it is verbatim.

50 See n. 85 in Lonsdale, "Kenyatta's Trials"; also, Lonsdale, Personal correspondence with the author, October 31, 2013.

51 KTT, vol. 6, pp. 1461–62 (February 13, 1953).

52 Pritt, in his closing arguments, does observe that because Somerhough persuaded Thacker not to allow the recordings to be subpoenaed, "all we know is that recordings were taken, *some were destroyed*, some were available, and we shall never know what they said" (KTT, vol. 7, p. 1898 [March 3, 1953]; emphasis added). However, "destroyed" and "doctored" are, of course, very different things, and one would expect Pritt to know the difference. Furthermore, it is interesting to note that Reiss's account of the doctoring, conveyed as it was via Fredricksen, would likely be considered hearsay were it offered in a court of law.

> MR. SOMERHOUGH: We have used them at one—in the Supreme Court—I could give you the name of the case—
> COURT: I would be prepared to take that risk, I would prefer to have this recording played over.[53]

We never learn the Supreme Court case to which Somerhough refers, but he appears ready to cite precedent in favor of using the recordings. But then he begins raising questions. First, about Reiss: "The position of Mr. Reiss as a witness seems to be obscure" (1458). As noted above, he presses this point, drawing on the provisions of The Indian Evidence Act to force Pritt to choose between having the recordings excluded or having them included contingent on the introduction of a potentially unpredictable and unprepared witness.

Second, Somerhough is actually the one to insist on the question of whether or not the recording is a document in the law, and his timing is intriguing. The end of the discussion about Reiss is punctuated by Pritt's compelling speech about the importance of the Kiambu meeting and, therefore, of the recorded evidence. Immediately after, Somerhough states, "Now that is clarified perhaps I might say we have to consider whether this is a document" (1462). Prior to this moment, everyone, Somerhough included, has been talking about the recordings in terms of documents, and at one point in response to Thacker, asking, "They are not documents?" Pritt replies confidently, "They count as documents in law" (1460). Somerhough does not object just then but waits until the moment Pritt seems to make headway in his case. Somerhough's role in this discussion is not as clear in Slater's account—from the transcript, we see that Somerhough not only raises the question at the moment of highest impact but repeats it in a way that plays on Thacker's admitted ignorance of the new technology. More than once, Thacker says something to the effect that he has no clue how magnetic recordings work: "I wish I knew more about this thing, I know so little about it, in fact I know nothing" (1457); "I am at sea" (1462); "Not for the first time I am asked to rule on something I do not know anything about, through sheer ignorance" (1463); "I am in difficulty, I cannot achieve impossibilities" (1463). Somerhough resourcefully capitalizes on these admissions: by insisting on the necessity of the document question, he gives the judge, who is lost "at sea," something with which to stay afloat; Thacker comes to agree, in other words, that the recordings must be evaluated according to the criteria for documentary evidence, but, because he "know[s] nothing," he repeatedly says he needs Reiss to lend his professional expertise. However, Somerhough replies, we cannot invite Reiss to lend such expertise without swearing him in. And to this, as we have seen, Pritt was vehemently opposed. Thus, the prosecutor, whose evidence generally was weak, manages to control and direct the conversation. Pritt seems at a loss, only asserting that "This is a document" (1462) and responding to Somerhough's subsequent challenge

53 KTT, vol. 6, p. 1458 (February 13, 1953).

with a technical description that leaves the judge only more certain that the recording does not qualify as a document (1463).

Once Thacker delivers his ruling on the recordings, the issue is dropped, although the Prosecution and Defense both return to it in their concluding statements.[54] Slater quotes both statements, as well as the statement on the matter made by the Supreme Court in their ruling on Kenyatta's appeal in 1954. Although sound and video recording on magnetic tape had been around for several decades, the Supreme Court judges, like Thacker, treat this as though it were a new and mysterious invention:

> Thus in relation to the tape recording, having stated originally that it did not bear physical marks, he [Mr. Pritt] went on to say that it might be contended that it bore marks by reason of the nature of the substance with which metal tape was coated having been changed by an electrical impulse. While this may be so, it would appear to us, in the absence of any technical knowledge, that it is at least equally possible that the effect of an electrical impulse on the magnetic tape is not to change the nature of the tape but rather to vary in some manner its properties; and we are by no means certain that a variation in the properties of a substance necessarily entails a variation in the substance or any marks upon the substance. [...] We do not consider that a sound track is a document within the meaning of the Indian Evidence Act. (qtd. in Slater 249–50)

The judges, like Thacker, refuse to look closely at the specific workings of the process of recording sound on magnetic tape, which involves altering through a magnetic impulse the arrangement of ferric oxide particles coating the tape and could conceivably be construed as bearing physical marks. The judges willingly admit their ignorance of this process, however, simply speculating "in the absence of any technical knowledge." In *Out of Africa*, Dinesen describes at one point the natural human attitude toward witchcraft, which bears an uncanny resemblance to the attitude of the judges toward the magnetic tape: "The human mind turns away its eye from witchcraft as from something unseemly. It may be forced to take an interest in the effects of it, but it will have nothing to do with the inside working, and no one has ever tried to squeeze out of a witch the exact recipe for her brew" (236). This is precisely how the judges in Kenyatta's case treat the audio recording: they simply speculate on the nature of the recording process as they are forced to take an interest in the effects of it, but they will have nothing to do with the inside working and refuse to squeeze out of modern techno-witchcraft the exact recipe for its brew.

But why? Why do the judges (including Thacker) refuse to seek out technical expertise or even legal precedent to better understand the legal standing of

54 For Thacker's full ruling on the recordings (including the question of Reiss's status as a potential witness), see KTT, vol. 6, pp. 1499–500 (February 17, 1953). For the concluding statements, see Slater, pp. 215–16 and pp. 231–32; and KTT, vol. 7, p. 1898 (March 3, 1953) and vol. 8, pp. 2027–28 (March 9, 1953).

what is, by the 1950s, not a particularly new invention? And why insist on determining whether or not the recordings meet the criteria used to evaluate documents? According to modern standards of evidence in Anglo-American jurisprudence, evidence is evidence, whether oral, documentary, or material (subject, of course, to the rules of authentication and hearsay); or, as Lord Chief Justice Sir Brian Hutton once observed, "if it is relevant, it is admissible" (qtd. in Twist 275).[55] Why is the category "document" so important to Thacker's assessment of the recordings? To answer these questions, we must consider the wider context of sound and video recordings in the law prior to and during the 1950s. Sound recordings had, of course, been in existence since the mid-1800s, and in the USA recordings were introduced as trial evidence as early as 1906.[56] Motion pictures were first submitted as evidence in 1915.[57] Recordings on magnetic tape did not emerge until after the 1930s when the technology was first developed by German scientists,[58] but subsequent decades saw increasing numbers of cases in which both video and audio recordings became acceptable forms of evidence in their own right, and not because they fit the criteria of a document.[59] In the UK, the early history of this technology is slightly less clear, but by 1940, in *Harry Parker Ltd* v. *Mason*,[60] a recording of an interview "containing proof of a fraudulent arrangement" was introduced at trial (English 158); a decade later, clearly, sound and video recordings were widespread enough globally to have been present at Kenyatta's speeches, and Somerhough even claims to have used such evidence in a case before the Supreme Court (the same court, possibly, that dismisses the evidence during Kenyatta's appeal).

One of the intriguing precedents for the use of audio and video recordings as evidence appeared just after World War II during the Nuremberg trials: eight years before Thacker wrestled with the question. Of course, Nuremberg involved the cooperation of Anglo-American and continental legal systems in prosecuting Nazi leaders, so the comparison to colonial Kenya can only get us so far. Furthermore, the Nuremberg Charter took a decidedly liberal position on the admissibility of evidence using the concept of "probative value" as the sole criterion (Twist 269), which contrasts with Kenyatta's

55 Hutton spoke in the context of the 1989 *Corporals Trial* in Belfast in response to a question about the admissibility of video recordings.

56 *Boyne City, G. & A. R. Co.* v. *Anderson*, 146 Mich. 328, 108 NW 429 (1906). See also Roper, "Sound Recording Devices Used as Evidence" (1960).

57 *Glyn* v. *Weston Feature Film Co. Ltd.* 114 LTR (NS) 354 (1915). See also Paradis, "The Celluloid Witness" (1965).

58 See Schoenherr, "The History of Magnetic Recording" (2002).

59 For a discussion of a few such cases in the USA up to 1960, see Roper, "Sound Recording Devices Used as Evidence" (1960). Also see *United States* v. *McKeever*, 169 F. Supp. 426 (SDNY 1958), which "established the conditions precedent to the admission of sound recordings" (Rychlak 4).

60 *Harry Parker Ltd* v. *Mason* [1940] 2 KB 590, CA.

case and the constraints of The Indian Evidence Act.[61] Nevertheless, the comparison bears mentioning, at the very least, because Director of Public Prosecutions Anthony Somerhough had previously served as a member of the Allied prosecution team at Nuremberg during which a documentary film was introduced as evidence. He does not mention this along with his unspecified experience with recorded evidence at the Supreme Court, but as a "Group Captain" he led a British unit that investigated war crimes (specifically, *medical* war crimes) committed in the Ravensbrück Concentration Camp.[62] Of course, Somerhough was not directly responsible for the documentary film that was used during the tribunal, but he nevertheless played an important role on the larger team that used the "novel witness" of film as part of their prosecutorial strategy (Douglas 450). Thus, he had direct knowledge of the new forms of evidence that the Allied prosecution, in 1945, introduced in order to provide unquestionable proof of the atrocities committed in the concentration camps. The film's use was somewhat controversial, partly due to the novelty of the technology (which could not be cross-examined by the defense as would happen with a human witness), but also due to the sensational effect of the images contained in the film—there was a tension, in other words between the "probative value versus the prejudicial effect" of the film (Twist 271).[63] In Kenyatta's case, the audio and video recordings of his speech would not have risked prejudicial effect due to their comparatively mundane content and, furthermore, would have been used not as proof of criminality but of the truth of Kenyatta's testimony. The point, essentially, is that, by 1953, Somerhough, Pritt, and Thacker found themselves in legal territory familiar to courts throughout the Western world in determining how new technologies fit into the established rules of evidence, but unlike these other courts Thacker turns atavistic rather than progressive: it is not simply that he relies

61 Article 19 of the *Charter of the International Military Tribunal* declares, "The Tribunal shall not be bound by technical rules of evidence. It shall adopt and apply to the greatest possible extent expeditious and non-technical procedure, and shall admit any evidence which it deems to have probative value" ("Agreement for the Prosecution").

62 See "Somerhough, Anthony George," in *Who was Who, 1951–1960* (1960); Heberer and Matthäus, *Atrocities on Trial: Historical Perspectives on the Politics of Prosecuting War Crimes* (2008), pp. 128–31; Weindling, *John W. Thompson: Psychiatrist in the Shadow of the Holocaust* (2010), p. 113; and Walters, *Hunting Evil: The Nazi War Criminals Who Escaped and the Quest to Bring Them to Justice* (2010), pp. 200–01.

63 In addition to Twist, see Douglas, "Film as Witness: Screening Nazi Concentration Camps before the Nuremberg Tribunal" (1995) and Picart, "Nationalities, Histories, Rhetorics: Real/Reel Representations of the Holocaust and Holocaust Trials and a Poethics of Film and Law' (2015). Although not about video or audio evidence as such, Jennifer L. Mnookin's "The Image of Truth: Photographic Evidence and the Power of Analogy" (2013) provides a fascinating analysis of the ways in which photographs became accepted as evidence in US law and, in turn, "helped to bring about broader changes in both courtroom practice and the conceptualization of evidence" (4).

on established law, but that he does so fully recognizing its limitations and that within the terms of the law the new technology does not even exist. Many other jurisdictions, including the UK and some of its former territories, have continued to use the term "document" in the laws of evidence but they have expanded it to include new forms of technological communication.[64] (Curiously, Kenya's Evidence Act uses the term "document" but does not define it.[65]) And, courts like that convened at Nuremberg opened the rules of evidence to include anything with probative value. Given Thacker's age at the time (having come out of retirement), intellectual rigidity, and negative predisposition toward the defendants, it is not surprising that he would evaluate a new technology according to a Victorian legal code that marked them as inadmissible. What is surprising, or at least ironic, is that Somerhough urges him in this direction; it makes sense for his case to do so, of course, but it also reinforces the atavistic impulses of colonial law that we have seen in the conflicted temporalities of indirect rule, in Dinesen's longing for a lost golden age of aristocratic glory, and now in the laws of evidence within which magnetic recordings are anachronistic and unassimilable.

Although he leaves out many of these details, Slater's core narrative not only critiques the conventions of colonial representation by claiming objectivity and then performing subjective selection, but he also critiques colonial law by catching it in this contradiction. On the one hand, the law's rejection of the audio recording could be seen as consistent with the law's traditional stance toward oral culture. Songs had been banned in the past for their subversive potential, and even the procedures of traditional African courts, though "allowed" to continue under the system of indirect rule, were sometimes slowly pressed toward modernity by having their procedures and laws written down. On the other hand, while colonial law's rejection of the recording is consistent with its rejection of oral culture, it inadvertently also rejects a product of its own narrative of progress. The "scientific inventions" of electronic media represent, in many ways, some of the most significant achievements of modern society. Such inventions are a natural product of the narrative of progress upon which colonial rule had been built. When confronted with this invention, however, the law rejects it, revealing two things: one, that the supposed primitive nature of oral culture is merely a myth as it has adapted more fluidly to "secondary orality" than has colonial culture; and, two, that colonial culture is the one in a state of crisis. The judgments in Kenyatta's trials occurred when the "crisis of modernity" myth was being widely deployed to account for the violence of Mau Mau. However, Slater seems

64 The UK's 1968 Civil Evidence Act, for example, states that "document" "includes, in addition to a document in writing—(a) any map, plan, graph or drawing; (b) any photograph; (c) any disc, tape, sound track or other device in which sounds or other data (not being visual images) are embodied so as to be capable (with or without the aid of some other equipment) of being reproduced therefrom" (11).

65 See "Documentary Evidence" (2011).

to claim that the pace of modernity proved too much for colonial culture, and in a moment of multiple crises the colonial legal establishment atavistically reverted to a dated definition of "document," refusing to recognize the very product of its own narrative of progress. Thus, while the discourse of a "crisis of modernity" comes to justify the colonial legal establishment's treatment of the Kikuyu people during the Emergency, Slater shows us that the law's refusal to admit sound recording as legitimate evidence is itself evidence that colonial society is the one experiencing a crisis of modernity. And, as we learned in the above discussion of the trial on Dinesen's farm, this crisis is not new, but has deep roots in the history of colonialism. The proponents of the colonial project ultimately underestimated the power of orality to adapt to and outlast change and to continue uniting people in communities that, by one means or another, sought freedom from colonial rule. Slater's selective retelling of Kenyatta's trial demonstrates how, in a moment of intense political crisis, oral culture was able to adapt, unite, and unmask the deep contradiction within colonial law: as colonialism fought a so-called atavism in the name of modernity, it retained its own atavistic longings by which it sought an escape from modernity over half a century earlier.

In the end, Kenyatta did serve his time in prison and the government did win the war against Mau Mau, but when the government's horrific abuses of prisoners in the "rehabilitation" camps (justified, of course, by the crisis myth) became public, the full contradiction of colonialism's claim to civilization and modernity became evident, precipitating Kenyan independence.[66] Furthermore, Kenyatta's trial ultimately made him a martyr to both KAU and Mau Mau, and after his release in 1959 he quickly rose again to prominence within the political leadership and became independent Kenya's first president. Strangely, however, Kenyatta continued to describe Mau Mau as symptomatic of a "crisis of modernity": although he benefited from Mau Mau's campaign, to the end he remained opposed to Mau Mau as he always claimed he was. In 1962, on the eve of independence, he declared in a public meeting that "Mau Mau was a disease which had been eradicated, and must never be remembered again" (*Suffering* 189). This was shocking to many and has contributed to Mau Mau's complicated and controversial legacy in post-independence Kenya. Additionally, the tension between "tradition" and "modernity" in terms of the law has continued to shape East Africa in the many years since independence and, consequently, the crisis of modernity has as well. Kenyatta's trial, and Slater's representation of it, thus continue to offer significant insights into the legacy of the early and late colonial periods and the crises and contradictions that destabilized colonial-created binaries (e.g., orality/literacy, uncivilized/civilized, illegal/legal and, ultimately, tradition/modernity), and, as we will see in subsequent chapters, their postcolonial variants.

66 See, in particular, Elkins, *Imperial Reckoning* (2005), p. 28.

CHAPTER TWO

A Song Whose Time Has Come: Northern Uganda, Apocalyptic Futures, and the Oral Jurisprudence of Okot p'Bitek

> The artist proclaims the laws but expresses them in the most indirect language: through metaphor and symbol, in image and fable. He sings and dances his laws.
>
> Okot p'Bitek, *Artist, the Ruler* (1986)

Two weeks before his unexpected death in 1982, at the age of 51, the poet Okot p'Bitek completed a collection of essays posthumously published as *Artist, the Ruler* (1986). As one of his final statements, the collection represents the most mature form of Okot's ideas about poetry's relationship to culture and society. When he passed away, Okot was also writing a new poem, titled "Song of Soldier," a response to the brutal Idi Amin regime, which ended in 1979. Though he never finished the poem, Okot was clearly thinking about issues of authority and its abuse, about the rule of law and the problem of African dictators who perpetuate cycles of colonial control and crisis. Whether or not literature can truly offer a remedy to such problems is a perpetual question globally, but Okot asserted at a crucial moment in East African history that alternative sources of morality, wisdom, and law could be articulated by Africa's artists. In the titular essay, Okot begins with the British poet Percy Shelley's claim that "poets are the unacknowledged legislators of the world," but he takes issue with Shelley's assumption that this is the case the world over (qtd. in Okot 39). Okot contends that throughout Africa poets and artists "are fully acknowledged, admired and feared for their sharp tongues" (39). He continues:

> I believe that a thought system of a people is created by the most powerful, sensitive, and imaginative minds that that society has produced: these are the few men and women, the supreme artists, the imaginative creators of their time, who form the consciousness of their time. [...] The artist

> proclaims the laws but expresses them in the most indirect language: through metaphor and symbol, in image and fable. He sings and dances his laws.

For Okot, the African poet is not simply an entertainer or cultural educator, but a fully acknowledged law-maker. Through poetry, songs, and dance—in other words, through orature—poets and other artists create and disseminate principles that form the foundation of a people's system of thought and action. Okot insists that the "artist creates the central ideas around which other leaders, law makers, chiefs, judges, heads of clans, family heads, construct and sustain social institutions." Thus, there are two types of rulers: those who "provide and sustain the fundamental ideas" of society and those who fashion these ideas into formal laws, who "put these ideas into practice in ruling or misruling society." Though formal laws are still the domain of conventional leaders here, it is a secondary domain that derives its substance and authority from those primary figures who articulate and *create* the moral and cultural vocabularies required before law can emerge. Robert Cover might identify the process Okot is describing as "jurisgenesis" ("Foreword" 11), or the dynamic law-creating impulse that produces "a language and a mythos—narratives in which the corpus juris is located by those whose wills act upon it" (9).

Okot speaks of the jurisgenerative powers of poets and artists in the third person from the position of critic and ethnographer, but a clear implication of his argument is that he himself, as an artist committed to African culture and identity, was a law-maker who sang and danced a "lexicon of normative action" upon which formal laws could theoretically be based (Cover 9). This fact encourages us to reread Okot's poems in terms of law and to examine his life and education as a process of jurisgenesis or of the emergence of normative regimes grounded in Acholi orature. Writing during and about the transition from the late colonial crisis of modernity examined in the previous chapter to the postcolonial period, Okot exemplifies the relationships among literature, orature, and law that are the subject of this book. Indeed, unlike Ngũgĩ, Farah, and others, Okot actually received formal legal training, and although such training is not a prerequisite for a law and literature reading of an author's work, it does set Okot apart as someone who was deeply invested in and conscious of the cultural dimensions and narrative structures of the law (including both indigenous and Western forms) at a time when independence opened the door to contest the colonial legal inheritance in East Africa.

What is particularly interesting about Okot, however, is that the "time" of his poems, or the period about and to which his poems speak most directly, is altered when we read them in terms of the law. Until an early version of this chapter was published in 2009,[1] no scholars had taken into account Okot's statements about law in readings of his poetry, reflecting a tendency

1 See Leman, "Singing the Law: Okot p'Bitek's Legal Imagination and the Poetics of Traditional Justice" (2009).

to privilege what we might call the Oxford perspective—i.e., one that follows from Okot's education in social anthropology at Oxford University—over the Aberystwyth perspective—i.e., Okot completed a degree in law at the University College of Wales, Aberystwyth before attending Oxford. Okot had a complicated relationship with Oxford and the discipline he studied there, even writing a critique of Western ethnography in *African Religions in Western Scholarship* (1971), but there is still a tendency to read his poetry—particularly *Song of Lawino* and *Song of Ocol*—ethnographically, as a catalog of Acholi culture and tradition representative of issues like identity, hybridity, language, the nation, tradition vs. modernity, authenticity, etc. that were central to early postcolonial theory.[2] Approaching his poetry in this way is certainly justified, and such readings have taught us a great deal about Okot and his importance in the canon of modern African literature, but they also suggest he has the greatest relevance at an earlier point in time, whereas today, in the era of globalization, international human rights, the Anthropocene, world literatures, etc., texts so bound to the terms and ideas of early postcolonial discourse appear to have mostly historical significance.

However, a perspective that takes seriously Okot's education in and statements about law not only provides us with a compelling case study of the dynamic relationship between law and literature in Africa, but more importantly it begins to reveal what Russell Samolsky would call the "apocalyptic future" of Okot's poetry, or the fact that his texts contain within them "various mechanisms or programs by which they target apocalypses to come," incorporating catastrophe into the field of their future reception (9). Specifically, Okot's poems target, in this sense, the catastrophe that is Joseph Kony and the Lord's Resistance Army. The LRA emerged in the late 1980s with the goal of overthrowing the Ugandan government and replacing it with a theocracy based on the biblical Ten Commandments. The group had early support from communities in Northern Uganda, but as their tactics became increasingly violent, they turned against the Acholi people and began abducting children and forcing them to fight or, for many of the girls, to marry LRA leaders. During the course of two decades, the LRA abducted over 60,000

2 Scholarship on Okot peaked in the 1980s and early 1990s, though interest in his work continues; for representative readings that discuss Okot in terms of early postcolonial concepts, see Heywood, "Modes of Freedom: The Songs of Okot p'Bitek" (1980); Ofuani, "The Traditional and Modern Influences in Okot p'Bitek's Poetry" (1985); Ojaide, "Poetic Viewpoint: Okot P'Bitek and His Personae" (1986); Osuagwu, "A Traditional Poet in Modern Garb: Okot p'Bitek" (1988); and Okumu, "The Form of Okot p'Bitek's Poetry: Literary Borrowing from Acholi Oral Traditions" (1992). For more recent discussions, see chapter 6 of Ramazani, *The Hybrid Muse: Postcolonial Poetry in English* (2001), which explicitly focuses on the relationship between Okot's poetry and the discipline of ethnography; Imbo, *Oral Traditions as Philosophy: Okot p'Bitek's Legacy for African Philosophy* (2002); and Usongo, "Cultural Identity and Literature: A Study of Okot p'Bitek's *Song of Lawino*" (2011).

children—some as young as 6 years old—and the violence displaced over two million people in Acholiland.

Military intervention did little to stop the LRA, and peace talks in the early 2000s met with limited success, although the violence eventually subsided and the LRA retreated from Uganda into neighboring states. Throughout the talks, however, and the reconciliation process that followed, the most fundamental challenges had to do with law and justice: first, whether international law (in the form of the ICC) or indigenous forms of law are best suited to addressing the LRA's crimes, and, second, whether or not "traditional justice" can heal communities wounded by the conflict. These are uncannily similar to questions revealed in Okot's poetry when we read them from a law and literature perspective. This is not to say Okot was prophetic in any literal sense, but something about his work, though written well before the LRA came into existence,[3] has enabled it to take on new significance, proleptically making legible events about which it could not have been written but for which it seems to be meant.

Indeed, evidence of this "apocalyptic future" can be seen, to a point, in the fact that there has been a resurgence of interest in Okot among scholars and activists writing about the LRA and the challenges of post-conflict reconciliation, all during a period when scholarly attention to Okot in the humanities has significantly declined.[4] Similar to the trends we see in the humanities, however, the role assigned to Okot in these studies is one of Oxford-educated ethnographer whose books *The Religion of the Central Luo* (1971), *African Religions in Western Scholarship* (1971), and *Acholi Proverbs* (1985), in addition to his poetry, are useful primers on Northern Ugandan culture. When seeking to understand and explain Acholi religion and cultural practice, what better authority than an ehtnographically-minded member of that community who understood it from within and was deeply committed to preserving it against

3 Though, coincidentally his collection *Artist, the Ruler*, which most clearly articulates his ideas about law, was published posthumously in 1986, the year before Alice Lakwena's "Holy Spirit Movement," the precursor to the Lord's Resistance Army, began its campaign against the Ugandan government.

4 There may be other examples, but the following books and articles—all written since 2006—reference Okot's work in the context of the LRA conflict: Harlacher et al., *Traditional Ways of Coping in Acholi* (2006), pp. 42–47, 51, 109, 155; Finnström, *Living with Bad Surroundings: War, History and Everyday Moments in Northern Uganda* (2008), pp. 4–5, 13–14, 27, 33–39, 49, 54, 65, 155, 159, 184, 189, 194, 199, 206, 207, 211, 213, 225, 234–35, 243, 244; Mino, "Dwog Paco: Tackling the Challenges of Reintegrating Ex-LRA in Kitgum District" (2009), pp. 6, 31; Horsley, "Our Lives, Our Stories: Storytelling Workshops in Uganda's Refugee Camps" (2011), pp. 148, 149, 150, 152; Hopwood, "We Can't Be Sure Who Killed Us: Memory and Memorialization in Post-Conflict Northern Uganda" (2011), pp. 9, 19; Moore, *Humanitarian Law in Action within Africa* (2012), p. 209; and Gauvin, "In and Out of Culture: Okot p'Bitek's Work and Social Repair in Post-Conflict Acoliland" (2013), who discusses Okot in detail throughout.

the incursions of Western influence? In an influential report on Acholi justice, Thomas Harlacher writes, "Much of our understanding of the traditional religion of the Acholi is owed to Okot p'Bitek" (42). This is perfectly reasonable (although there is some danger of treating Okot like a "native informant"), but I also think Okot has much more to offer. Sverker Finnström comes close to explaining what when he observes, "Despite being more than thirty years old, the poems P'Bitek's [*sic*] wrote about Lawino and her husband Ocol, describing the encounters of development and modernization with the local moral world, seem *strikingly up to date* regarding the present understanding among informants about the situation in Acholiland" (206; emphasis added). What Finnström describes are texts that appear simultaneously *of* and *ahead of* their time, but he does not fully explain why.

I agree with Finnström and others who see Okot's words as having renewed significance, but I wish to take this a step further to argue that the apocalyptic future of Okot's writings has been only partially realized. Okot's appearance in conversations about the LRA is evidence of this future, but the reasons for and details of this capacity go beyond his status as a reliable authority on Acholi culture. I argue, instead, that we must read Okot as many things: poet, ethnographer, cultural critic, musician, footballer; most importantly, however, we must read him as lawyer, judge, and law-maker. In this chapter, I first describe Okot's direct connections to the legal field in more detail and also briefly discuss the history of colonial law in Northern Uganda to provide some context for a pre-LRA understanding of his statements about law. I then focus my attention on Okot's two most famous poems, *Song of Lawino* and *Song of Ocol*, and demonstrate how a legal reading draws the LRA catastrophe into the field of their current reception. We can also read Okot's later poems, including *Song of Malaya* (1971), *Song of Prisoner* (1971), and the unfinished "Song of Soldier" in terms of law, but it is in the companion songs of Lawino and Ocol, along with his essays in *Artist, the Ruler*, that we see his fullest expression of the forms of oral jurisprudence and, therefore, the fullest expression of the apocalyptic future of his work. Although Okot imagines orature being enacted to resolve crises within the intimate jurisdictions of family and home in the era of early postcolonial critique, I ultimately demonstrate that Okot's ideas have implications far beyond the local and personal and beyond their moment of composition, resonating with renewed energy in the context of contemporary questions about local, national, and international law and justice.

Artists and Rulers in Northern Uganda

Born in 1931 in Gulu, Uganda, Okot entered a world structured by the competing cultures of colonialism and the Acholi people. Okot's parents had been baptized as Christians and were involved with missionary schools and societies in Northern Uganda, but they also "firmly retained the traditional way of life" (Lubwa 2). According to Lubwa p'Chong, Okot's father and mother "participated in the chiefdom and clan rituals, dances and ceremonies" and both parents were highly proficient in orature (2). His mother, Lacwaa, "was a famous dancer and composer of songs"; and Opii Bitek, his father, "was an accomplished story-teller and dancer from Patiko chiefdom." From his birth, Okot was surrounded by and immersed in Acholi orature and, over time, as his "creative spirit was nurtured," he developed his own artistic gifts. After primary and secondary school, Okot attended Kings College, Budo, in Kampala, and there began writing songs and stories and was awarded his first literary prize. He then attended the Mbarara Teacher Training College in western Uganda from 1951 to 1952, during which time he wrote his only novel, published in 1953 in Acholi as *Lak Tar Miyo Kinyero Wi Lobo* ("I laugh only with my teeth, but my heart is bleeding," published in English as *White Teeth*). After completing his studies at Mbarara, Okot taught at the Sir Samuel Baker School in Gulu for several years, became involved in local politics (he was nominated for the Acholi District Council), and began writing the poem *Wer pa Lawino*, which he would later revise and then translate into English as *Song of Lawino*. At the time, however, the poem was rejected by publishers in Uganda and Okot set it aside.

In addition to his academic activities and growing literary talents, Okot was also an accomplished footballer and had joined the Ugandan national team while studying at Mbarara. In 1956, the team went on a tour of the United Kingdom where they played several games, often barefoot,[5] and afterward Okot remained in England to enroll in a postgraduate education program at the University of Bristol. He completed his work at Bristol in a year and then turned his attentions to law. What made him decide to study law and to study in Wales is unclear since he never wrote about it himself. However, the records we have suggest his experience was largely positive. In 1976, J.A. Andrews, a law professor at the University College of Wales, Aberystwyth (now Aberywsyth University), published a brief history of the Law School. Identifying the post-World War II years as a "second golden period" for the school, Andrews notes the great successes of their professors and students from the United Kingdom. He then states: "To them must be added some very distinguished overseas graduates, for the fifties and sixties witnessed a substantial influx of students from East and West Africa, the West Indies and, above all, Malaysia. [...] They made a very big impact on the life of Aberystwyth. They worked hard, often in difficult circumstances, and have seen their work rewarded" (5). Okot was among these "distinguished overseas graduates," and, given accounts of his exuberant personality, he no doubt contributed a great deal to the life of Aberystwyth during his years as a student from 1957

5 Archival footage from a Pathé News report about a match with the Wycombe Wanderers in 1956 can be seen here: www.britishpathe.com/video/sports-news-1/query/Uganda. (URL active as of March 2020.) I have reviewed this footage with Okot's daughter, Juliane Okot Bitek, and we agreed that the Ugandan player entering the field at 0:07–0:08 appears to be her father.

to 1960.[6] Lubwa p'Chong describes "the great enthusiasm with which Okot embarked on the study of law" (6), and Mary Llewelfryn Davies, whose spouse, the late D. J. Llewelfryn Davies, was Dean of the Law School at the time of Okot's attendance, recalls that Okot was "charming" and "an excellent law student who took a leading part in the life of the Department."[7]

Although Okot did not write about his experiences at Aberystwyth, his transcripts show that he excelled in law school.[8] In addition to completing the required classes, he opted for third-year subjects that earned him Honors when he graduated with an LLB in 1960. Okot also registered at one point with the Middle Temple, one of the four Inns of Court in London, and had begun "to keep terms and eat dinners, with a view of being 'called to the Bar'" (Lubwa 6). According to Lubwa p'Chong, Okot even "spent three months at the International Court of Justice at the Hague, as part of his studies in International Law." In other words, Okot was well-situated to excel in the legal profession just as he had excelled as a student. Three years of professional education, significant achievements, respect from his peers: Okot had built a foundation for a successful career and clearly developed at least a basic expertise in the law. Why, then, did he abandon it? One interesting response to this question appeared in 1983 when Humphrey J. Ojwang wrote an elegiac drama titled *Okot p'Bitek on Trial: A Biographical Play* (first performed in 1983, published in 1993). The short play imagines the afterlife as a place where recently departed souls are brought before a tribunal to answer for their life's activities (14). In Okot's case, the play eventually reaches the conclusion that he achieved great things and left an important legacy among his students, his community, and more broadly within African letters, but a prosecutor during the tribunal first proposes that Okot was "wasteful" in his life, particularly in terms of his failure to put his extensive legal education to use. The prosecutor states, "I submit that Okot the lawyer died the moment he was born and I consider that wastage" (17). Okot's "Defense Counsel" counters this charge by arguing that no education truly goes to waste: "I submit that Okot's legal education enabled him to have an objective approach to life and see both sides of arguments throughout his career" (19).

The play is a clever and sincere tribute to Okot, and this moment constitutes one of the few extended meditations anywhere on the meaning of Okot's legal education. However, I submit that the prosecutor and defense counsel are both wrong and that Ojwang missed an opportunity to consider the more substantial meaning and lasting impact of Okot's study of the law. Okot obviously did abandon the legal profession, as that profession is conventionally

6 Edward Blishen of the BBC, for example, met Okot in 1967 and noted the poet's "mischievous high spirits," describing him as "dynamic, awkward, witty," "explod[ing] incessantly" into laughter (3).
7 Personal correspondence with the author, September 19, 2006.
8 I am grateful to Professor Richard Ireland of the Aberystwyth Law School and the administrative staff who helped me locate these records.

understood or defined, but his education did more than make him a more objective thinker (and, certainly, we could even question "objectivity" as an inevitable outcome of legal education). I argue that his formal training in law gave him a new appreciation for and interest in the nature of indigenous law in Africa, and he subsequently joined the legal profession, in a sense, as it was defined from within Northern Ugandan culture. Recognizing this enables us to see his turn to ethnography and then back to poetry in relationship to law, or as a means toward the end of better understanding African law and culture. Lubwa p'Chong relates an experience Okot had in one of his honors subjects during his final year of law school that sheds light on the first stage of this turn:

> One day the Professor of Legal History was discussing "Trial by Ordeal"; a method of determining guilt or innocence by subjecting the accused person to fire, water or other serious danger, the result being regarded as divine or preternatural. Okot immediately remembered that this was also being practised in Northern Uganda. The professor advised that in order to pursue this interest further, Okot should, on completion of the law studies, proceed to Oxford University to read Social Anthropology. (6)

As noted earlier, Okot's education at Oxford, where he studied with British luminaries Godfrey Lienhardt and E.E. Evans-Pritchard, tends to receive more attention in scholarship of his work, and the impact of that education is evident in the clear ethnographic strains and themes in *Song of Lawino*, in particular.[9] However, it is important to recognize that *legal* anthropology is what first caught Okot's attention. Questions of law led Okot to Oxford where he hoped to understand his own cultural legal traditions more completely. However, Okot's experience at Oxford, compared to that at Aberystwyth, was quite negative. Okot was eager to study with world-renowned figures like Evans-Pritchard and Lienhardt but he was soon disappointed as he encountered the still resilient rhetoric of temporal difference by which anthropology sought "to constitute its own object" (Fabian 1). Okot writes, "[I]t was the insulting language they and others who came from other universities used which caused me so much suffering. The world was divided into two: the 'Civilized West' and the rest. These were *savages, primitives, uncivilized, crude, rude, un-progressive, etc.* This often led to bitter exchange in lecture rooms and during seminars" (qtd. in Lubwa "A Biographical Sketch" 7; emphasis

9 In addition, Okot also collected oral artifacts in books such as *Horn of My Love* (1974) and *Acholi Proverbs* (1985); he wrote directly about Northern Ugandan culture in *Religion of the Central Luo* (1971); and he even composed a critique of Western ethnographic methods in *African Religions in Western Scholarship* (1971). Jahan Ramazani's chapter on Okot in *The Hybrid Muse* (2001) provides a fascinating analysis of Okot's poetry in relationship to these writings and to ethnography more broadly, noting how Okot both draws upon and criticizes the discipline, the history of which is bound up in the discourses and practices of colonial power, particularly in the development of the legal system of indirect rule.

in original). This is, of course, the very narrative that was the initial justification for British colonialism and was later adapted and formalized by Henry Maine in the system of indirect rule. Furthermore, it was anthropology, as a discipline, that served such a crucial role in the development of that system in Africa, and it is perhaps not surprising that the residues of that role were still found at this time (probably 1960 or 1961) despite the fact that Uganda, along with so many other African countries, was preparing for independence. To Okot's credit, discovering anthropology's complicity in the colonial project did not dissuade him from completing his studies. Indeed, he embraced the challenge his professors presented to him and committed himself to studying Ugandan culture from within its own terms, using but also repudiating the methods he learned from his Oxford professors.

In 1963, Okot completed his (437-page) B.Litt. thesis at Oxford titled "Oral Literature and its Social Background among the Acholi and Lango." This was partly the basis of his later book *The Religion of the Central Luo* (1978). For Jahan Ramazani, the thesis and book are both evidence of the impact of ethnography on Okot's life and work.[10] However, if we take Okot's experiences in law school into account, we might conclude that when Oxford failed to fulfill Okot's intellectual desires, which had been stimulated by his studies in law, he turned to oral culture. This is not the directionless or erratic movement of someone who "wasted" his education, but, I argue, a deliberate movement through different modes of studying, understanding, and practicing the law. Aberystwyth introduced Okot to a conventional Western legal education, albeit in a location that was still the product of imperial relations and motivated him to study law from an African perspective. Rather than provide this perspective, Oxford made Okot aware of the narratives and myths at the heart of colonial law, and of Western law more broadly, wherein the world is divided along the lines of civilized and uncivilized. It was not until his late essay, "Artist, the Ruler," that Okot made explicit his ideas about the relationship between poetry and law, but it is my contention that his turn at Oxford toward the orature of Northern Uganda was a continuation of his effort to understand law from within the terms of African culture.[11] Like

10 See the previous footnote.

11 Indeed, this can be seen in his thesis, most particularly in chapter 10, "'Poetic Justice' through Orak Dance Songs," and chapter 11, "Proverbs." In chapter 10, Okot observes that "customs like other social codes are an apparatus for compelling or forbidding certain behavior" (315–16), and he examines "orak songs," which ruthlessly satirize and shame individuals who engage in forbidden behaviors. "To be the subject of an orak song is not a thing to be proud of," Okot writes, "no one desires it" (315). In this way, the songs are a form of sanction that "enforce […] standards of daily conduct" (316). Of Acholi and Lango proverbs, Okot states, "They are 'the instructions of wisdom, justice and judgment and equity'" (319). The songs and proverbs are not law in the formal sense, but they are examples of oral jurisprudence, or orature that serves as a "lexicon of normative action" (Cover, "Foreword" 9).

many nationalist and négritude writers, Okot strongly believed that "the nations of Africa should be built on African not European foundations" (Heron, "Introduction" 5), and Okot's commitment to oral culture and indigenous forms of law was central to his search for such a foundation.

This search forms an important—and perhaps even deliberate—contrast to that of the architects of indirect rule who argued, similarly, that African society should be built upon African foundations. In describing the need for the system of indirect rule, Frederik Lugard observed—as had Maine—that direct rule would destroy native institutions, and instead of preparing Africans for eventual self-rule would merely teach them the "duty of obedience" (219). "We can then only offer an alien system," Lugard continued, "evolved by Western nations to suit wholly different circumstances moulded on European and not on native habits of thought" (219–20). Thus, to avoid this, Lugard detailed and advocated a system that he claimed to be molded on African, rather than European, habits of thought. Of course, Okot's turn toward indigenous culture is very different from Lugard's—one has the explicit aim of resisting colonial power and the other of reinforcing it. However, by contrasting the two approaches to "African foundations," we can better see how Okot's ideas about law, particularly in his poems *Song of Lawino* and *Song of Ocol*, can be read in relationship to the history of colonial law. Indeed, given the role that anthropology played in the development and administration of indirect rule and the fact that Okot studied that very discipline at Oxford, it is, I argue, hardly a coincidence that his rejection of anthropology took the form of a fuller immersion in indigenous culture, as if to show that his professors and their forerunners who shaped indirect rule got it wrong: they were wrong in what they codified as "customary" law, they were wrong in assuming African "traditions" stood in opposition to "modernity," and they were wrong in their interpretation of the meaning of "native crisis." For colonialists, this crisis meant that Africans were unable to cope with modernity; for Okot, the crisis meant that colonial modernity itself was fundamentally disruptive and invasive. Because of this, the preventative impetus of indirect rule ultimately failed: premised upon a misinterpretation of the violence of colonial subjects, indirect rule continued to foster the instability it was supposed to avert.

This failure takes an interesting form in Northern Uganda, and it is worth considering the specific development of indirect rule in Acholiland in order to situate properly Okot's response through the "indirect language" of poetry (*Artist* 39). A number of explorers had traveled through Northern Uganda prior to the 1890s, but Acholiland was not incorporated into the Ugandan protectorate until 1898 (Finnström 60). Perhaps reflecting Lugard's racially charged view that direct rule is "at first temporarily unavoidable among the most backward of all" (218), colonial rule in Acholiland appears to have been very direct at the beginning, or, if not direct, then most certainly exploitative. "Colonial control," writes Sverker Finnström, "in the form of imposed taxes, confiscation of firearms, and forced recruitment of porters and labor became the order of the day" (60). A group under the leadership of the Lamogi clan staged a rebellion in 1911, and although they failed to drive the British out and were eventually stopped, the act made a clear statement. This was the kind of violence that Maine and Lugard interpreted as evidence of the disruptive influence of modernity, but, as this case illustrates, the only disruptive influence was colonial exploitation, which the myth of modernity was meant to conceal. There has been very little published about this time period in Northern Uganda, but it would not be difficult to imagine the narrative of "native crisis" being used to justify a new approach to administration in the wake of the Lamogi rebellion. At a certain point, two districts were established in Acholiland under the larger "Native Administration," and then in 1937 the districts were combined into one "Acholi District," which included six counties, each overseen by a colonial-appointed County Chief.[12]

When the District was first created, F.M. Barrell, the District Commissioner, sought to reorganize the Native Administration along more indigenous lines, believing that some of the Acholi customs—such as settling quarrels "by paying compensation rather than fighting"—would prove more effective than British customs (Girling 196). "Every effort was made by the British Administration Officers to 'make it [the customary system] function efficiently and to mould it to the needs of modern Government'" (199). This was the classic form of indirect rule: preserving native institutions and assimilating them within the colonial administrative structure. However, by 1943, the colonial leaders decided that conventional indirect rule "was impossible and an administrative system based on 'new principles' was introduced" (199). Reflecting in practice the contradictory movement in colonial culture both away from and toward modernization, the methods of rule in Northern Uganda first attempted to privilege what colonial officers identified as custom, but when that failed they resorted to the method of imposing a modern system rather than adapting "the traditional order to modern conditions" (199).

There are likely many reasons why a strict form of indirect rule was "impossible," but Thomas Harlacher explains one of the most important: "The relatively decentralized socio-political order that characterized precolonial Acholi was not convenient for the colonial authorities. For administrative purposes, they much preferred a more hierarchical and neatly structured system" (30). Authorities introduced this more convenient and efficient system, but they still retained the appearance of indirect rule by using the "titles of precolonial authority figures," even if the offices themselves were new, as a way of trying to convince people that their traditions were being preserved. It is unlikely the Acholi people were deceived so easily, and they surely retained a memory of the early history of the Lamogi, which revealed the true nature

12 Girling notes, "A *County Chief*, or *Rwot*, in the present day [i.e., 1960] Native Administration, is not necessarily drawn from any of the former chiefly families in the area. As it happens, at present three of them are. They were already in office in 1937 and they were not disturbed. Subsequent appointments have been made without reference to this fact" (197).

of the colonial project from the beginning.[13] That nature was also revealed in the fact that "fear" was the fundamental principle of administration, as articulated by a Divisional Chief in 1949–50 (when F.K. Girling conducted his field research for *The Acholi of Uganda* [1960]).[14] The Chief, an officer of indirect rule, which was supposed to protect the Acholi from the harmful effects of progress, insisted that fear was necessary to achieve progress: "You see we must rule by fear. The people are lazy, they do not realise what good things the Government is doing for them. How can we Acholi progress unless we grow cotton, pay our taxes and dig latrines, as the Government wants us to do?" (qtd. in Girling 198). The District Commissioner, a British officer, "agreed that fear was still the main sanction of the government." It is no surprise that Girling also describes an Acholi man expressing frustration at the government's unwillingness to understand the people's reasons for ignoring certain regulations (198). Indirect rule ultimately fostered the discontent it was supposed to prevent.

Northern Uganda's experience with indirect rule reveals, as one might expect, that there are significant differences between the theory of indirect rule and its implementation. And this is not simply because theory and practice often struggle to match up, but more importantly because the theory of indirect rule was founded upon a misreading of "native crisis" and, therefore, had no relationship to initial conditions on the ground. As the legal formalization of the colonial myths of modernity, indirect rule sought to perpetuate colonial rule by resolving the contradiction between the idea that Western modernity justified colonialism and the fact that Africans and others often rejected modernity. However, simply interpreting resistance as a crisis of modernity does not change the oppressive nature of colonial modernity itself, and we see the consequences of this in Northern Uganda. When Okot encountered the still resilient myths of colonial modernity in his classes at Oxford University, he recognized their fictionality as well as the harm that they had caused and would continue to cause if allowed to perpetuate. His poetry and his writings on Acholi, Langi, and Luo cultures constitute an attempt to understand indigenous African societies from within their own terms and to imagine ways in which what remained of indigenous culture, such as oral jurisprudence, might be brought to bear on the problems and crises created by the contradictory myths and exploitative practices of

13 The importance of this event can be seen in the fact that the rebellion is still commemorated today. See "'Lamogi Rebellion against British Rule Was Justified'—President Museveni" (2015).

14 It is important to note that Girling's book—one of the few about Acholiland at this time—was based on a doctoral thesis he completed in 1951 at Oxford University. Like Okot, Girling studied anthropology under the supervision of E.E. Evans-Pritchard. Although I recognize Girling's likely bias and colonial perspective, I believe the basic details about the development of indirect rule that we find in his book are more or less reliable.

colonial rule. Okot recognizes that African culture certainly changed in its contact with colonialism, and his demonstration of the value of oral law is not without qualifications and complications, but he also sees within Acholi culture a normative world that could rival the false forms of custom and tradition that indirect rule claimed to preserve. We see the product of his negotiations with both indirect rule and oral jurisprudence most clearly in his poems *Song of Lawino* and *Song of Ocol.*

Lawino v. Ocol: A Song of Law

George A. Heron, in his book-length study of Okot's poetry, analyzes *Song of Lawino* in terms of the "rhetoric of apostrophe," suggesting that this technique demonstrates the "formal influence of oral literature on Okot's practice as a writer of poetry" (25). Heron notes that Lawino's "apostrophe" principally addresses her abusive, Westernized husband Ocol, but she also speaks of Ocol in the third person to an audience (13–14). Lawino seems to appeal to this audience—her "clansmen"—for advice, but Heron claims that her real intention is simply to involve her people in ridiculing her husband (15). Though Heron's analysis does much to demonstrate the influence of oral poetry on Okot's poems, I argue that there is more to the dramatic context. Lawino's address is being made for a particular occasion—i.e., that of an "open court" being held to resolve the dispute between Lawino and Ocol, an event overseen by a clan head or group of elders (*Roco* 111). The Acholi call this *wang oo*, which refers to "both the central fireplace where people gathered" in the village "and the activities that took place on such occasions," including entertainment, instruction, but also dispute resolution (Harlacher et al. 37–38). Acholi elders would use *wang oo* as a forum for preventing and correcting misbehavior, but "when conflicts had already overtly erupted, they were openly discussed and resolved at the *wang oo*. Such sessions were practical lessons in conflict resolution as both sides had the opportunity to explain the causes and course of the conflict from their perspective" (38).

Lawino is the first to explain her side of the conflict, and as she narrates her husband's various offenses, she shifts between addressing Ocol directly and speaking of him to the attendees of the open court. She begins, "Husband, you now despise me / Now you treat me with spite / And say I have inherited the stupidity of my aunt" (34). She then turns her attention from Ocol and states:

> My clansmen, I cry
> Listen to my voice:
> The insults of my man
> Are painful beyond bearing.
> My husband abuses me
> together with my parents;

He says terrible things about my mother
And I am so ashamed (35)

This pattern of address continues throughout the poem. Understanding the larger dramatic context in this way allows us further to identify specific legal elements in the poem as they correspond to practices and beliefs in Acholi society.[15] At this extreme local level, indigenous legal practices were least impacted by British policy In fact, Thomas Harlacher describes how during the colonial era two offices—*rwodi kweri* ("chiefs of the hoe," responsible for organizing communal digging and resolving land disputes) and *atekere* (a figure who presided over traditional rituals)—were created by the Acholi people, apparently without the knowledge of the British administration (32–33). The continued existence of these offices can be attributed in part to the fact that they were not "on the payroll of the colonial or post-colonial governments" (33). "This might have given space," Harlacher continues, "for the evolution of these offices over time to meet peoples' ever changing needs." This is one example of Acholi law adapting and going underground when faced with the proscriptive and contradictory procedures of colonial law. Indirect rule claimed to have appointed "traditional" chiefs to oversee the affairs of people in rural areas, but, as the Divisional Chief freely admitted to F.K. Girling, the basis of their rule was fear. Rather than turn to such leaders, the Acholi sought justice and order in alternative—or rival, as Ngũgĩ would say—forms of law that functioned independently of the colonial system. This changed the context of certain aspects of Acholi law, making them potentially subversive. Though we do not specifically encounter *rwodi kweri* or *atekere* in *Song of Lawino*, the *wang oo* is precisely the forum in which an *atekere* might play a role, and if we accept that Lawino has convened such a forum among her clansmen then we can also read the poem as part of the tradition of subversive law. At the time of its writing, *Song of Lawino* essentially initiated a conversation with—or, more properly, a challenge to—indirect rule and the myths of modernity and crisis that were its foundation.

In her *Song*, Lawino criticizes her spouse for his "apemanship,"[16] and for abusing her, but she goes beyond critique by attempting to restore him to his rightful place within their society. She attempts to enact, in other words, the Acholi concept of justice. In a Western-style legal system, were Ocol to break the law, he would be punished accordingly, whether by fine, imprisonment, or

15 In terms of my approach it is interesting to note that Taban lo Liyong's retranslation of *Song of Lawino* is entitled *The* Defense *of Lawino*. Furthermore, he calls the chapters "Submissions," and "Submission One" is subtitled "Opening the *Case*" (v; emphasis added). While I have certain reservations about Taban's translation, which he—a student, colleague, friend, and outspoken critic of Okot—insisted was meant to correct aspects of Okot's translation, I find it interesting and supportive of my argument that he uses this terminology.

16 This is Okot's term for the blind acceptance and performance of Western culture at the expense of African culture. See Okot, *Africa's Cultural Revolution* (1973), p. 5.

in the most serious cases, even death. In an Acholi court, however, depending on the particular offense, Ocol would have to submit to a process of atonement and reconciliation (and possibly pay compensation) that would cleanse him and the community of his crimes and ultimately restore him to his original place in society. As Morris and Read note, "[In general], a characteristic of customary law in Uganda [...] was the importance of compensation paid by the wrongdoer [...] in many circumstances which in English law would give rise to criminal action" (*Uganda* 255–56). What is interesting about Ocol's offense, however, is that he has not done anything of which we are made aware that would register as a crime in English law. This is a matter that *only Acholi law can handle*. But what, then, is the matter? What has he done that requires the convening of an open court? Clearly, Ocol has verbally and emotionally abused Lawino, but the problem, as she makes evident, goes much deeper.

Justice for the Acholi is founded upon an earnest belief in the importance of societal unity and must be understood in its spiritual context. A report on Acholi justice, prepared by the Liu Institute for Global Issues (LIGI), explains, "A communal society, the Acholi valued first and foremost the unity of the clan. As a result, each member of the social unit was expected to fulfill different but complementary productive, reproductive, and cultural roles" (*Roco* 11). Lawino constantly addresses Ocol's neglect of his cultural roles, often by demonstrating that while he was a respected *man* before abandoning Acoli culture, he is now "A dog of the white man" and "a woman" trying to please her husband, the white man (115, 116). Her invocation of conventional gender categories reveals Ocol's behavior as contrary to the roles he is supposed to perform *as a man*.[17] This disruption of the social order thereby threatens the stability of their home and, ultimately, their society. Such cultural roles have implications for both the material and spiritual worlds which, for the Acholi, are intimately related. Law and transgressions against it have consequences extending beyond temporal existence. Ancestors and spiritual forces help in "maintaining the unity of the clan," and it is of serious concern when a member of the clan offends such forces (*Roco* 10). Indeed, to put it another way, offenses against spiritual forces lead to a state of crisis, requiring urgent means of resolving the problem. On several occasions, Lawino points to the fact that Ocol has committed such an offense:

17 Okot struggles with the concept of traditional gender roles, however, for although he is often associated with Lawino's call to return to indigenous culture, Ocol's later response becomes extremely persuasive when he argues for the liberation of women from traditional patriarchal dominance (see *Song of Ocol* 130–34). It is Okot's "traditional" portrayal of Lawino that has led some feminist critics to dismiss her as a mere stereotype (i.e., as a "Mother Africa" figure), but Ocol's response seems to complicate the issue (see Stratton 43–44). Furthermore, Lawino's reliance upon law and the implications this has in terms of contemporary relevance would seem to argue against her dismissal on the basis of oversimplification and stereotype.

> For when you insulted me, Saying
> I was a mere village girl,
> You were insulting your grandfathers
> And grandmothers, your father and mother! When you compared me
> With the silly *ojuu* insects
> That sit on the beer pot,
> You were abusing your entire people. (119)

Frequently, Lawino expresses fear for Ocol's status and for the continued existence of their ways of life: "I am concerned / About the well-being of our homestead!" (111). Ocol's crime is not simply apemanship, but that through apemanship and the neglect of his cultural roles, he has offended his family, his ancestors, and the gods, whose wrath could bring misfortune and unhappiness to the entire clan. "Thus one person's actions always had ramifications for his or her family and clan who in turn assumed collective responsibility for the offence" (LIGI 10). *Individual* responsibility is typically emphasized in societies with a "strong centralized authority"—such as that of the Buganda (Mugerwa 285)—whereas among the Acholi and other societies where a "supreme political authority" or centralized power has not necessarily been the rule it is "more likely that the clan will step in" to assume responsibility (289). Lawino is faced with a serious crisis and, by going to such lengths to save Ocol and preserve the homestead, is assuming such responsibility and notifying the community of the need to do so collectively.

Ocol's abuses against his wife and, thus, his ancestors may constitute a "wrong against the dead," which would be an instance of *kii* (or *kir*), an abomination or taboo that brings *cen*, a form of spiritual punishment (*Roco* 12). *Cen* is described as a phenomenon in which the individual who has committed a wrong (as well as his/her family and community) suffers from the visitations of an "angry spirit" in the form of nightmares, sickness, or mental illness. Okot also identifies *cen* as the manifestation of a "vengeance ghost" (*Religion* 108). In *Religion of the Central Luo*, Okot distinguishes between diseases resulting from a "free *jok*" (an unrestricted spirit force) and angry ancestors, stating that "guilt was a dominant factor" in causing the latter (114). He explains, "The ancestors were angry because they had been neglected, because somebody among the living had not done his or her duty." Lawino's very point is that Ocol has not done his duty, and her descriptions of him resonate with accounts of *cen*: she says, for example, that her husband is "half-crazy" (41); that his language is like that of a "witch" (67); and, after Ocol violently chases away a diviner, the people ask, "What ghost has captured / The head of Ocol?" (95). When *cen* appears, it is imperative that the wrongdoer proceed through a deliberate process of restitution to satisfy the demands of justice by appeasing spirit forces and protecting him/herself and the community.

It is important to note that much of our current information about this process, including that provided by the LIGI report, has become available in response to the LRA conflict as a way to facilitate the reconciliation process. Before continuing our analysis of the poems, it is worth pausing to point out a few parallels. Ocol's "crimes" may seem minor when compared to those of the LRA: the LRA and its elusive leader Joseph Kony committed numerous atrocities, including the abduction and forced enlistment of an estimated 66,000 children. Through the course of the conflict, which began roughly in 1986 and continued for the next two decades,[18] over two million people were also internally displaced—in other words, homesteads were disrupted and destroyed (Harlacher et al. 1–4). Despite the difference in the severity of their crimes (although, as we will see, Ocol predicts the apocalyptic destruction of Acholiland, and Kony quite literally carries it out), Ocol and Kony are both guilty of bringing *cen*. For example, former LRA abductees are seen as having been contaminated with *cen*, or the "vengeful spirits of those they have killed" (Harlacher et al. 5). In this way, "victims and perpetrators are often the same person," and consequently the appropriate means of administering justice—even the appropriate *definition* of justice—has been the subject of "intense debate" (*Roco* ii). Despite Lawino's dramatic criticisms of her husband, she sees him as perpetrator and victim as well: he is responsible for *cen* and, therefore, needs the cleansing process through which she is leading him, but he is also a victim of the colonial mentality that sees Africa as expendable because of its inferiority to the West. Although there are complications with the idea of "traditional justice," as Okot reveals in the next stage of the process, it is significant that the fundamental problem toward which Lawino points is, in a sense, the same problem the ICC, the Ugandan government, and so many others have sought to address in the context of the LRA: Lawino is sensitive to a situation that threatens Acholiland and has turned to the internal juridical resources of her own culture with a hope that they will prove equal to the challenge. Whether or not they actually are equal, in the end, is a fascinating question and is one of the reasons Okot's text does more than simply confirm the ideas of those who have argued that Acholi "traditional justice" is better suited to promoting reconciliation than international law.

Once Lawino has made her allegation—i.e., that Ocol has threatened the community by committing a wrong against the dead—she must follow an established set of procedures in order to prove the crime and cleanse its effects: these include "the establishment of truth, the voluntary nature of the process (particularly on the behalf of the offender), the payment of compensation to restore what was lost, and finally the restoration of social relations and unity of the family and clans" (*Roco* 14). Once a dispute has been identified, therefore, the truth or facts of the matter must be established. "The process of establishing the facts of a particular conflict was considered [...] essential to resolving the conflict" (*Roco* 15). As mentioned previously, at the *wang oo* the disputing parties "had the opportunity to explain the causes and course of the conflict from their perspective" (Harlacher et al. 38). Lawino's long

18 Arguably, it is still ongoing: although the LRA has largely ceased its attacks (as of 2020) and moved away from Northern Uganda into nearby regions, Joseph Kony has yet to be apprehended.

lament can be read as the initial step of establishing the facts of her case in accordance with the Acholi legal process. She outlines Ocol's abuses and the various ways in which he has offended her, offended their ancestors, and threatened the stability of the homestead. "My husband pours scorn / on Black people," she declares (35). Additionally,

> Ocol rejects the old type.
> He is in love with a modern woman,
> He is in love with a beautiful girl Who speaks English. (36)
>
> My husband says He rejects me
> Because I do not appreciate
> White men's foods,
> And that I do not know How to hold
> The spoon and the fork. (56)
>
> My husband quarrels bitterly. He says
> I do not know hygiene
> And I do not know
> How to look after the sick.
> [...]
> He says
> He is sick of my superstitions and fears. (91)

Although some of these insults may seem somewhat benign, they are all evidence, or truth-establishing facts, of the destructive nature of Ocol's behavior. He has not killed anyone or burned anyone's home or destroyed anyone's cattle, but his blatant hatred of their culture has the potential to bring *cen* and ultimately kill the very social order that makes their lives, homes, and means of livelihood possible—something Ocol confirms in his response when he celebrates the "passing of / The Old Homestead" (147). Lawino sees this attitude spreading—"There is not a single true son left," she says (117)—and she uses the Acholi legal process and the dispute with her husband to draw attention to the crisis facing the homestead. In this, she also affirms (or at least expresses the belief) that Acholi oral law has contemporary relevance and, as part of a fluid oral culture, is capable of adapting to and dealing with this kind of threat. Whether or not the elders have the ability to join Lawino in this belief and address the questions she raises is never made clear in the text. Because Ocol ultimately rejects the process (as we shall see), we never learn what the judgment might have been. Furthermore, traditional mediators were limited in their power with regard to enforcing judgment. As Girling says, "The efforts of the ruler were directed not to enforcing law, but to maintaining peace within the domain [...]. The success of the *Rwot*'s [or chief's] attempt at mediation depended on the willingness of the parties to a dispute to accept his decision" (104–05). Just like the elders who oversaw the Kyama in Isak Dinesen's *Out of Africa*, those whose presence is implied by the text would be playing a primarily advisory role. They may be capable, ultimately, of offering a judgment, but they lack the means of enforcing that judgment, relying instead on the concept of "willingness." This brings us to the next step in the legal process, that of the willing or voluntary confession on the part of the offender.

"The voluntary admission of guilt was considered a necessary act for moving forward," although mechanisms exist for prompting "voluntary confession" (*Roco* 16). "Part of the logic of Acholi cosmology is to illicit [*sic*] fear and shame if one broke a social norm and to encourage people to take the appropriate steps towards restoration" (*Roco* 14). In addition to establishing the facts of the dispute, Lawino's song serves these two purposes: she shames Ocol and, in so doing, encourages him to confess his guilt voluntarily and allow the process of reconciliation to proceed. The first occurs throughout her argument. As quoted earlier, Lawino says Ocol behaves "like / A dog of the white man" (115), and later she asks, highlighting her very purpose, "Do you not feel ashamed / Behaving like another man's dog / Before your own wife and children?" (116). Several times she returns to the point that Ocol is embracing an inferior and humiliating position by imitating the ways of white men:

> Like beggars
> You take up white men's adornments, Like slaves or war captives
> You take up white men's ways.
> Didn't the Acoli have adornments?
> Didn't Black people have their ways?
> Like drunken men
> You stagger to white men's games,
> You stagger to white men's amusements. (49)

Lawino's language not only reveals the humiliation of Ocol's habits, but terms such as "beggar," "slave," "drunken," and "stagger" emphasize the fact that Ocol's mimicry of the white men, inhabiting an identity that is not his own, has weakened him. At another point, she reminds Ocol of his previous strength as a "Prince / of an ancient chiefdom" and the descendant of renowned ancestors, but then she turns to her clansmen and laments, "Let us all cry together! / Come, / Let us mourn the death of my husband, / The death of a Prince" (116–17). This rhetorical maneuver of alternately offering praise and insult is meant to shame Ocol and thereby persuade him to see how far he has fallen and how deeply he has betrayed himself and his people.[19]

19 Scholars have noted the influence of Acholi "Orak" songs in *Song of Lawino* and this pattern of praising and shaming Ocol is evidence of that influence. See Okumu, "The Form of Okot p'Bitek's Poetry: Literary Borrowing from Acoli Oral Traditions" (1992). In his Oxford thesis, Okot explained the normative function of the Orak songs/poems: "Any act, behavior or spoken word, so long as it is a breach of, a divergence from the straight and narrow path of custom is seized upon as a subject for these poems. Very few of them sing praises; the so-called love songs are often a combination of praise and insult. [...] The fear of being a subject of these songs act [*sic*] as an important sanction" ("Oral Literature" 314–15).

In chapter 2, Lawino addresses the issue of her husband's infidelity. Though she admits to being somewhat jealous that Ocol has run off with "Clementine" (or "Tina," for short), she also demonstrates her resilience in the face of this insult by attributing it to the male nature: "Who has ever prevented men / From wanting women?" (40). But she then turns her shaming on "the woman with whom I share my husband" (40). Lawino says that Tina's "lips look like bleeding" (because of her red lipstick), and,

> Her head is huge like that of the owl,
> She looks like a witch,
> Like someone who has lost her head And should be taken
> To the clan shrine!
> Her neck is rope-like,
> Thin, long and skinny
> And her face sickly pale. (39)

Lawino insists that she is not insulting Tina and that she truly feels sorry for her; but, in her language, Lawino explicitly and implicitly suggests something more sinister. Heron writes, "[Tina's] long hair which makes her head look huge and the lipstick she uses give her the kind of eccentric appearance which might have led to accusations of witchcraft" (*The Poetry* 94). In fact, Lawino states explicitly that Tina "looks like a witch," and later makes an unfounded accusation that amounts to rumor-mongering, referring specifically to the phenomenon of *cen*:

> Perhaps she has aborted many!
> Perhaps she has thrown her twins
> In the pit latrine!
> Is it the *vengeance ghosts*
> Of the many smashed eggs
> That have captured her head? (39; emphasis added).

Heron suggests that Lawino here and elsewhere is turning the colonial practice of "dirty gossip" against her enemies, but she seems to be turning the law against Tina as well ("Introduction" 14).[20] Lawino insults but ultimately offers reconciliation to Ocol; she tries to place Tina in the precarious position of being a suspected witch. This is no small matter: were Acholi law to be followed, Tina could come to great harm and even be killed. Indeed, punishments for suspected witches, according to Okot's own research, were incredibly violent: the offender was either impaled with a long stick through the length of the body, had a nail driven through the skull, or "was given a good beating with clubs" (Okot, *Religion* 125). Under British rule, customary courts were banned from making accusations of witchcraft, but there is

20 In *African Religions in Western Scholarship*, Okot describes the practice of "dirty gossip" as the tendency of Western scholars to exoticize, exaggerate, and demean African culture (22).

evidence that the practice returned after independence. Okot claimed in 1971 that neither he nor anyone he spoke to (when conducting research for *Religions of the Central Luo*) had seen, caught, or killed a witch, but more recent research has revealed that "there was quite a bit of witch cleansing in the 1960s," when Okot first wrote his poems, and there have been other cases as recently as the 1980s (Allen, "The International" 158).[21] The point is that Lawino's words have the potential for very serious and harmful consequences. She is the hero throughout the text, and readings that see her as an advocate for Acholi culture are justified, but she is far from one dimensional. Okot shows her complexity and, by extension, the complexity of the idea of "traditional justice." In LRA discussions, there has been a tendency to romanticize Acholi justice as naturally forgiving and oriented toward reconciliation in contrast to the punitive measures of international law. In reality, as Tim Allen discusses in his critique of this tendency, these are stereotypes that neglect the complex reality of the Acholi normative world and there are "serious risks in local customs and rituals being interpreted by outsiders as inherently benign" (159). In his poetry, Okot depicts, and confronts, these things as an insider in the *voice* of another insider, revealing the potential for healing and justice but also the potential for great harm.

In addition to the harm of having Tina killed as a witch, Lawino also risks harm by threating to commit a curse. Lawino's shaming ritual is, again, a strategy to humiliate Ocol and prompt a kind of renewal, but, as insulting as her language is, she never actually utters a curse because to do so in Acholi society would constitute an "abomination" similar in its effects to that committed by Ocol (*Roco* 17). Lawino herself recognizes this as she discusses the effects of mother's and uncle's curses, saying that if one of these are uttered toward you, "Know that you are in deep / trouble" (98–99). Curses are generally avoided, although they are "often committed by a husband or wife who has exhausted all other avenues of communication or resolution" (*Roco* 17). Lawino has not yet exhausted such avenues (she is in the process of doing so) and, given her concern for the homestead, is likely not ready to commit a curse. For a curse "symbolically jeopardizes the well-being of the family and therefore of the entire clan." Okot examined the curse in *Religion of the Central Luo*, stating:

> The curse [...] was a deliberate act by a person who found himself or herself in an intolerable social position. It was a desperate act by a weak person against others who infringed on his or her rights, privileges, status and interests. The curse was the last resort that a person turned to, and it drew urgent and immediate attention to a serious social situation when conflict and tension had reached a boiling point. (145)

Furthermore, Okot explains that if a "rude son, one who neglected his duties to his parents and other old persons [...] persisted in his unpleasant ways he

21 See also Ray Abrahams, "A Modern Witch-Hunt among the Lango of Uganda." *Cambridge Anthropology* 10.1 (1985): 32–45.

might be cursed." Clearly, Ocol is such a "rude son" and it may be that Lawino is trying to elicit fear by demonstrating how close she is to cursing. Interestingly, Okot examines "*the wife's curse*," which is committed by throwing out a pot, dish, or handful of ash from the stove and declaring, "*Uyaa! An mono pe adano?* Oh! Am I not a human being?" (147). Like other forms of abomination, the wife's curse is followed immediately by "ill-health and misfortune," and the community responds with a combination of sympathy and fear. "By this act the woman brought an already highly strained relationship to a point of total rupture," and forced the familial dispute to the level of "lineage or even clan importance" (147–48). The curse is thus something of a paradox: a provision of the law, it can serve the needs of justice as a last resort, but it is only a last resort because it stands outside the law.

Though frowned upon as an act of extreme desperation, the wife's curse does offer "an opportunity for a settlement of serious problems by a solemn ceremony" (148). Okot concludes, "The wife's curse posed a permanent threat for husbands with a tendency to trouble their wives. Everyone knew that if a man persisted in troubling his wife she might commit *kir*." Lawino can be seen, then, as making clear both to her husband and her people that she is close to invoking such a curse and forcing their society into a virtual state of emergency. In fact, she actually hints at the wife's curse at one point saying:

> If you annoy the girl
> She will strike the ash
> Then you will get
> Exactly what you ask for! (99)

She does not go so far as to say, "if you annoy *me*," but the threat is nevertheless clear. Like her insinuations about Tina's alleged witchcraft, Lawino's gestures toward the curse suggest that she is not a simple and idealized advocate of Acholi culture. She offers Ocol forgiveness and reconciliation; but, in the process, she also implies that if Ocol does not accept, she will make matters even worse. This could still be seen as an expression of faith in Acholi justice because the curse essentially raises the stakes and demands further attention from leaders in resolving the crisis, but it is also evidence of the ambivalence of the system: Okot appears to recognize that in its most extreme acts of eradicating harmful ghosts Acholi law may bring others into being.[22]

22 Of course, this is by no means a problem specific to Acholi law, and one could point to extreme provisions in nearly every legal system worldwide that have the potential to create new problems in the act of resolving others. The US prison system might be one example. However, given how enthusiastic many advocates and activists have been in promoting a romanticized version of Acholi justice in Northern Uganda in response to the LRA, it is important in drawing out the potential of Okot's contribution to understand his awareness of the specific dangers of the legal principles upon which Lawino relies.

Chapter 13 is Lawino's summation, her final word, the last chance she offers her husband to make things right. It consists entirely of an invitation to Ocol to submit voluntarily and return to his true place in the homestead. She begins:

> But Ocol, my husband,
> If you are not yet utterly dead
> And fit only for the stomach of the earth,
> If your heart-string
> Is not yet completely cut,
> If your ghost
> Has not yet escaped and got completely lost,
> If some blood is still flowing
> However faintly,
> Take courage,
> Take a small amount of millet porridge, Let them prop you up,
> Drink some fish soup
> Slowly, slowly
> You will recover. (117)

Lawino then outlines several rituals, each specifically designed to cleanse Ocol of a delusion or condition that developed through his apemanship. To clear his throat, he must "Chew the root of *omwombye*. / It is very bitter"; to unstop his ears, she prescribes "simsim oil"; to "remove the blood" that has clotted and blinded his eyes, "the ripe seeds of *labikka*"; "raw eggs mixed in millet flour" to make him "vomit / The shyness that [he] ate in the church"; and salt water to gargle and cleanse his mouth from "The abuses you learnt / From your white masters" (118–19). Here, again, Lawino's narrative resonates with recent debates about the efficacy of traditional reconciliation rituals in the post-LRA environment. The cleansing rituals she prescribes are similar in detail and purpose to those that have been used in Northern Uganda in recent years, including: *nyono tonggweno* ("stepping on the egg"), *lwoko pik wang* ("washing away the tears"), and *mato oput* (a reconciliation ceremony after a killing) (Harlacher et al. 65–91).

Once Ocol has been "completely cured," Lawino directs him to pay respects to his ancestors and seek forgiveness and blessing from the elders and his mother: "Let the elders / Spit blessing on you / Let them intercede for you" (119); "Let her spit blessing in your hands" (120). This blessing (which reminds one of the *possibility* of the curse, the blessing's performative opposite) signifies that the offender has acted correctly in seeking forgiveness. For Ocol, such blessings would indicate that his offenses against his wife and his people no longer had any power and that he could rejoin society (thereby healing both himself and the homestead) with a clear conscience. Lawino concludes by asking Ocol to let her show him the "wealth in [his] house," and she ends by reiterating a proverb that she has used throughout: "Let no one uproot the / Pumpkin" (120). Heron explains, "Pumpkins are a luxury food.

They grow wild throughout Acoliland. To uproot pumpkins, even when you are moving to a new homestead, is simple wanton destruction" ("Introduction" 7). Okot explains further: "Old customs which are harmless and may even be useful should not be uprooted. [This proverb] is used a great deal by old men who feel that the young educated men may throw the entire Acholi culture overboard" (*Acholi Proverbs* 37). Thus, Lawino's parting words entreat Ocol to desist in his destructive path, emphasizing the fact that there is much yet useful and beautiful in Acholi culture. Ultimately, she proves that she has done her part. It is now up to Ocol to confess and submit.[23]

In *Song of Ocol*, which marks the next step in the legal process, Ocol does confess willingly. He does not deny his wife's accusations. But he does not make his "confession" with the intent of seeking forgiveness. He rejects Lawino's invitations and, in the process, shamelessly confirms her depiction of him. His words are biting and swift. "Woman," he begins curtly, refusing even to use Lawino's name or address her as his wife, "Shut up! / Pack your things! / Go!" (121). He believes the homestead is at its end. Though slightly shorter than Lawino's song and only written in English, Ocol's response has a similar form with lengthy chapters (9 total to Lawino's 13) of dramatic monologue. The tone is at times vibrant, if bitter, and at others dejected. Ocol's language is less idiomatically Acholi, with fewer cultural references and oral intertexts, but there are still traces of a shared cultural vocabulary. However, in his state of crisis, Ocol wields this vocabulary as a weapon in striking back against his wife:

> Woman
> Your song
> Is rotting buffalo

23 The Acholi version of *Lawino* is one chapter longer than the English version and, thus, ends in a slightly different manner. As is evident in the fact that Okot first wrote the poem in 1956, expanded it later from 30 to nearly 200 pages, and then wrote an English version that differed in significant ways from the Acholi, the poem was constantly evolving (an indication, perhaps, of its relationship to orature). Okot's omission of the last chapter in the English version may have been part of this revisionary process. However, when asked why he stopped at chapter 13, Okot spoke of the difficulty of translating Acholi into English, which often required him to build un-poetic cultural explanations into the work. "The translation was so painful," he said, "I just could not go on" (Interview 293). Taban lo Liyong also asked "why he had not completed the translation. He said he was tired" ("On Translating"). In his criticisms of *Lawino*, Taban insists that Okot only translated whatever was "striking, dramatic, and sarcastic," leaving out the deeper, more philosophical portions of the poem, including chapter 14. In 2001, Taban published a more literal translation of the Acholi original and included the final chapter. Primarily, the chapter restates Lawino's arguments and departs somewhat from the tone and direction of the rest of the work, addressing issues of development near the end. Whatever Okot's reason for leaving out the last chapter, in the context of Acholi law, there is a logic to having the poem end at chapter 13 when Ocol's response is clearly invited.

Left behind by
Fleeing poachers,
Its nose blocked
With house-flies
Sucking bloody mucus [...]

Song of the woman
Is sour sweet,
It is pork gone rancid,
It is the honeyed
Bloodied sour milk
In the stinking
Maasai gourd. (123–24)

The imagery of decay reinforces Ocol's ultimate argument that the homestead is, or will soon be, dead. Ocol has fully embraced the colonial narratives of time and modernity, believing that the various aspects of Acholi culture that Lawino has described are worthless because primitive and that Africa must progress, urbanize, and build its foundation on the Western inheritance in order to move into the future.

At one point, Ocol turns from Lawino and addresses a larger East African audience, describing the "backwardness" of the Kalenjin, for example, and asserting that their "barren empire / Remained 'closed' to progress" (136). To Lawino, Ocol later says,

Weep long,
For the village world
That you know
And love so well,
Is gone,
Swept away
By the fierce fires
Of progress and civilization! (147)

Although Okot writes in *Artist, the Ruler* that "the African of tradition [...] is not interested, in the least, about the end of time" (44), Lawino's fears about the end of the homestead have a kind of apocalyptic tone. She is not concerned with the end of the world, as such, but with the end of the Acholi world. Ocol, who is no longer the "African of tradition," confirms that fear with apocalyptic imagery culled from his new Christian beliefs, characterizing as "fierce fires" the forces of modernity that will destroy "the village world." Indeed, in contrast to the preservationist nature of Lawino's appeal and her proverbial refrain about pumpkins, Ocol wishes to cleanse Africa by destroying all aspects of African culture and identity: "To hell / with your Pumpkins," he declares (126). "We will uproot / Every sacred tree / And demolish every ancestral shrine."

Moments such as these reinforce the apocalyptic future of the poems in the context of LRA violence. As noted earlier, Ocol and Joseph Kony are quite different in terms of the actual crimes they commit, although the spiritual consequences are similar. However, Ocol's potential offenses become increasingly serious in his response, and parallels with the LRA start to emerge: just as Ocol channels a kind of Old Testament furor in predicting the destruction of the "village world," the LRA originated in and was driven by an apocalyptic form of Old Testament/Christian-inspired spiritualism. Kony's predecessor, Alice Auma, formed the Holy Spirit Movement (HSM) to fight the recently established government of Yoweri Museveni. Auma, mixing Christian mythology with Acholi witchcraft, claimed to be a medium possessed by multiple spirits who directed her, including the spirit of a dead officer named "Lakwena."[24] (Auma, therefore, referred to herself as "Alice Lakwena," and she tends to be better known by this name.) The HSM had some military success as they attempted to advance toward Kampala in 1986, but they were eventually driven back by government forces, and, in the disarray that followed, Joseph Kony stepped in and formed the LRA. Like Auma/Lakwena, Kony claimed to be possessed by powerful spirits—embracing and deliberately identifying the "ghosts" that had captured his head—and, like Ocol, had an apocalyptic vision for the future of Uganda, which he intended to rule according to the Ten Commandments. Additionally, Kony succeeded in decimating the sacred trees, ancestral shrines, and social unity of the Acholi world. The violence of the LRA conflict—also perpetuated by the Ugandan army, which committed numerous atrocities against the Acholi people—disrupted the homestead that Lawino was so desperate to protect. The cult-like philosophies of the LRA would seem to be largely at odds with the idealistic claims of "civilization" and "progress," but Ocol invokes such ideals in articulating his vision of the apocalyptic destruction of African culture; similarly, Kony invokes Christian ideals in carrying out that very destruction.

As readers, we are supposed to sympathize somewhat with Ocol, recognizing, as does Lawino, that he is a victim of a colonial mentality and, indeed, of the colonial crisis of modernity which both craves and fears modernity. Ocol is deeply torn and his hatred of all things African becomes a hatred of self: "Mother, mother," he asks, "Why, / Why was I born / Black?" (126). However, today there is something uncanny and frightening about Ocol's apocalyptic declarations now that we have seen them fulfilled by the LRA. Significantly, among the many aspects of Acholi culture Ocol hopes to destroy are the creators of Acholi law:

24 In her fascinating study, *Alice Lakwena and the Holy Spirits* (1999), Heike Behrend writes, "The HSM conducted a war against war. Since it understood itself to be a Christian movement, in common with the Christian moral theologians in Europe, it had to ask itself whether warlike violence can be harmonized at all with Christian teaching. In point of fact, Lakwena attempted to conduct war and nonetheless adhere to Christian commandments. […] Lakwena [the spirit] was not a warmonger; for him, war was a necessary evil in order to achieve a new and better society" (57).

We will arrest
All the village poets
Musicians and tribal dancers,
Put in detention
Folk-story tellers
And myth makers,
The sustainers of
Village morality (129)

Although activists and others in Northern Uganda have been eager to promote the virtues of traditional justice, one of the problems Allen points out is that of authority: even if the reconciliation rituals are legitimate and not invented (in the Hobsbawm/Rangerian sense),[25] a legitimate authority figure must perform them. Allen summarizes a study conducted in 1999 by the Agency for Cooperation and Research in Development (ACORD) on the potential of traditional rituals; ACORD "concluded that traditional structures were weak and fragmented; that many of the 'elders' were themselves not sure how to carry out traditional rituals; that there was widespread disagreement about who were the *real* traditional leaders, and that few people considered the traditional structures a key priority" ("The International" 151; emphasis in original). These problems are the product of two things: 1) the legacies of indirect rule, which replaced legitimate authority figures with colonial-appointed chiefs, thus laying the groundwork for a future of uncertainty about who can speak for the Acholi; and 2) the LRA conflict itself, which tore communities apart, drove them from their homesteads, and thereby dismantled the social structures within which traditional authority may have had meaning. Okot anticipated such a state of affairs through Ocol's self-hating prediction: Ocol (and, therefore, Okot) knew that destroying a society's laws and law-makers was necessary if one were to destroy the society fully. Ocol threatened this, and Kony made it happen.

If the destruction of those who create law is one of the most damaging effects of colonial history and the LRA conflict, and if the "apocalyptic future" of Okot's poems allows them to speak to that conflict in some way, then we must ask: what is to be done? If Okot's texts anticipate and allow us to diagnose the effects of the LRA conflict, do they offer any solutions? The short answer is, no, they do not offer any solutions, but it would be a sign of overly simplistic reading on our part to look for solutions, at least in any straightforward sense. Indeed, the form of the debate between Lawino and Ocol explicitly refuses resolution: Ocol finishes his statement at the *wang oo* without remorse or reconciliation, rejecting Lawino's invitation and holding fast to his anti-African position (which is marked, as noted, by a kind of pathos as he reveals the extent to which he has internalized colonial alienation and descended into self-hatred). The conversation ends there. Like the other texts

25 See Hobsbawm and Ranger, *The Invention of Tradition* (1983).

I will examine in subsequent chapters, Okot's poems are radically open-ended: there is no closure, no satisfying resolution. Lawino appears to have failed, although she still has the option of committing the wife's curse; but Okot never wrote a follow-up song, so we can only speculate on whether or not this would happen. It is, thus, possible to read Lawino's failure as evidence of the failure and, therefore, irrelevance of the justice process in which she has placed so much faith.

However, it is important to see *Song of Ocol* as Okot's own effort to elicit shame and fear in those around him who had become victims of the colonial crisis of modernity. In her song, Lawino makes certain charges against Ocol; either she is telling the truth, or she is exaggerating and lying. Were Ocol to deny her charges, we would not be certain of the truth. Were Ocol to confess and submit willingly, there would be no need for his detailed response. However, Ocol does not deny her charges. Instead, he confirms her portrait of him. We learn that she has been telling the truth and, further, that his condition is worse than she imagined. Okot had to write Ocol's response as he did to justify the response and, more importantly, to elicit fear in his readers and shame in those who, like Ocol, had fallen prey to the destructive logic of colonial modernity. Reconciliatory justice is still necessary, but it is imperative that society act quickly because there is a point at which, as with Ocol, individuals can be lost. Furthermore, the open-endedness of the dispute corresponds to and reinforces the other aspects of the poems that draw out and attempt to negotiate the complexities of Acholi law. Okot does not endorse this law or "traditional justice" in a simplistic way, nor does he romanticize that law, though some have accused him of doing so more generally with respect to Acholi culture.[26] Lawino makes a compelling case for the value of Acholi traditional culture, but she also reveals some of its weaknesses and potential pitfalls: specifically, that Acholi justice can facilitate reconciliation and forgiveness, but it can also be vindictive, channeling the fury of aggrieved persons into highly punitive and socially destructive acts. We might say that Okot does express a kind of faith in Acholi justice and what it can achieve, but it is a tentative, cautious faith that recognizes that Acholi justice must be used carefully and with an awareness of its potential dangers.

Additionally, Lawino's apparent failure looks less like failure when we examine it not only in the context of Okot's statements about law in *Artist, the Ruler* but also his statements about temporality and progress. After he identifies the oral artist as a law-maker in *Artist, the Ruler*, Okot devotes the next two chapters to questions of temporality in African thought. Given the fact that orature emerges throughout East African history to contest the

26 Ngũgĩ argues, for example, that Okot risks romanticizing and idealizing culture and is, therefore, "in danger of emphasizing culture as if it could be divorced from its political and economic basis" ("Introduction" to *Africa's Cultural Revolution* xii).

temporal narratives that lie under colonial law and its residues, it is hardly a coincidence that Okot gives successive attention first to oral jurisprudence and then to questions of temporality. In the first essay, "Time and History," Okot insists that the concept of history and the idea of a distant past are of no concern to the "African of tradition" who only remembers "those events and personalities that explain, make meaningful and justify the present" (42). Of course, "tradition" is not an entirely straightforward concept, so we might take issue with Okot's generalization here,[27] but within the terms of his larger narrative critiquing the negative effects of colonial mimicry, the figure of the African of tradition plays an important role. In terms of models of temporality, the worldview of such a figure has a very different relationship to time than those who teach and embrace the colonial perspective. In fact, Lawino devotes a chapter of her *Song* to the difference between Ocol's obsessive Westernized time-keeping (i.e., "Time is money" [67]) and the Acholi model of pragmatic temporality, or time-keeping as dictated by practical necessity (i.e, "There is no fixed time / For breast feeding" [68]).

For Okot, this difference indicates the irrelevance of colonial myths of time for Africa. In "The African Historian," the essay following "Time and History," Okot writes that for "traditional" Africans "there is no concept of history moving 'forward' towards a future climax, or towards the end of the world" (48). He takes this a step further, however, and asks, "But what of the concept of 'progress,' 'development' as understood especially by our political leaders?" In other words, he ties the temporal narratives of colonial culture to the neo-liberal narratives of progress in the postcolonial period, and his conclusion is that "progress," as colonialism defined it for Africans, is meaningless. "But who, in his right senses, would like to catch up with the so-called West?" he asks. Instead, Okot offers an alternative definition of progress, which I argue is implied by the open-ended structure of the *Song of Lawino / Song of Ocol* dispute. "If 'progress' has any meaning," Okot writes, "then it means making life more meaningful. This, in turn, means ensuring the maximum participation of every individual in the productive activities of the society here and now: in politics, economics, artistic and all other fields of human endeavor" (48–49). By calling an open court and inviting Ocol's participation in a productive activity of the here and now,

27 The classic articulation of the complex nature of "tradition" is, of course, Hobsbawm and Ranger's *The Invention of Tradition* (1983), although Ranger later revised some of his ideas in "The Invention of Tradition Revisited: The Case of Colonial Africa" (1993). Okot's insistence that "traditional" Africans were unconcerned with history might invite some criticism, although I would compare his effort to ground a historical consciousness or narrative of time in African thought to the work of the Subaltern Studies collective who sought to do away with historical methodologies that treated European history as a necessary template; or, as Dipesh Chakrabarty put it much more succinctly, they sought to "provincialize Europe" (*Provincializing* 254).

Lawino is giving "progress" new meaning, or is inscribing it within a new regime of intelligibility designed to make sense of the crisis of Acholi society. Although Ocol's participation does not necessarily resolve that crisis, he does participate. In that sense, Lawino is not a failure, and those aspects of Acholi justice that brought Ocol to the table and encouraged him to take part are vindicated. This suggests, further, that a similar approach to progress may be essential to post-conflict reconciliation in Northern Uganda. Okot ultimately does not solely privilege Acholi justice, and similarly, his works, if we can access their potential apocalyptic future in the wake of LRA violence, would suggest a broadly inclusive process that would ensure "the maximum participation of every individual," including perpetrators, victims, and advocates of traditional and international forms of justice. This is not to say that Okot's poems should be forced into the LRA conversation and reduced to a policy treatise, but perhaps it is possible, given the renewed significance of the texts, for them to be read in a way that could inform, problematize, or at least raise questions about the central issues of the reconciliation process, particularly if so many scholars are already turning to Okot in writing about Northern Uganda. If we are to read him responsibly and allow the "maximum participation" of his texts rather than treating them as a kind of native informant, we will find he has much more to say and much more to offer those interested in questions of justice in Northern Uganda and, indeed, in comparable contexts throughout the global south.

An Idea Whose Time Has Come: Kony 2012 or Okot p'Bitek?

In 2012, more people than ever suddenly became interested in Joseph Kony and the question of justice: on March 5 of that year, the US-based non-governmental organization (NGO) Invisible Children released a 30-minute video titled "KONY 2012." The film begins with the captivating declaration, "NOTHING IS MORE POWERFUL THAN AN IDEA WHOSE TIME HAS COME." Seven seconds in, the phrase "HAS COME" transforms into "IS NOW." Filled with anticipation, the viewer is left asking, "*What* idea?" As is well known, even now, years after the film became one of the most successful viral videos in history, the answer is that 2012 is the year Joseph Kony *will be stopped*. Nearly overnight, the film was viewed and shared by millions of people throughout the world (over one hundred million, in fact, according to YouTube) who suddenly knew the name *Joseph Kony*. They also knew he was bad. And they knew he had to be stopped (preferably by the US military). Invisible Children was unprepared for the tidal wave of support that gathered so immediately behind the idea whose time had come, and almost as quickly as it gained what would prove to be an unsustainable momentum, the well-intentioned campaign began to weaken and eventually crumble in the face of extensive criticisms from Ugandans, scholars, activists, and others who pointed out several fatal flaws in the film's representation of the conflict in Northern Uganda.[28] Prominent among the criticisms is an idea that can be summed up in one word: belatedness. Why, in other words, is this passionate, compelling, and wildly successful call to capture Joseph Kony appearing now? As many who had followed, studied, and worked to end the conflict knew, Invisible Children was coming to the problem relatively late. By 2012, Joseph Kony was no longer operating in Northern Uganda, and his followers had dwindled to a few hundred soldiers.[29]

Despite this belatedness, Kony 2012 caught the world's attention, largely because most people did not know it was belated, and the gripping narrative of innocent children threatened by an evil African warlord simply demanded justice. The LRA war had already become one of the major crises in East Africa that had drawn the attention and contributed to the direction of international law. In 2005, the International Criminal Court issued its first arrest warrants, and first among them was one for Joseph Kony. Because this was its initial case, writes Tim Allen, "The ICC had much to prove [...]. Doubtless 'the situation concerning the Lord's Resistance Army' seemed like a relatively simple case to start with, one that would help establish the court's credentials" (*Trial Justice* 82). However, the case was much more complicated than initially assumed—in part, because of tensions with those who favored "traditional" rather than international justice—and Kony much more difficult to apprehend. Although the LRA had weakened, Kony was still at large in 2012, and, no doubt because of this, one of the many prominent individuals to support Invisible Children's campaign was the ICC Chief Prosecutor Louis Moreno Ocampo (who appears in the Kony 2012 film).[30] For someone who had long called and fought for Kony's arrest, it was a great relief to see global awareness of the LRA leader's crimes and support for aggressive intervention in the region, even if it was coming a little late. If nothing else, for better or for worse, Kony 2012 put East Africa and its complicated relationship to international law once again in the spotlight.

28 Given the massive global response to the film, the criticisms are also particularly capacious in number, although some of those that had the greatest impact early on would include the Ugandan journalist Rosebell Kagumire's YouTube video "My Response to Kony 2012" (2012); Teju Cole's series of tweets on March 8, which he discussed in more detail in a follow-up article, "The White-Savior Industrial Complex" (March 21, 2012); and, among others, Dinaw Mengistu's "Not a Click Away: Joseph Kony in the Real World" (March 12, 2012).

29 After the immediate wave of criticisms, the Kony 2012 campaign tried to recover by releasing a second video (called "Kony 2012 Part II: Beyond Famous") that attempted to take a more nuanced and historically accurate approach to the crisis in Northern Uganda, but it received significantly less attention, with 2.8 million views compared to the over 100 million views of the first film.

30 Although Kony is still at large as of the writing of this book, in 2015, Dominic Ongwen, one of the LRA leaders, was apprehended after he surrendered himself in the Central African Republic and he was immediately handed over to the ICC. He became the first LRA member to appear before the court. See "LRA Commander Dominic Ongwen Appears before ICC in The Hague" (2015).

In the years since its precipitous rise and fall, the Kony 2012 phenomenon has been the subject of a number of studies on a range of issues from the problems of "military humanitarianism" and naive youth activism to lessons that other NGOs and companies can learn from Kony 2012's social media strategies.[31] What I find interesting, however, are the unusual temporalities at work both internal and external to the Invisible Children campaign, which had a particular form of justice as its ultimate goal. Like other humanitarian campaigns, Kony 2012 was marked by a nearly apocalyptic sense of urgency and immediacy: nothing is more powerful than an idea whose time is *now*; the time to act is *now*; donate *now*. Such aggressive presentism presumes the moral validity of its claims, thus pushing aside time-consuming critical thought, debate, and historical reflection in favor of immediate and decisive action. Along with the charge of belatedness, in fact, one of the most damaging criticisms of Kony 2012 was that it dehistoricized "a murky reality of globalized war into an essentialized black-and-white story" (Finnström, "KONY 2012" 130).[32] This story inadvertently repeated colonial assumptions about Africa as being temporally stunted (i.e., "not yet" able to solve its own crises) and not having a history worth noting. The campaign's belatedness, in fact, was a symptom of this lack of historical perspective: had Invisible Children better understood the history of the LRA and the wider issues of increased militarization in central Africa, then perhaps it would have recognized its place in the timeline and advocated an approach better suited to the needs of Northern Uganda in 2012. However, that would also likely have meant a significantly less attractive campaign.

The forms of urgency and immediacy, belatedness and historical blindness that characterized Kony 2012 form an important contrast to the writings and ideas of Okot p'Bitek. Whereas the apocalyptic urgency of Kony 2012 was ultimately undone by its belatedness (among other problems, of course), Okot's texts, which would normally be considered outmoded or anachronistic, found their way into more nuanced discussions about the LRA and the challenges

31 See, for example, Finnström, "'KONY 2012,' Military Humanitarianism, and the Magic of Occult Economies" (2012); Gregory, "Kony 2012 Through a Prism of Video Advocacy Practices and Trends" (2012); Drumbl, "Child Soldiers and Clicktivism: Justice, Myths, and Prevention" (2012); Bal et al., "Do Good, Goes Bad, Gets Ugly: Kony 2012" (2013); and, among many others, Cronin-Furman and Taub, "Solving War Crimes with Wristbands: The Arrogance of 'Kony 2012'" (2014).

32 Similar criticisms were made of the Save Darfur campaign, which also relied on a rhetoric of urgency and immediacy in trying to prompt action. In a short film made for the campaign, for example, celebrities and world leaders such as Matt Damon, Don Cheadle, Archbishop Desmond Tutu, and others stand silently holding and then dropping a series of cards on which are written pleas for an end to the killing. They typically end with a card reading, "Ceasefire Now." See "Celebrities Speak Out for Darfur" (2007). Mahmood Mamdani's book *Saviors and Survivors: Darfur, Politics, and the War on Terror* (2010) pointed out and sought to remedy the lack of historical perspective in the Save Darfur campaign.

of post-conflict reconciliation. Kony 2012 claimed to present an idea whose time had come, but I argue that it was Okot's ideas whose time had come and whose time *has* come both in the sense that Okot's ideas about law, justice, and the challenges of progress and modernization suddenly took on new life or had the potential to take on new life in the context of LRA discussions, but also that the time has come for scholars of LRA issues to recognize this potential; to see Okot as more than a trusted cultural authority, indeed to see him as a poet/law-maker whose artistic legislations were simultaneously *of* and *ahead of* their time, offering ideas that rival those of others in the debate about what is at stake in choosing local or global forms of justice and whether or not true progress can be realized in the here and now. Furthermore, Okot is just one example of the potential for texts that draw on the authoritative discourses of oral jurisprudence to speak to the larger legal and political crises of the global south and modern law more generally. I examine other examples in subsequent chapters, but there remains a great deal to be done not only to develop a better understanding of Okot's potential contribution to debates about international law but also the potential contribution of other writers, artists, experts in orature, etc. whose works blur the boundaries between the legal and the aesthetic and open new ways of approaching the legacies of colonial temporality in modern law today.

CHAPTER THREE

Between Formal and Infinite Time: Labor Law and Revolutionary Futures in Kenyan Popular Performance

> We have stolen his land. Now we must steal his limbs. [...] Compulsory labour in some form is the corollary of our occupation of the country.
>
> Ewart Grogan, *From the Cape to Cairo* (1902)

> Peasants do not write, they are written about. The speech of humble folk is not normally recorded for posterity, it is wrenched from them in courtrooms and inquisitorial trials.
>
> Shahid Amin, *Event, Metaphor, Memory* (1995)

In 1977, Ngũgĩ wa Thiong'o was promoted to the position of Associate Professor of Literature at the University of Nairobi. One of his colleagues, Okot p'Bitek, expressed concern that Ngũgĩ's promotion indicated his official absorption into the "institutions of education and power in Kenya" and that, as a result, "he could no longer be interested in incorporating popular and oral culture into his work or the literature curriculum" (Gikandi, *Ngũgĩ* 195). Okot was, of course, an advocate of popular culture, and oral culture in particular, and just as Ngũgĩ worried that Okot focused too much on the cultural at the expense of the economic and political, Okot worried that Ngũgĩ had now conformed too much to the institutions of power for politics' sake at the expense of the popular, the cultural, and the oral. However, as Simon Gikandi observes, Okot's "fears were soon proven unfounded." At this time, Ngũgĩ had been working with Ngũgĩ wa Mĩriĩ, a researcher in adult literacy at Kenya's Institute for Development Studies, on writing a new play in collaboration with Kikuyu villagers and workers at the Kamĩrĩĩthũ Cultural Centre at Limuru. The play, *Ngaahika Ndeenda* (translated in English as *I Will Marry When I Want* [1977]), was the product of what has often been called an "experiment" in rural theater: a play composed and performed through the collective efforts of Kenyans who had little or no formal training in writing, musical composition, or acting. The community built the Cultural Centre in order to promote education, literacy (in Gĩkũyũ, not English), and cultural traditions within the village, and *I Will Marry When I Want* was the Centre's first major achievement. Integrating indigenous songs with a plot representing the struggles of everyday Africans, *I Will Marry When I Want* gained the immediate attention of the Kenyan people. Word spread, and, Gikandi writes, "as throngs of workers, peasants, and students boarded buses and trucks to see the performance of *I Will Marry When I Want*, p'Bitek was impressed enough to declare the experiment at Kamĩrĩĩthũ the most important event on the African literary and cultural scene in the postcolonial period." Gikandi continues, "For the first time, p'Bitek told an Oral Literature Seminar at the University of Nairobi, intellectuals had taken culture to the people and the people were teaching them the terms by which they understood and represented cultural experiences and expressions."

The success of this effort of learning the terms of representation and cultural experience from the people did not go unnoticed by the Kenyan government. It was not long after the play's performance that Ngũgĩ was arrested and detained for a year in Kamiti Maximum Security Prison without trial or formal charges, although it was understood that his offense had everything to do with the success of Kamĩrĩĩthũ. Ngũgĩ's detention no doubt further reinforced Okot's realization that his colleague was far from being accepted by Kenya's institutions of power, except in the sense of having been accepted as an inmate in one of the state's most *institutional* mechanisms of power, the prison. Moreover, Ngũgĩ's detention further reinforced his own commitment to the Kenyan people—the poor, the workers, the oppressed—and to African arts.

While in prison, after reflecting deeply upon his experiences at Kamĩrĩĩthũ, Ngũgĩ famously decided to abandon English in favor of Gĩkũyũ as the primary language of his literary works, later articulated in *Decolonising the Mind* (1986). He wrote his first Gĩkũyũ novel *Caitaani Mũtharaba-inĩ* (*Devil on the Cross* [1982]) while in prison (and on prison-issued toilet paper) and has since published multiple works in Gĩkũyũ, including his most recent novel *Mũrogi wa Kagogo* (*Wizard of the Crow* [2005]). Critics have recognized that this crucial turn to Gĩkũyũ marks a stylistic and ideological break in Ngũgĩ's oeuvre from the Anglo-Modernist realism of *Petals of Blood* (1976) and his earlier novels to the later novels which were written in Gĩkũyũ and draw heavily on African orature.[1] Although oral conventions figure in his earlier works to a limited

1 See, for example, Simon Gikandi's "The Postcolonial Wizard" (2008); Evan Mwangi's "Gender, Unreliable Oral Narration, and the Untranslated Preface in Ngũgĩ wa Thiong'o's *Devil on the Cross*" (2007); Alamin Mazuri and Lupenga Mphande's "Orality and the Literature of Combat: The Legacy of Fanon" (2000); Christopher Wise's "Resurrecting the Devil: Notes on Ngũgĩ's Theory of the Oral–Aural African

extent, his later works, beginning in particular with *The Trial of Dedan Kimathi* (1976) and *I Will Marry When I Want*, increasingly recognize the power of orality and experiment with blurring the boundary between the written and the oral in narrative and performance. However, there is a third dimension of Ngũgĩ's turn—language and orality being the first two—that demands greater attention, and it is directly related to Ngũgĩ's experience in both Kamĩrĩĩthũ and Kamiti: not only does Ngũgĩ turn to the Gĩkũyũ language and the aesthetics and politics of orature around the time of his detention, but he also turns his attention to the law. As I argue in this chapter, the coincidence of orature, performance, and the law in Ngũgĩ's work is not a coincidence at all, but a product of the fact that African orature is a powerful means of challenging and *rivaling* the laws of the State, in which the residues of colonial law's temporalities persist.

Such temporalities manifest themselves in a variety of ways in the postcolonial period. In the forms of emergency law, for example, we witness the contradictory pattern of progress being protected through the disruption and suspension of progress, and for this reason I consider indirect rule to be a kind of emergency law. The "normal" rule of law that colonialism offered its colonies was suspended in the face of a threat, which required an exceptional form of law (indirect rule) to restore order and peace. And, as with most forms of emergency law, indirect rule was theoretically a temporary solution that became permanent. In particular, the narratives of time and modernity that authorized indirect rule became deeply ingrained in various colonial and later postcolonial forms of governance. In the events surrounding Ngũgĩ's detention, for example, we see variations on these narratives and the crisis of which they were a part: Ngũgĩ's detention order was authorized by an emergency regulation which had its roots in the colonial period,[2] and rather than embrace the work of the Community Centre, which focused on education, job training, democratic participation, etc. (i.e., what one might call modernization), the government ultimately destroyed the Centre and built a technical/vocational school in its place.

There is nothing inherently wrong with such a school, of course, but in the Kenyan context it was a symbol of colonial-inherited forms of modernity, the purpose of which was to inhibit actual progress or to inhibit progress defined from within the "terms by which [the people] understood and represented cultural experiences and expressions" (Gikandi, *Ngũgĩ* 195).

The government's choice to build this school underscores the central term around which these debates and contestations circled, and in which can be found one of the more penetrating forms of the colonial crisis of modernity:

Novel" (1997); and F. Odun Balogun, *Ngũgĩ and African Postcolonial Narrative: The Novel as Oral Narrative in Multigenre Performance* (1997).

2 A facsimile of Ngũgĩ's detention order, authorized under "The Public Security (Detained and Restructed Persons) Regulations 1966," appears at the beginning of *Detained: A Writer's Prison Diary* (1981).

labor. After Ngũgĩ's release from detention but before the Community Centre was destroyed, the Kamĩrĩĩthũ group reunited to write a second play, titled *Maitu, Njugira* (*Mother, Sing for Me*). The principal concern of this play is the history of labor law in Kenya. Alongside the "native question," to which indirect rule was a response, and the "land question," the "labor question" was considered one of the most important in the colonial period. Indeed, as Ewart Grogan wrote somewhat dramatically (and, to a degree, ironically) in 1902, "We have stolen his [the African's] land. Now we must steal his limbs. [...] Compulsory labour in some form is the corollary of our occupation of the country" (377–78).[3] Land law and labor law were, therefore, two

3 Grogan, along with Lord Delamere, was one of the most influential settlers in colonial Kenya from 1904 until independence. He died in 1967. This quotation has become famous, or perhaps infamous, as an expression of the openly cruel motivations of colonial land and labor acquisition. It is typically attributed to "Colonel Grogan," a Kenyan settler, who was speaking specifically about the settler's open and malicious theft of Kikuyu land and limb. Most references to Grogan's statement, however, either do not include a source citation or refer back to Walter Rodney's influential *How Europe Underdeveloped Africa* (1972). See Loomba, *Colonialism/Postcolonialism* (2015), p. 132; Podmore, *British Foreign Policy since 1870* (2008), p. 30; Rwegasira, *Land as a Human Right* (2012), p. xviii. Rodney also does not include a source citation, and it is my suspicion that most iterations of the quotation since Rodney's book have cited Rodney's text and, consequently, repeated his phrasing. It is a minor matter, but nevertheless important to understand that Grogan has not only been misquoted, in a sense, but largely misunderstood. The quotation comes from the revised edition of his book *From the Cape to Cairo*, which he published in 1902, *before* he ever set foot in Kenya. His book primarily recounts his famous expedition as the first person—or, at least, first European—to traverse on foot the whole of the African continent from the south to the north. As was typical of colonial travel memoirs, however, the author pauses to comment on pressing colonial questions, including, obviously, that dealing with labor, but his focus was explicitly on South Africa, not Kenya. Furthermore, in the pages leading up to his confession that they have stolen African land and will now steal his limbs, Grogan expresses strong criticisms of the colonial project. He asks, "Why are we in Africa?" and then laments "that we, the strenuous, the snob-ridden, the crude dross-hunting victims of a hideous mesh of blatant greed and misery meek, have ever crossed their path" (376). Later, he writes, "I have seen too much of the world to have any lingering beliefs that Western civilization benefits native races. Socially, physically and morally its advent is their death-knell" (377). He then observes that, despite this danger, "we have taken up the task," and, therefore, they need to understand what that means: i.e., we have stolen his land; now we must steal his limbs. He is not endorsing this theft; rather, he is recognizing that what they have done is wrong, but they are essentially in too deep. We have committed half of the crime, he seems to say: we have no choice now but to keep going. Contemporary readers will surely still find these statements distasteful—was it really necessary to keep going? Why could they not just have given the land back? Nevertheless, Grogan's views are significantly more complex than generally assumed. Despite this early critical perspective on colonialism, however, Grogan would go on to acquire significant

parts of a larger project by which the colonialist took land from the African, claimed it as his own, and in an act of cruel irony then forced the African to return to the land in a different capacity as a laborer within a capitalist economy. Furthermore, indirect rule framed them both: for how could enterprising settlers build an agricultural economy on their newly acquired lands when native workers experienced the kind of disorder and social unrest that indirect rule was supposed to prevent? A docile, well-ordered native population makes for a more effective labor population. This was one of the goals of indirect rule in parts of Africa—including Kenya[4]—and yet we see the colonial crisis again rearing its contradictory head: indirect rule was supposed to protect Africans from the harmful effects of contact with modernity, but labor—including, often, *compulsory* labor—which indirect rule helped make possible, was "a central element in the civilizing mission of European rule" (Anderson, "Kenya" 498–99). Forcing Africans to become laborers was justified, in other words, because it would put them on the path to progress (indeed, on Maine's path "from Status to Contract").[5] The system designed to protect Africans from modernity made possible a system designed to introduce them to modernity. What's more, as we saw in Chapter 1, labor was the preferred antidote to the "disease" of Mau Mau, or the psychic distress colonialists claimed was caused by the overwhelming

amounts of land in Kenya, requiring the use of native labor. For more on Grogan, see Edward Paice's biography, *Lost Lion of Empire: The Life of "Cape-to-Cairo" Grogan* (2001).

4 Although indirect rule was not implemented in the same manner in Kenya as it was in other colonies (see Chapter 1), many of the contradictory narratives still circulated and provided the basis for other forms of law, including emergency law as we saw in the previous chapter. On indirect rule's relationship to labor, however, Bruce Berman writes, "The preservation of indigenous structures of authority was seen as essential for the transformation of precolonial labour and production in the direction required by imperial needs without provoking social collapse and bitter struggle" (*Control and Crisis* 209). At the same time, however, this transformation led to significant "contradictions in the political economy": "The greater the pressure put on the indigenous authorities to reshape the underlying society, the greater the danger of their collapse; while to equip them to manage the economic sphere meant 'modernization' into a bureaucratized, subordinate extension of the colonial state, a process that progressively destroyed their traditional legitimacy" (209).

5 Even though labor was often forced in colonial Kenya, workers were still given contracts. This entitled them to wages, which distinguished their employment from simple slavery, but, more importantly, it gave settlers greater power and allowed them to maintain the appearance of legitimacy in controlling their workers: i.e., anyone who tried to abandon their employment "opportunity" was in breach of contract and, therefore, could be legally punished. In Chapter 1, we saw one example of the unfair use of contract law in Isak Dinesen's response to the Kyama. See also Anderson, "Kenya, 1895–1938: Registration and Rough Justice" (2004).

pace of modernity, which indirect rule was supposed to prevent. What these contradictory narratives of modernity and justification sought to conceal, of course, was a project of control: indirect rule was less about protecting Africans from modernity than protecting colonialists from resistance; and colonial land and labor laws were designed not to modernize Africans but to exploit them for economic benefit. And just as the residues of indirect rule lingered during the postcolonial period, so too did the exploitative objectives of the labor system. One of the strongest condemnations of this system and its history is found in the play *Mother, Sing for Me*, and one of its most effective methods of critique is oral jurisprudence.

This chapter examines Ngũgĩ's collaborative drama in the 1970s and 1980s, a period that marks a crucial turning point in Ngũgĩ's career and demonstrates the extent to which his critiques of the postcolonial state and its laws rely heavily upon oral culture. I focus, first, on the play Ngũgĩ co-authored with Mĩcere Githae Mugo, *The Trial of Dedan Kimathi* (1976), and then turn to the second and lesser-known of the two Kamĩrĩĩthũ plays, *Maitu Njugira*, or *Mother, Sing for Me*, which was first written and rehearsed in 1981–82 but is still unpublished.[6] *The Trial of Dedan Kimathi* and *Mother, Sing for Me* both draw heavily on oral conventions and, in fact, the latter is arguably more a musical than a conventional play given its extensive incorporation of songs from different Kenyan language traditions. Both plays are also interested in colonial law and its residual effects in the postcolonial period.[7] Ngũgĩ's post-detention novels also draw on oral conventions, are interested in labor questions, and could be read from a perspective that recognizes orature's relationship to law,[8] but for my purposes I choose to focus on his

6 I am grateful to Ngũgĩ wa Thiong'o for generously providing me with a copy of the English version of the play and for sharing his insights into its context and production. As of 2020, the play is still not published, although one of the Gĩkũyũ performances was recorded and is available on YouTube. See "MAITU NJUGIRA: A PLAY BY NGUGI WA THIONGO WHICH WAS BANNED BY MOI" (2016).

7 I could certainly have included *I Will Marry When I Want* in this study beyond simply recognizing its important place as a product of the Kamĩrĩĩthũ project. It is also heavily invested in orature, blurs temporal boundaries, and raises questions about law, particularly in terms of contracts and land ownership. It is an important work to which law and literature scholars should give more attention, but I leave it out here given the much more explicit forms of law and oral jurisprudence found in *Kimathi* and *Mother, Sing for Me*, and because much less is known about the latter play.

8 *Devil on the Cross* (1982), for example, was not only written during Ngũgĩ's detention, but it opens with an oral-inspired narrator who identifies himself as the "Prophet of Justice" and describes how the people of Ilmorog pleaded with him, the Gĩcaandĩ Player, to tell their story. He accepts, and the subsequent narrative is, thus, the story he tells (see pp. 7–9). *Matigari* (1989) is the story of a former Mau Mau freedom fighter who, after independence, comes out of hiding in the forests to wander the country "in search of truth and justice" (59). The novel had such an impact in Kenya that it, like Ngũgĩ's other works, stimulated

drama in this transitional period of his career. Literary critics tend to give more attention to Ngũgĩ's novels than his "experiments" with drama, as if to suggest, as the term "experiment" does, something anomalous about this area of his work.[9] I wish to speculate, however, that were it not for the harsh response of the government in shutting down the Kamĩrĩĩthũ Centre and performances of both *I Will Marry When I Want* and *Mother, Sing for Me*, Ngũgĩ very likely would have gone on to produce many more plays, perhaps even focusing more on popular drama than fiction. His dramatic period is, therefore, less an anomaly than a suggestion of what might have been, a utopian imaginary whose promise went unfulfilled at the hands of a paranoid government threatened by any sign of collective movement among its people. "Kamĩrĩĩthũ," Ngũgĩ writes in *Decolonising the Mind*, "had given palpable form to a vision of Kenya's future—a Kenya for Kenyans, a self-reliant Kenya for a self-reliant people, a vision embodying a communal ethos of democracy and independence" (61). That the promise was unfulfilled does not mean, however, that it never can be. In keeping with the larger argument of this book, therefore, I will also discuss the continued relevance of Ngũgĩ's short-lived dramatic career and investments in oral jurisprudence. In particular, I will briefly discuss *Kenyan Tea Workers* v. *Unilever plc and Unilever Tea Kenya Ltd* [2015], in which a group of Kenyan laborers sued their UK-based employer for failing to protect them from attacks after the 2007 presidential election. These and other incidents represent continued efforts to grapple with the legacies of colonial law's underlying narratives, and although Ngũgĩ's drama has not reemerged in the same way Okot's poetry has, it nevertheless presents a concerted engagement with colonial law and temporality through oral performance that can shed light on cases like *Kenyan Tea Workers*.

In this chapter, I first describe key aspects of the history of labor law in Kenya, discussing its origins in the early years of the colony when settlers

---

a response from the forces of law and order, who actually issued an arrest warrant for the novel's main character, whom they believed to be real. And in Ngũgĩ's most recent novel, *Wizard of the Crow* (2006), which Gikandi and others have shown to be heavily invested in oral traditions, the dictator of the fictional country of Aburĩria issues various Acts and laws to support his oppressive rule and, at one point, has an epiphany about the power of sovereign command (in the spirit of Austinian positive law): "When he saw that his signature on paper or a word from his mouth could bring about the immediate cessation of a life, he there and then truly believed in his omnipotence. He was now sovereign" (233). All of this is simply to say, of course, that many of the themes and issues in Ngũgĩ's plays that I examine in this chapter could also be traced through his novels and read from a law and literature perspective. For a recent treatment of Ngũgĩ's novels *Weep Not, Child* (1964) and *A Grain of Wheat* (1967) in relationship to colonial emergency law, see Morton, *States of Emergency: Colonialism, Literature and Law* (2013), pp. 119–45.

9 See, for example, Gĩchingiri Ndĩgĩrĩgĩ's *Ngũgĩ wa Thiong'o's Drama and the Kamĩrĩĩthũ Popular Theater Experiment* (2007).

(like Isak Dinesen) were trying to build a strong agricultural economy, to its development through and past the period of independence when the promises of a free and equal society remained perpetually unfulfilled. Although labor is only one area of any society's system of law (and has an important relationship to land law in the colonial context),[10] in Kenya during both the colonial and postcolonial periods it dominated the political and economic scene. By using oral jurisprudence to critique colonial labor laws, Ngũgĩ and his co-authors seek to define a "regime of intelligibility" from which new forms of justice, law, and labor might emerge. That *Mother, Sing for Me* is also marked by peculiar modes of temporality, including formal open-endedness and futurity, reinforces the extent to which the play is attentive not only to land and labor but also the deeper narratives of time and modernity that gave meaning to colonial law throughout its history. I preface my analysis of *Mother, Sing for Me* with a reading of Ngũgĩ's earlier play *The Trial of Dedan Kimathi* (1976). Like *Mother, Sing for Me*, *Kimathi* is explicitly about law and shares an interest in orature's capacity to work on and with residual forms of colonial legality. More importantly, Ngũgĩ and Mĩcere write that the play must be seen as "breaking the barrier between formal and infinite time," and this allows us to see how *Mother, Sing for Me* engages in a similar kind of temporal disruption. Paired with *Kimathi*, my reading of *Mother, Sing for Me* will convey the development and trajectory of Ngũgĩ's increasing use of orature and collective work to critique and rival the legacies of colonial land and labor laws and, at the same time, to continue

10 Ngũgĩ, of course, does address issues of land throughout his work, but his focus in *Mother, Sing for Me* is ultimately on labor law, for reasons that will become clear through the course of this chapter. Other texts written around this time address land more directly, however, and would be worth thinking about in this context: for example, Ismael Mbise's novel *Blood on Our Land* (1974) delves into land issues in colonial Tanzania. In particular, Mbise tells the story of his own Meru people in the years leading up to the famous Meru Land Case (1951). In that case, Meru resisted the colonial "alienation" of their lands, ultimately appealing to the United Nations to intervene. Although they lost, the case received widespread attention nationally and internationally, giving force to the independence movement within the country as well as drawing attention to the plight of subjugated peoples globally. Mbise critiques the practice of colonial land alienation (technically, the "voluntary" transfer of real property from one person to another) and depicts a somewhat romantic view of the pre-colonial Meru world in which land and law were inseparable: "Tradition itself was tantamount to law. For what indeed was law but a traditional formality agreed upon and adhered to by our predecessors. Our predecessors who had gone before us, yet lived with us through *land*. All the tradition, all the formality, all the life gone, present and coming, were united by *land*. Land was the material foundation of people's lives" (5; emphasis in original). In addition, Mbise depicts the land/labor connection, showing how settlers forced Africans from their lands but then forced them to return to work the land as if alien to it. For more on the Meru Land Case, see Japhet and Seaton, *The Meru Land Case* (1967) and Spear, *Mountain Farmers* (1997), pp. 209–35.

exploring ways of suspending colonial time within which the myths of labor originated and, in the postcolonial period, continued to flourish.

Labor Law and Exceptional Power in Colonial and Postcolonial Kenya

The history of labor law in Kenya is, of course, impossible to cover in any comprehensive way in a chapter such as this, and, in fact, volumes have been written and will no doubt continue to be written on the subject.[11] What I hope to cover here are some of the key moments of that history that pertain to Ngũgĩ's plays. In particular, I am interested in identifying the relationship between labor law and emergency law, two areas of legislative and regulatory praxis that would seem to have little to do with one another. However, not only are there important intersections between the two areas of law in Kenyan history, but by understanding the unfair labor practices as manifestations of exceptional power we can go beyond a general critique of such practices to a deeper understanding of the particular mechanisms and cultural myths that structure and legitimate Kenya's autocratic labor laws. With this understanding, we will then be better prepared to understand the nature and strategic effects of the myths of labor and time that Ngũgĩ and his co-authors confront and reinvent.

In his book *The Jurisprudence of Emergency: Colonialism and the Rule of Law* (2003), Nasser Hussain argues that the history of colonial law has been characterized and conditioned by the continual need to declare states of emergency or to suspend the normal rule of law in the face of some internal or external threat for the sake of restoring law and order. This "jurisprudence of emergency," he argues, focusing on the case of colonial India, demonstrates that emergency powers are not an exception to the normal rule of law, but, in fact, "the rule of law and emergency, norm and exception, the standard and that which contravenes it, must be viewed as powerfully and intimately connected" (134). In the colonial situation, and increasingly throughout the "modern" world, as Giorgio Agamben and recent history have demonstrated,[12] exceptional powers are part of the "normal" rule of law. Many of Hussain's arguments apply to colonial law in Kenya, partly because many of the laws were the same—i.e., many of the great legal codes written for colonial India, including the Indian Penal Code, the Indian Evidence Act, and the Indian Contract Act, were transported and

11 See, for example, Ghai and McAuslan, *Public Law and Political Change in Kenya* (1970); Clayton and Savage, *Government and Labour in Kenya: 1895–1963* (1974); Stichter, *Migrant Labour in Kenya: Capitalism and African Response, 1895–1975*; Collier and Lal, *Labour and Poverty in Kenya, 1900–1980* (1986); and, among many others, Aluchio, *Trade Unions in Kenya: Development and the System of Industrial Relations* (1998).

12 See Agamben, *State of Exception* (2005).

dropped wholesale into East Africa in the late nineteenth century—but also because colonial authorities in Kenya similarly felt the need to suspend the normal rule of law and exercise exceptional power to maintain order and control. In fact, it could be argued that there was never a "normal" rule of law established from the beginning in Kenya as the governing myth of Africa as pre-modern required exceptional measures to bring about modernity and, simultaneously, as we have seen, to prevent modernity from disrupting native social structures. Labor was an important area where exceptional measures were used because settlers and colonial authorities believed two things: one, that Africans were naturally idle and therefore needed forced labor in order to become civilized and industrious; and, two, that a cheap labor force was necessary to bring order to the land through the growth and development of a strong agricultural economy. Writing on the labor issue during his tour of East Africa in 1906, Winston Churchill, who was then Under-Secretary of State for the Colonies, asserted, "I am clearly of the opinion that no man has a right to be idle, whoever he be or wherever he lives. He is bound to go forward and take an honest share in the general work of the world. And I do not except the African native" (43). This "gospel of labor," writes David Anderson, "was a central element in the civilizing mission of European rule, frequently referred to by settler farmer and government official alike as the justification for *stringent labor laws*" ("Kenya" 498–99; emphasis added). While not (yet) strictly emergency laws, such laws (in the early 1900s) were exceptional in the severity of their requirements and punishments, and in the latitude and protections provided for settlers, who abused and exploited workers. Anderson argues that "colonial states [...] readily colluded with capital in providing the legal framework necessary for the recruitment and maintenance of labor in adequate numbers and at low cost to the employer" (498). Furthermore, he continues, "The emphasis of the law was to protect the contractual interests of the employer rather than the employee, and the penal sanctions were designed to act as a strong deterrent against workers who were thought to be largely ignorant of the burden of contract law" (500).

As I argued in Chapter 1, despite the narrative of progress that depicted Europe as a "progressive society" that had made the transition "*from Status to Contract*," contracts were used in colonial Kenya to reinforce status relationships (Maine 170). Colonial practice undermined its own justificatory myth of progress because it was driven more by the desire for capital and control than an altruistic desire to promote so-called civilization. The labor laws put in place in early colonial Kenya, including the 1902 Native Porters and Labour Regulation and the 1906 Master and Servants Ordinance, assumed that a "primitive" labor force required "primitive" labor laws; labor law shared this assumption with the system of indirect rule, but differed in its stated goal of promoting modernity rather than keeping it at bay. In practice, writes Anderson, "the rights of the master were enforced in *draconian* terms, whereas relatively few protections were offered to the servant" ("Kenya" 502; emphasis added). The rights of the masters were rights of contract, which entitled them to demand labor at rates that overwhelmingly favored their interests and to enforce their demands with harsh punishments; and such "draconian" practices were not unlike those of emergency laws, which gave sweeping powers to those in authority and deprived others of rights and protections. Over time, some administrators began to recognize the need to protect native laborers, and they gave instructions in 1908 to magistrates to investigate disputes to make sure that workers were not being treated unfairly; but, writes Anderson, "These directives [...] had little impact" (503).

The first concrete intersection between labor and emergency law came during World War I. Amendments were made to the masters and servants ordinance periodically, and several came during the war. These changes, observes Anderson, "were considered as *emergency acts*, and so needed no approval from London" (503; emphasis added). The wartime changes "served to tighten the constraints upon employees and to add to the severity of the punishments imposed, making desertion a cognizable offense, allowing the police to arrest deserters without a warrant, and increasing the penalties for breach of contract" (503). Anderson notes that these changes were thought to be necessary to "maintain recruitment for the dreaded Carrier Corps," a combat division comprised of Africans whose mortality rates, primarily from disease and malnutrition, were significantly higher than those of other corps fighting in East Africa. With the end of the war and the end of recruitment needs, however, the emergency measures remained in place. States of emergency are often declared because of an internal or external threat of some kind and the purpose is to utilize exceptional powers in order to protect the state and its citizens. The people forfeit their rights *temporarily* in the face of a crisis, and it is understood that those rights will be restored. When the temporary suspension of law becomes permanent, however, all citizens, or all members of certain groups within the state, become potential threats and are treated as potential criminals. This is how laborers were treated in colonial Kenya, particularly after the wartime acts became permanent: as potential deserters (a criminal offense), laborers were threatened with harsh punishments and deprived of basic rights. Within a few years, this criminalization of the worker became even more apparent with the introduction of the *kipande*, or the internal passbook system that restricted workers' ability to move and work freely within their own country.

The Registration of Natives Ordinance was put into place throughout the colony in 1920 and required all men over 15 years of age to register with the local administration and receive a "finger-print certificate of identity" (Anderson, "Kenya" 506). Describing this certificate, Anderson writes, "This document [...] provided basic personal details and acted as a record of employment. [...] [B]y 1931 nearly 2 million *kipande* had been issued." Some officials argued that the passbook would protect the rights of native workers by "making it harder for settlers to defraud them of their wages," but "in effect this law restricted the workers' freedom of mobility to a far greater degree than had any provision under the master and servant ordinance" (506). A worker could not move from one place of employment to another without the signature of his current employee, so employers could refuse their signature or even make a note criticizing the worker, thus making it difficult for him to find employment elsewhere. If a worker left without a formal signature, it was considered desertion, which was, of course, seen as a punishable offense and could be reported immediately to the police. Furthermore, the *kipande* facilitated the formation of police state practices because any official could inspect a worker's book and report any discrepancies in the work history to the authorities for possible prosecution.

Under an official State of Emergency, a government assumes special powers and, depending on the reasons for the emergency, imposes restrictions such as forced curfews, detention without trial, constraints on movement (often with police-checks on roads and other transportation routes), censorship, the prohibition of organizations and public meetings, etc. The *kipande* essentially put such restrictions into effect at a time when there was no need for emergency regulations, except in the sense that settlers wanted protections against Africans who did not like working for them. "Whenever an African was outside the reserves, working, resting, or travelling," write Anthony Clayton and Donald Savage, "he was liable to arrest and prosecution on a criminal charge if he could not produce his *kipande*" (133). "A cook without a *kipande* crossing a road after 10 p.m. to see a friend might be liable for a month in prison." Ultimately, this system (which required men to wear the passbook in a metal container worn around the neck "like the badge of a dog's collar as some Africans observed" [132]) "struck deep at the African sense of self-respect [...]; a demand for the abolition of the *kipande* formed from then on a principal item on the platform of African 'protest'" (132). Although eventually abolished in 1946, the *kipande* added to the culture of exploitative exceptionality that came to characterize labor law in Kenya through the colonial period and following independence. For this reason, it continued to be a powerful symbol in the people's memories, making its way, for example, into the storyline of *Mother, Sing for Me*.

Despite the *kipande*'s abolition in 1946, an actual emergency several years later would add further to the exceptional nature of labor problems and the rule of law in Kenya. As described in Chapter 1, above, the dominant response to Mau Mau among settlers, the colonial government, and many outside observers was to characterize the movement as a violent, atavistic retreat to savagery—Mau Mau was a crisis or a "psychic disease" brought on by a failure to cope with the changes of modernity (which the system of labor was intended to promote and the system of indirect rule was intended to prevent). The most immediate response to the threat of Mau Mau was the widespread detention of massive numbers of the Kikuyu people in central Kenya. Many were given rushed trials in emergency courts—which resulted either in sentences of permanent detention or execution—and others were simply detained without trial. The *kipande* system introduced one form of detention and control in colonial Kenya, and detention without trial was also authorized under an emergency law enacted at the outset of World War II (the Emergency Powers [Colonial Defence] Order in Council), and under the emergency laws enacted during the Mau Mau conflict.

Detainees in Mau Mau camps were subjected to forced manual labor, although "paid manual labor" was promised as part of the process of rehabilitation (Lonsdale, "Mau Maus of the Mind" 410). The working and living conditions in the camps were highly unsanitary and prison overseers were extremely abusive, often brutally assaulting prisoners. "Violence," writes David Anderson, "had become intrinsic to the system" (*Histories* 325). The use of labor as a punitive device went beyond the prison camps, however, as Governor Baring "unleashed a policy of forced communal labor" on the Kikuyu reserves (Elkins 116). This was one of the policies aimed at keeping the Kikuyu people who were not in prison from assisting or joining Mau Mau. "Under Emergency law," Caroline Elkins writes, "the Kikuyu had to work unpaid ninety days a year on communal projects like bracken clearing, trench digging, and the much-hated land terracing program. If they refused, they could be fined up to five hundred shillings or imprisoned for six months. [...] The colonial government argued that communal labor was for the benefit of the Kikuyu community, and that the Africans actually enjoyed it" (117).

Although harsh, this was not the worst policy to befall those who had been neither charged nor convicted but were simply Kikuyu and, therefore, potential victims of the crisis of modernity from which Mau Mau was said to suffer. To add to the abuses of forced manual labor, the colonial government began creating "emergency villages." In 1954, the War Council began burning and razing existing villages in the Kikuyu reserves and forcing the people—mostly women, children, and the elderly—into compounds heavily guarded by the loyalist Home Guard police force and enclosed with barbed-wire fences, supposedly for their protection. "By the end of 1955, less than eighteen months after the measure's introduction, 1,050,899 Kikuyu were removed from their scattered homesteads throughout Central Province and herded into 804 villages, consisting of some 230,000 huts" (Elkins 235). In many of these villages, there were no huts and villagers were forced to build their own homes. Colonial authorities, under fire from critics, including Labour Party members in the English Parliament, insisted that the villages presented an opportunity to promote civilization among the Kikuyu through education and the "gospel of labor." However, Elkins writes, "Despite the self-satisfied and optimistic rhetoric of Britain's colonial planners, villagization was intended as a punitive strategy to contain, control, and discipline Mau Mau women" (240). The central component of this strategy, aside from forced relocation, was forced labor. They began with building hundreds of huts and were then forced to dig trenches around the villages, which they lined with sharpened sticks and covered with barbed wire. However, "The hard labor began when the villages were finally completed" (242). In one village, for example, the women and others able to work were forced day after day to dig deep trenches at the edge of the forest on Mount Kenya. There were no breaks allowed, no singing, talking, or eating, and the Home Guards were notoriously abusive. Many villagers died of "exhaustion, brutality, and hunger," and the Guards forced the others to bury the dead in the bottom of the trench.[13] In short, the villages were another demonstration of exceptional power that criminalized an entire category of people and, in effect, imprisoned them through forced labor without formal charges or any evidence of wrongdoing. And, as we saw in Chapter 1, all of these policies were justified through the colonial crisis of modernity narrative.

This history is necessary for a full understanding of the critique that Ngũgĩ levels at labor law. Most obviously, *The Trial of Dedan Kimathi* and *Mother, Sing for Me* confront this very history, portraying the lives of workers under oppressive colonial and postcolonial regimes. More importantly, however, the history of the intersections of labor and emergency law are relevant to a reading of Ngũgĩ's plays because *Kamĩrĩĩthũ itself was an emergency village*. The very people with whom Ngũgĩ began the theater project were direct inheritors of the abusive policies of the emergency period and the very site was a product of forced labor. In *Detained*, Ngũgĩ briefly describes the history of the village and how toward the end of the emergency the government decided to turn the *temporary* villages into "permanent features to facilitate the creation of an African landed middle class through land consolidation and the enclosure system, while retaining the villages as permanent reservoirs of cheap labor for both the 'white' highlands and for the new African landlords" (74). Even years after independence, Ngũgĩ continues, "Kamĩrĩĩthũ has not changed much from its emergency origins. Poverty is still the king. [...] And of course Kamĩrĩĩthũ is still a reservoir of cheap labor for the new Kenyan landlords and Euro-American multi-nationals." It is no coincidence, in other words, that the plays Ngũgĩ produced at Kamĩrĩĩthũ took the form they did, given the complex history that the village experienced and symbolized. To enact on that site new narratives that contested those of the state and to make "palpable" a democratic vision of Kenya's future was to challenge the very roots of colonial history and the very foundations of contemporary Kenya's legal system, which, like its predecessor, used exceptional powers to mediate its control of labor in pursuit of capital.

13 Ngũgĩ vividly portrays the experience of digging these trenches in his novel *A Grain of Wheat* (1967).

'Between Formal and Infinite Time': *The Trial of Dedan Kimathi* and *Mother, Sing for Me*

In their Preface to *The Trial of Dedan Kimathi* (1976), co-authors Ngũgĩ wa Thiong'o and Mĩcere Githae Mugo state that although their play is inspired by the actual trial of Mau Mau's most famous general, it is not, nor does it attempt to be, historically accurate in the sense of reflecting the factual happenings of Dedan Kimathi's trial under an emergency colonial court in 1956. Ngũgĩ and Mĩcere were colleagues in the Literature Department at the University of Nairobi, and following a long series of conversations about anti-imperialist struggles throughout the world the two professors determined to collaborate on a play that, they wrote, "reconstruct[ed] imaginatively our history, envisioning the world of the Mau Mau and Kimathi in terms of the peasants' and workers' struggle before and after constitutional independence" (iv). They explain further: "The play is *not* a reproduction of the farcical 'trial' at Nyeri. It is rather an imaginative recreation and interpretation of the collective will of the Kenyan peasants and workers." Ngũgĩ and Mĩcere's dismissal of the actual trial as "farcical" suggests an important irony: the supposed "facts" of colonial history, including those of Kimathi's trial, are the real works of fiction, the real performances, whereas this "imaginative recreation" is, in a sense, more truthful and more accurate in its portrayal of Kimathi's struggle—and the *meaning* of that struggle—from the perspective of the oppressed. In *Kimathi*, therefore, Ngũgĩ and Mĩcere employ a historical *method*, rather than strict historical representation, that challenges the dominant, institutional narrative about Mau Mau and, further, attempts to shatter conventional narratives of colonial time. Indeed, Ngũgĩ and Mĩcere write, "The action should on the whole be seen as breaking the barrier between formal and infinite time, so that past and future and present flow into one another" (2). As dramatists employing a historical method, Ngũgĩ and Mĩcere break apart progressive, and thereby oppressive, conceptions of history in such a way that will provide a "new angle of vision" and bring the dead (in the sense of institutionally suppressed) Kimathi to "new life" (Thomas, *New Historicism* 111). From the very beginning of the play, they attempt to suspend a linear, progressive notion of history, and bring the past, present, and future into a horizontal relationship. Walter Benjamin observes that the "awareness that they are about to make the continuum of history explode is characteristic of the revolutionary classes at the moment of their action" (261). Furthermore, these classes recognize that certain moments of the past are "charged with the time of the now" and can be "blasted out of the continuum of history" (261). In both *Kimathi* and *Mother, Sing for Me*, the past moments of Mau Mau and pre-colonial Kikuyu history are charged with the time of the now and through the shattered barriers between formal and infinite time can escape the continuum of history to authorize revolutionary action in the present.

Of course, for Ngũgĩ, Mĩcere, and later the Kamĩrĩĩthũ players, orature plays a central role in this revolutionary and counter-temporal process. In chapter 3 of *Penpoints, Gunpoints, and Dreams* (1998), in which he describes the immediate reception of *Kimathi* and the politics surrounding its performance in the Kenyan National Theatre, Ngũgĩ begins by describing the relationship between African artists and the State. He writes,

> If before the emergence of the state, the domain of culture embodied the desirable and the undesirable in the realm of values, this was expressed through performance. The community learnt and passed on its moral codes and aesthetic judgments through narratives, dances, theatre, rituals, music, games, and sports. With the emergence of the state, the artist and the state became not only rivals in articulating the laws, moral or formal, that regulate life in society, but also rivals in determining the manner and circumstances of their delivery. (36)

Like Okot, Ngũgĩ recognizes the fact that African artists are those who knew and disseminated normative principles to their people. Mĩcere understood this potential as well. Mĩcere later authored two books on African orature and human rights, in which she analyzes the legal and human rights principles inherent in many African oral cultures, including those of the Kikuyu.[14] "Through proverbs, sayings, stories and illustrations," she writes, councils of elders in Kikuyu society would "show what needed to be done to remedy a given situation" in order to protect "the rights of the aggrieved in the community" (*African Orature* [1991] 20). "The Orature artist," she asserts, "was a staunch advocate and defender of human rights," as such rights were defined within the Kikuyu cultural tradition (21). Knowing Ngũgĩ and Mĩcere's shared recognition of the legal ideas and principles that can emerge through the deep structures of orature, we can better understand the implications of their oral appropriations in *Kimathi* in relationship to the explicit legal themes of the play and, more broadly, in the critique of colonial myths of progressive time. We see all of these themes converge in the opening of the play.

The Trial of Dedan Kimathi begins with the eponymous character's arraignment in a colonial emergency court and then shifts abruptly to a performance of "Black people's History," which is, essentially, a history of labor (4). This moment conveys the essential argument of the play, namely that colonial law has determined the official version of Kenyan history and that if post-colonial Kenya is to become truly independent its laws must be founded on the history of "the struggling, oppressed class" of African workers and peasants (Benjamin 260).[15] The first scene of the play, identified as the "Opening," is

14 The first, *African Orature and Human Rights* (1991), develops a theory of orature and human rights using Kikuyu oral traditions as a case study, and a later volume, *African Orature and Human Rights in Gikuyu, Shona, and Ndebele Zamani Cultures* (2004), broadens the analysis to include other cultural traditions.

15 As Shahid Amin writes in *Event, Metaphor, Memory*, "Peasants do not write, they are written about. The speech of humble folk is not normally recorded for posterity, it is wrenched from them in courtrooms and inquisitorial trials" (1).

brief and repetitive—a white judge in a court during the State of Emergency in 1956 presides over a courtroom and addresses the prisoner, Dedan Kimathi. The judge reads the charge and asks how the prisoner pleads. Kimathi refuses to reply so the judge repeats the charge and the question. Kimathi is charged with possessing a firearm without a license, which is a violation of "section 89 of the Penal Code [...] under Special Emergency Regulations," and is a capital offense (3). The judge then asks, "Guilty or not guilty?" Kimathi remains silent. Kimathi's refusal to speak gives us an immediate sense of his defiance of the colonial system—standing in a room surrounded by armed guards and angry settlers, Kimathi maintains a "quiet dignity" and refuses to participate in the farce of law to which he is being subjected.

This stark, procedural opening falls into "sudden darkness" before turning into the "First Movement" of the play.[16] The courtroom scene of the "Opening" in many ways invokes the history of colonial law as a "jurisprudence of emergency" (Hussein). In immediate contrast to this, the "First Movement" follows by beginning with a darkened stage that is then filled with the sound of drums, which crescendo into a "frantic, frenzied and intense climax" before twilight dawns and a crowd of peasants enter the stage singing a protest song in Swahili:

Tutanyakua	[We will take
Mashamba yetu	Our farms
Tupiganie	We should fight for
Uhuru wetu	Our freedom
Natukomboe	And we redeem
Elimu yetu	Our education
Tutanyakua	We will take
Viwanda vyetu	Our factories
Utamaduni	Culture
Ni mashamba yetu	Is on our farms
Damu na jasho	Blood and sweat
Zatiririka	Flow
Tutakomboa	We will redeem
Udongo wetu! (4)	Our land!][17]

16 Rather than identify the components of the play as Acts and Scenes, Ngũgĩ and Mĩcere identify them as "Movements," of which there are three. Simon Gikandi reads the "movement" structure in temporal terms and argues that because the movements are "defined by disjuncture," the "play produces knowledge through the dramatization of temporal conflicts" (*Ngũgĩ* 178). However, "movement," as a discrete component within a larger aesthetic structure, also brings to mind musical compositions. While Gikandi's temporal reading is still applicable as time is essential in music and the play stages a clear concern with "formal and infinite time," as I discuss, the invocation of musical structures in the play's "movements" may be a way of further reinforcing the oral and aural qualities of the play.

17 My translation, with the assistance of Benjamin Kirato, to whom I am deeply grateful.

Following this song, the same peasants "enact the flashback of Black people's History," portraying four "phases" of that history from slavery to more recent struggles against imperialism (4). As part of the same performance that began with the above song, this enactment of black people's history is placed in explicit contrast to the play's opening—colonial law, in other words, is being compared and contrasted to other means of telling history and *enacting* principles for guiding collective action. Indeed, the fact that Ngũgĩ and Mĩcere use the term "to enact," which can denote both "to perform" and "to ordain, decree," i.e., make into law, suggests the extent to which this can be read as a comparison of legal traditions ("Enact"). On the one hand, emergency law is the classic form of colonial law, including indirect rule, as I have argued earlier. Within such a system, capital punishment for possession of a handgun is perfectly legal. On the other hand, the song and historical enactment that open the first movement suggest, indirectly—which is how, according to Okot p'Bitek, the African artist "sings and dances his laws" (*Artist* 39)—that in black people's history may be found principles of and justification for collective action, indeed, for "inaugural violence" that, according to Derrida, is "able to justify, to legitimate, or to transform the relations of law, and so to present itself as having a right to law" (34). Phase I of the performance of black people's history depicts the slave trade, the time when Africans were sold, often by their own or rival chiefs, to white slave traders; phase II depicts a group of slaves laboring under heavy burdens; phase III depicts a "labour force of blacks" working on a plantation under a "ruthless black overseer" and "white master"; phase IV depicts "An angry procession of violent blacks" who are prepared to fight against imperial domination and who chant: "Away with oppression! / Unchain the people!" (5). Following the chant and another brief protest song, the main action of the play begins.

The direct message of this performative prelude is that black people's history has been a history of struggle, of fighting against slavery and oppression. In the matter of a few minutes, Ngũgĩ and Mĩcere locate the beginnings of the present struggle—the 1950s in the diegetic world of the play, and the 1970s in the play's moment of production—in the slave trade. Furthermore, by beginning with the slave trade, Ngũgĩ and Mĩcere draw attention to the issue of labor. Each phase of this opening performance traces the persistence of forms of slavery into the late colonial period when the "angry procession" demands an end to the exploitation and oppression that characterize colonial labor practices. This point is reiterated throughout the play, particularly in Kimathi's speeches. Finally, though the content of the performance of black people's history makes certain points, the form makes an essential point as well: this story is performed to music, not simply told; as Ngũgĩ himself states, it is through performance that the African artist rivals the state in articulating and disseminating the law, and the form of the performance in this way invokes orature's "lexicon of normative action" (Cover, "Foreword" 9). Ngũgĩ and Mĩcere's performance of black people's history both challenges official history by turning to the oppressed class for historical knowledge and provides a narrative that connects past struggles with present. This narrative can then justify action in the present, becoming, in effect, a source of energy for new notions of normativity and law, for acts of inaugural violence that can lead to new, or renewed, forms of legitimacy and social order.

The main action of the play begins after the procession's protest, which concludes with a "Staccato burst of machine gun fire" (directed by whom and at whom is unclear—is this an attack by or on the liberation movement?) and a few voices shouting, "Uhuruuuuuuu–uu!" (6) The audience witnesses events within the controlled spaces of the courtroom and prison as well as events outside as the leader of the liberation movement in Kimathi's absence attempts to rescue him from his "trials." There is, of course, the main trial, first depicted in the "Opening," and then Kimathi's three additional trials in prison. The sub-headings in the text mark these sections out, using "First Trial," "Second Trial," and "Third Trial" instead of "scene," just as the larger sections of the play are marked "Movement" instead of "Act." These are "trials" in the sense of crucibles through which he must pass, rather than official trials by law, and serve to characterize Kimathi as a martyr and savior figure. For my purposes, these trials are less important than the courtroom trial, although they do raise some interesting questions about the coercive networks that developed in the post-independence period as businessmen, politicians, and even church leaders colluded with foreign governments and corporations to continue the exploitation of African resources and labor. In his three trials, Kimathi receives visits in prison from representatives of each of these classes, all of whom try to persuade him to plead guilty and give up his vision of liberation in favor of compromise. As an African Business Executive tells him, "Partnership in progress: that's the new motto" (45). Kimathi, of course, refuses these temptations as he recognizes that the myth of progress will only perpetuate the crises and injustices of colonial rule. As dialogues portrayed in a semi-fictional past that speculate on a future that is the audience's present, these trials, in connection with the explicit critiques that Kimathi makes in his courtroom speeches, expose the compromises (in the negative sense) that took place just prior to independence that created many of the economic and legal inequities under which laborers in the 1970s still suffered.

In the courtroom, Kimathi offers an even more explicit criticism of the colonial legal system. The beginning of the "Second Movement" returns to the moment depicted in the "Opening" when the judge repeats the charge a second time. Kimathi questions the court's authority to judge him, insisting, "I will not plead to a law in which we had no part in the making" (25). The Judge, named Shaw Henderson,[18] replies, "Law is law. The rule of law is the basis of

18 The Judge's name is significant because it combines the names of Robert Patrick Shaw and Ian Henderson, both members of the Kenya "Special Branch," which was an arm of the police force that fought against Mau Mau. Furthermore, Henderson led the final pursuit of Kimathi that resulted in the leader's arrest and he

every civilized community. Justice is justice." The conversation continues with Kimathi challenging the very concept of law as it is defined within and by the "imperialist court":

> KIMATHI: Whose law? Whose justice?
> JUDGE: There is only one law, one justice.
> KIMATHI: Two laws, two justices. One law and one justice protects the man of property, the man of wealth, the foreign exploiter. Another law, another justice, silences the poor, the hungry, our people. (25–26)

Kimathi's bold challenge to the court excites the Africans attending the trial and angers the settlers. At face value, this critique of colonial law is relatively straightforward. Colonial law is bad because it protects those in power and facilitates their exploitation of Kenya's resources by controlling the masses through both physical and economic forms of coercion.[19]

This is a valid critique, of course, but a closer reading reveals a more subtle challenge to colonial law. When Kimathi retorts that there are actually "two laws," he is saying that colonial law is "two-faced" and contradictory, but the reference to a bifurcated system of law also alludes (indirectly) to the system of indirect rule. Indirect rule was *literally* a system of two laws—one for Europeans in urban areas and one for Africans in rural areas, and it became a source of severe oppression rather than protection. Mahmood Mamdani argues that the colonial-appointed chiefs who were given authority to administer customary law were notorious for abusing their authority as

---

documented the entire experience in *The Hunt for Kimathi* (1958). Shaw continued to work for the Kenyan government in the post-independence period and was notoriously harsh in his tactics as a member of the Special Branch, known for his "wild campaigns of terror" (Ngatia). Shaw is said to have facilitated the dictatorial tactics of both Kenyatta and Moi, and rumors maintain that Moi eventually tired of Shaw and had him killed.

19 It is perhaps because of the apparent simplicity of this claim that some critics have dismissed *Kimathi* as less sophisticated than Ngũgĩ's other works. Simon Gikandi, for example, observes, "*The Trial of Dedan Kimathi* is perhaps not a good play in an aesthetic sense, but it is the drama that enables Ngũgĩ to finally make the transition from the liberal ideology of Makerere to the Marxism that produced works such as *Petals of Blood* and *Devil on the Cross*" (*Ngũgĩ* 176). By treating the play as a mere transitional marker in Ngũgĩ's oeuvre due to its apparent lack of aesthetic value, Gikandi risks oversimplifying it and, thereby, overlooking the significance of its indirect and subtle qualities. Like many critics, for example, Gikandi sees *Kimathi* as an attack on State power. He writes, "Ngũgĩ's plays attest to the fact that it is in performance, rather than mere writing and reading, that the compromised narratives of state power are contested and discredited" (162). While I agree with Gikandi's basic point about performance, he discusses "power" here and elsewhere in a vague and abstract sense when the play itself gives both direct and indirect attention to the specific mechanisms by which the State exercised its power, or the specific mechanisms that narratives of State power sought to maintain—i.e., the mechanisms of the law.

they carried out the "day-to-day violence of the colonial system" (22). He continues:

> Not only did the chief have the right to pass rules (bylaws) governing persons under his domain, he also executed all laws and was the administrator in "his" area, in which he settled all disputes. The authority of the chief thus fused in a single person all moments of power: judicial, legislative, executive, and administrative. This authority was like a clenched fist, necessary because the chief stood at the intersection of the market economy and the nonmarket one. The administrative justice and administrative coercion that were the sum and substance of his authority lay behind a regime of extra-economic coercion, a regime that breathed life into a whole range of compulsions: forced labor, forced crops, forced sales, forced contributions, and forced removals. (23)

This description of what Mamdani later calls "decentralized despotism" is not only also a fitting description of the consolidation of powers in a state of emergency, but it makes an important connection between this system of governance and the market. By controlling the population in this manner, colonial authorities were able to control the flow of labor and other economic variables in order to maximize their own profits and further solidify their authority. This is precisely what Kimathi's character in the play is describing: a system of law bifurcated along racial and economic lines designed to make one group wealthy through the oppression and forced labor of the other.

After he rejects the Judge's law and argues that there are two laws facilitating the oppression of the Kenyan people, Kimathi draws our attention to a third law:

> I recognize only one law, one court:
> the court and the law of those
> who fight against exploitation,
> The toilers armed to say
> We demand our freedom. (27)

Kimathi claims to recognize a law separate from the bifurcated laws of the colonial state. This "one law," however, sounds figurative—it is not a literal law that he recognizes, but the guiding ideology of the workers who seek liberation. Freedom is the law, resistance to injustice is the law. A higher, natural law, perhaps, not unlike the law Antigone famously invokes in Sophocles' play as justification for her resistance to Kreon's command. However, the Kikuyu word for revolution is *twika*, and, by some accounts,[20] prior to colonial rule, the authority to administer Kikuyu law was passed from one generation to the next every 30 or 40 years through what was called the

20 Specifically, I draw primarily on Jomo Kenyatta's *Facing Mount Kenya* (1938) in characterizing the myth of *itwika*, recognizing, of course, that Kenyatta himself engages in an act of mythmaking in recounting precolonial Kikuyu history.

itwika ceremony. Kimathi's "law of those who / fight against exploitation" may be nothing more than a subversive appropriation of the colonial rhetoric of legality, but it is worth considering the echo of *itwika* in the Mau Mau leader's invocation of a law that guides revolution. Moreover, it is not just in Kimathi's speech, but in the crucial subplot of the Mau Mau woman and two youths that the spirit of *itwika* appears. Furthermore, *itwika* is the key myth used in *Mother, Sing for Me* to challenge colonial myths of modernity.

The subplot in *Kimathi* is led by an unnamed woman who maintains the Mau Mau fight in Kimathi's absence. Early in the play, she encounters a boy and a girl fighting over a small amount of money. The girl is first seen running from the boy, and he catches her and demands money she owes him, threatening, "I will kill you for it" (15). The woman steps in, separates the two, and chastises them for fighting over something so petty. From this point onward, the boy and later the girl return periodically in the plot, as the woman teaches them that fighting between themselves will only destroy them as a people and that they need to unite against colonialism and exploitation. At one point, the woman gives the boy a loaf of bread and entrusts him with the responsibility of delivering it to a fruitseller in front of Kimathi's prison. The boy and the girl accidentally smash the bread and discover a handgun baked inside. They consider getting rid of it, but ultimately resolve to do their part in helping the resistance movement. They disguise themselves as Maasai, put the gun back in a loaf of bread, and attempt to deliver it to Kimathi themselves. They fail to do so, but run into the woman again, who informs them that plans have changed and they three are the only ones who can help Kimathi at this point. They enter the courtroom the next day, the woman "dressed to kill," as she says, in order to signal Kimathi and the two youths still disguised as Maasai (61). When the woman gives the signal, the youths draw the gun and begin firing. Kimathi is supposed to escape in the confusion, but the action ends there, and the play concludes with the boy and girl at the center of a group singing a final freedom song.

This subplot is structured in the manner of a *Bildungsroman*, with two young people coming of age in a time of conflict and crisis. They are both orphaned, and both experience the narrative of development, growing from their "state of nature" existence on the streets into maturity as "man" and "woman," Adam and Eve carrying forbidden fruit,[21] members of the new generation of freedom fighters. The fact that they go through this process together makes a point about the necessity of unity in the fight. As the woman tells them, re-appropriating a Christian maxim for revolutionary purposes, "United, our strength becomes the faith that moves mountains" (60). More than illustrating

21 Almost literally, in fact, as handguns were forbidden under emergency regulations—they commit the very same crime with which Kimathi is charged. And the fact that the woman disguised herself as a "fruitseller" seems to reinforce the Adam and Eve/loss of innocence motif; it was she who "sold" forbidden fruit to the young man and woman by persuading them to join the liberation movement.

the importance of unity, however, the use of a developmental narrative brings the play into conversation with other texts similarly interested in the relationship between law and "*Bildung*." Joseph Slaughter has argued that the developmental narrative has a complex relationship with notions of human rights, and one could argue that Ngũgĩ and Mĩcere have re-appropriated the *Bildung* narrative for their purposes as they have Christian mythology and rhetoric.[22] However, I argue that although *Kimathi*'s narrative of development asserts a "revolutionary rhetoric of liberty, equality, and fraternity" (Slaughter 5), similar to that of human rights discourse and other *Bildungsromane*, it does so against a backdrop of Kikuyu nationalism and within a dramatic frame that breaks "the barrier between formal and infinite time" (Ngũgĩ and Mĩcere 2). One of their purposes, in other words, is to think outside the box of colonial temporality; indeed, to demolish the box by blasting apart the continuum of history and allowing past, present, and future to run freely into and through one another.

In the context of this anti- or counter-temporal objective, then, the developmental narrative, which relies upon notions of linear progress, is either contradictory or impossible. How do we make sense of the "progress" of the boy and the girl within a context of non-linear temporality? I argue that the narrative of the youths' development functions within the terms of the liberation struggle and Kikuyu forms of generational succession. In other words, while the youth would seem to develop in a dramatized version of the *Bildungsroman* and, therefore, of colonial narratives of temporality, they actually embody the fractured boundary between "formal and infinite time" because they represent the future in two senses: first, within the diegetic world of the play, they are the future of the Mau Mau movement, the inheritors of Kimathi's armed struggle; and, second, they correspond to those in Ngũgĩ's and Mĩcere's day who are being called upon to stop fighting amongst themselves and, like the boy and girl, unite in overcoming oppression and exploitation. The youths also embody the past in the sense that their succession to a position of responsibility echoes formal practices of succession—the *itwika* ceremony—used in Kikuyu society. This echo grounds the developmental teleology of the play in Kikuyu culture rather than in narratives of liberty and human rights inherited from Enlightenment thought.

In *Facing Mount Kenya* (1938), Jomo Kenyatta describes the history and mythology of the *itwika* ceremony in extensive detail. It is important to recognize, of course, that Kenyatta's version of the ceremony was not

22 In *Human Rights, Inc.* (2007), Slaughter argues that "the *Bildungsroman* is exemplary in the degree to which its conventions overlap with the image of human personality development articulated by the law" (4). The coming-of-age novel and human rights law, he states, "are mutually enabling fictions: each projects an image of the human personality that ratifies the other's idealistic visions of the proper relations between the individual and society and the normative career of free and full human personality development" (4).

strictly historical and, in fact, is likely to be rather mythologized and even romanticized. His account no doubt had some basis in precolonial tradition, but, more importantly, it recreated the myth in a way that influenced later generations. It is likely, in other words, that Ngũgĩ's portrayals of and references to *itwika*—indirectly in *The Trial of Dedan Kimathi*, directly in *Mother, Sing for Me*—owe their form to Kenyatta. The word "twika" refers to a revolution or breaking away, and *itwika* is the oral procedure of passing on both the laws and the authority to administer the laws of Kikuyu society (180). According to John Lonsdale, *itwika* was a ritual through which a "new generation was said to 'redeem the country', *kuura bururi*—as a legal witness might disprove a false accusation" ("Contests" 210). The story of the youths in *Kimathi* does not follow the *itwika* ceremony in any exact procedural sense, but their narrative embodies the redemptive and normative spirit of the ceremony, which, according to Kenyatta, was banned by the colonial government in 1925. Despite this banning, Kenyatta wrote in 1938, "The spirit of *itwika*, namely, the changing of government in rotation through a peaceful and constitutional revolution, is still ingrained in the minds of the Gikuyu people" (189).

In Kenyatta's narrative, the original *itwika* ceremony took place many years before colonialism when an age group identified as the "Iregi" decided to do away with their oppressive king and change their government "from a despotism to a democracy" (180).[23] Groups of elders convened and through a series of long deliberations came up with a "constitution" that included nine primary articles. Kenyatta records number seven as follows:

> In order to keep up the spirit of the *itwika*, and to prevent any tendency to return to the system of despotic government, the change of, and the election for, the government offices should be based on a rotation system of generations [...] It was further decided that one generation should hold the office of government for a period of thirty to forty years, at the end of which the ceremony of *itwika* should take place to declare that the old generation had completed its term of governing, and that the young generation was ready to take over the administration of the country. (182)

Kenyatta goes on to describe the details of the ceremony, involving magicians, ritual animal sacrifice, and a ceremonial feast, and states that the constitution was drafted into song form and disseminated throughout the land using call-and-response singing. The woman and the two youths in *Kimathi* do not carry out the specific requirements of the *itwika* ceremony (although they do sing a call-and-response revolutionary song at the end of the play), but the spirit of generational succession described in article seven is very much a fitting description of the spirit of generational succession that the *Bildung* subplot conveys. Furthermore, the last *itwika* ceremony took place sometime

23 Lonsdale also notes that there has been some speculation that *itwika*, with its goal of redeeming the land, "sometimes represented an attempt to ward off or recover from famine" ("Contests" 210).

between 1890 and 1898. Kenyatta states that the next *itwika* was supposed to take place around 1925, but when the governing generation began "singing and dancing *itwika* ceremonial songs and dances to mark the termination of rule by the *mwangi* generation" the British colonial government declared the ceremonies illegal and "seditious" (189). If the *itwika* ceremony had taken place in 1925, then the next ceremony would likely have taken place sometime in the 1950s, precisely when *Kimathi* is set. Indeed, historians have shown that the revolutionary mythology surrounding *itwika* "exercised an immense influence on the Mau Mau fighters," and this is no doubt one reason why the Mau Mau characters in *Kimathi* also seem guided by *itwika* mythology (Kagwanja 60). After the 1950s, the next *itwika* would have been on the horizon in the late 1970s when Ngũgĩ and Mĩcere wrote their play and would have taken place in the 1980s when the Kamĩrĩĩthũ Theatre group wrote and began performing *Mother, Sing for Me*, as I discuss below. Although *Kimathi* does not incorporate songs as extensively as *I Will Marry When I Want* and *Mother, Sing for Me*, its use of a Kikuyu coming-of-age narrative alongside the plot about Kimathi's trial, in which the Mau Mau leader declares his commitment to a *revolutionary* law, invokes in subtle but significant ways the mythology and spirit of Kikuyu oral jurisprudence. The play seeks to instruct its audience in becoming the next generation to take up leadership and authority to ensure an end to oppression because, as Kenyatta writes, "submission to a despotic rule of any particular man or a group, white or black, is the greatest humiliation to mankind" (189).

It was in part because of this play, in addition to Ngũgĩ's other achievements, that the Kamĩrĩĩthũ villagers approached Ngũgĩ about contributing to the Community Education and Cultural Centre, which can be seen as seeking to fulfill the juridical mandate of *itwika* with which *Kimathi* ends. It was in the year following *Kimathi*'s publication that *I Will Marry When I Want* (1977) was first performed, but I see *Mother, Sing for Me*, the second of the two Kamĩrĩĩthũ plays, as explicitly continuing *Kimathi*'s effort to "break the barrier between formal and infinite time" (2). Furthermore, *Mother, Sing for Me* shares *Kimathi*'s interest in the history of labor in Kenya, but it stages a much more direct critique of labor law and its legacies of crisis in postcolonial Africa, challenging the myths of colonial temporality through the same modes of oral expression and imagination found in *Kimathi*. In addition, *Mother, Sing for Me* uses the *itwika* mythology and related forms of orature to articulate new "regimes of intelligibility" (Mbembe 339) and explore the conditions needed for the emergence of a new normative order to rival that of the postcolonial State.

The history of labor law in Kenya as described earlier, established a model of labor that relied upon exceptional power, coercion, and the unfair use of contracts: to be a laborer was to be produced as a particular kind of subject, conditioned by the exceptional powers granted to employers through uneven contracts and a system of law that buttressed the exploitative practices of the capitalist system. Labor was not freely given in exchange for fair wages and equal treatment, but was extracted, like a natural resource, individual by individual as cheaply and efficiently as possible. In contrast to this, at a site that was a concrete product of this history of exceptional labor law (because Kamĩrĩĩthũ was, originally, an "emergency village" that remained a source of cheap labor after independence), a group of workers and peasants came together and defined a collective cultural experience that, effectively, declared their autonomy from the State. It was not a secessionist movement, but the government seemed to react as though it were. It was, however, a successful "experiment" in applying the principles of collective work inherent in oral culture and thereby generating a model of labor that presented a promising, democratic alternative to the individual-oriented, exploitative labor model of the State. And this is what the State feared most—"not crime or brigandage" (both rampant problems in Kamĩrĩĩthũ prior to the Community Centre's success),[24] but something capable of doing violence to the existing system of law and order by legitimating itself and "presenting itself as having a right to law" (Derrida, "Force of Law" 34).

The fact that Kamĩrĩĩthũ must be understood in terms of labor (and of law because it is labor guided by the democratic vision of oral and Marxist forms of collective order) is evident from Ngũgĩ's descriptions of the experience. Ngũgĩ and his university colleague Ngũgĩ wa Mĩriĩ had written a rough framework for the first play in April of 1977, but over the next two months the villagers significantly altered the script, rewriting and reworking the story so that the end product was much changed from the original outline. Rehearsals began in June and, Ngũgĩ explains:

> The six months between June and November 1977 were the most exciting in my life and the true beginning of my education. I learnt my language anew. *I rediscovered the creative nature and power of collective work*
>
> *Work, oh yes, work! Work, from each according to his ability for a collective vision, was the great democratic equalizer.* Not money, not book education, but work. Not three-piece suits with carnations and gloves, not tongues of honey, but work. Not birth, not palaces, but work. Not globe-trotting, not the knowledge of foreign tongues and foreign lands, not dinners at foreign inns of court, but work. Not religions, not good intentions, but work. Work

24 In fact, Ngũgĩ talks about positive effects that the Community Centre had on some of Kamĩrĩĩthũ's social problems. As more and more people became involved in the Centre's activities, he writes, "I saw with my own eyes an incredible discipline emerge in keeping time and in cutting down negative social practices. It was the women's group [...] who imposed on themselves a ban on drinking alcohol, even a glass, when coming to work at the centre. This spread to all the other groups including the audience. [...] For a village which was known for drunken brawls, it was a remarkable achievement of our collective self-discipline that we never had a single incident of fighting or a single drunken disruption for all the six months of public rehearsals and performances" (*Detained* 77). Ngũgĩ also describes the case of a young man who had tried to commit suicide several times, but then overcame his depression through involvement at the Centre where he became known and loved for his beautiful singing voice.

> and yet more work, with collective democratic decisions on the basis of frank criticisms and self-criticism, was the organizing principle which gradually emerged to become the cornerstone of our activities. (*Detained* 76–77; emphasis added)

Labor in the world outside Kamĩrĩĩthũ and in the history of Kenya since the early 1900s was the opposite of a democratic equalizer—conditioned by the "jurisprudence of emergency," labor was used as a means of structuring hierarchies, accumulating capital, and depriving Kenyans of their rights and of the possibility of self-determination. Here in Kamĩrĩĩthũ *work* had become "the great democratic equalizer." Collective work built the Centre, defined its mission, wrote the play, and performed it for the community. Labor was not extracted from inferiors by superiors; rather, work was a creative enterprise freely given which provided all with an equal opportunity to contribute in their own way to fulfilling the vision of the Centre and meeting the needs of the community.

I should acknowledge at this point that there is a risk of being overly romantic about what happened in Kamĩrĩĩthũ, just as there is a risk of romanticizing oral culture as utopian in its promotion of collectivity in contrast to the dystopian culture created by the "big men" of the postcolonial state. The terms that Ngũgĩ uses in describing his experience may reflect idealizing and romanticizing on his part, perhaps leading us to question the real significance of the cooperative work that led to *I Will Marry When I Want* and, later, *Mother, Sing for Me*. At the same time, however, the work worked. Cooperative work built the Centre, wrote the plays, staged a series of highly successful rehearsals and performances, and breathed new life into a community that had been struggling for economic, emotional, and cultural survival. And, of course, the government panicked. This "alternative vision" of labor, which rivaled that supported and employed by the State, posited in a very real way the possibility of democratic revolution, a democratic "vision of Kenya's future," as Ngũgĩ described it, and this frightened the government (*Decolonising* 61). The state demonstrated this fear most obviously in Ngũgĩ's detention, which is often described as though it were a simple brute show of force in the manner of a kidnapping (which, in truth, it was). However, technically, Ngũgĩ's arrest was legal. His detention was authorized under the Public Security (Detained and Restricted Persons) Regulations 1966, which, as Ngũgĩ discusses in *Detained*, was a hold-over from colonial emergency laws dating back to 1897. In responding to Kamĩrĩĩthũ, the State used emergency law to deny the promise of democratic labor, an alternative path to modernization, which would disrupt the State's existing autocratic model of labor relations. Fortunately, Ngũgĩ's detention was only temporary, but his encounter with the law in this way had more than a temporary impact on his thinking as well as on the Kamĩrĩĩthũ players, with whom Ngũgĩ reunited in 1982 in writing and rehearsing *Mother, Sing for Me*. Like *The Trial of Dedan Kimathi*, *Mother, Sing for Me* is, in some respects, a history play, or a play concerned with Kenya's history and the concept of history itself. However, *Mother, Sing for Me* becomes even more explicitly concerned with Kenyan *legal* history in particular, which is partly a product, I argue, of Ngũgĩ's direct encounter with the authoritarian uses of the law at Kamiti prison.

As noted, *Mother, Sing for Me* is made up of two parts: the first is set in colonial Kenya on a settler farm in the 1920s and 1930s, while the second is set on the same farm several years later. Though still technically in the colonial period, the second part of the play is supposed to evoke the era of postcolonial crisis.[25] The play focuses on a group of Kenyans working for a settler named Kanoru who abuses them, enacts strict punishments for dissent and disobedience, and rapes one of his workers, a woman named Nyathira. At Kanoru's side are Nyabarra, his African overseer, and other servants who receive increasing levels of power as they demonstrate loyalty to Kanoru. The play opens with the workers being tortured and a long series of texts of colonial laws—most having to do with labor—being dictated, translated, and visually projected (on a screen) to the workers and audience. Kanoru enters on a rickshaw and through Nyabarra demands to know who prompted the workers to burn their *kipandes*. An informant identifies the perpetrator, a mechanic named Kang'ethe, and Kanoru oversees his trial and eventual execution.[26] Another worker, Kariuki, is chosen to replace Kang'ethe as mechanic and is given his bloody overalls to wear. Kanoru's abuses continue, but resistance develops again. Kariuki discovers a piece of paper in the overalls with the letters "KCA" on them, suggesting that Kang'ethe belonged to the Kikuyu Central Association, Kenya's first national liberation organization. Kariuki meets an old man who is deaf and mute but instructs him in building guns and introduces a central motif of the play: holding a single stick, the old man breaks it; but holding a bundle of sticks

25 In a conversation I had with Ngũgĩ in 2011, he stated that they set the second half of the play in the colonial period as a way of protecting themselves by partially concealing the critique of the current government. They had hoped to avoid what had happened with *I Will Marry When I Want* when the government reacted so violently to the play's overt criticisms of contemporary Kenya.

26 The fluid, almost dream-like quality of the play in terms of pacing and its extensive use of mime and song (to reach a broader non-Kikuyu speaking audience, as I will discuss) make the play seem, at first, more symbolic than historically mimetic. The fact that the transition from Kang'ethe's accusation to his trial happens so quickly and with very little change in setting and scenery aside from Kanoru putting on judge's robes could suggest on a symbolic level that colonial law was little more than an arm of settler capitalism disguised as justice. While this was true, it is also worth noting that not only did settlers often "dispense justice" on their farms without the involvement of the colonial government, but at one time the government actually considered making settlers judges so they could decide cases on their farms instead of having to take every dispute to the district court (see Anderson, "Registration and Rough Justice" 513). Perhaps this simply would have made official what was already taking place on the farms.

fastened together, he is unable to break them. If the people are united, in other words, nothing can break them. Kariuki becomes the new leader, and, in time, the workers burn their *kipandes* again and succeed in overthrowing Kanoru in a series of scenes that, historically, correspond to the Mau Mau movement. The first half of the play ends with Kanoru's yes-men, Mwendanda (the informant) and Muhuunjia (the rickshaw driver who became a priest) attempting to befriend the liberated workers and promising they will help them abolish the oppressive labor laws.

The second half begins almost exactly as the first with the workers being tortured, laws banning strikes and requiring identity papers being dictated and projected, and the farm's owner being brought in on a rickshaw. The only difference is that the farm, previously called "Kanoru's Farm," is now called the "Anglo-American Fruit Storage Company," and the man in the rickshaw is Mwendanda, an African. Mwendanda behaves as abusively as Kanoru, and the people's leader, Kariuki, whom Mwendanda has disfigured and kept in prison, returns in the end with the stick motif: single, the sticks break easily; bound together, they cannot break. The play thus concludes with the cyclical suggestion of revolution, that, just as the people overthrew the colonial regime, they can now overthrow the postcolonial regime as well.

Clearly, *Mother, Sing for Me* shares symbolic and thematic space with *The Trial of Dedan Kimathi*, but with more of a direct focus on the plight of workers and on the deep history of contemporary labor problems. That history is introduced, in part, by the slideshow that opens the first and second halves of the play. The slides chronicle the various mechanisms that were put in place to control labor in Kenya and, more broadly, highlight the constitutive role of law in the colonial project.[27] Gary Boire has written that "law is colonialism's first language," and, in effect, the first language we encounter in *Mother, Sing for Me* is that of the law (231).

One of the first laws projected (and read in English and then translated into Kiswahili and Gĩkũyũ for the benefit of the workers) is the Anti-Slavery Decree of 1800. This would seem to start off on a liberative rather than oppressive foot, but it only reinforces the irony of what is to come—whereas slavery was technically abolished, subsequent laws simply made different forms of slavery legitimate. Such laws projected on the slides include: Labour Ordinances 1896–1919; Vagrancy Law 1896; Native Pass Ordinance 1900; Hut

27 In using these slides, it is very likely that Ngũgĩ was influenced by Bertolt Brecht's technique of *Verfremdungseffekt*, or distancing effect, which often involved the use of supertitles. The "distancing effect" was a technique of his epic theater intended to prevent the audience "from simply identifying itself with the characters in the play. Acceptance or rejection of their actions or utterances was meant to take place on a conscious plane instead of, as hitherto, in the audience's subconscious" (Brecht 91). That Ngũgĩ had Brecht in mind while working on the play is indicated by the two epigraphs included with the English translation of *Mother, Sing for Me*: two poems from Brecht, "Motto" and "The Anxieties of the Regime."

Tax Ordinance 1901; Native Porters and Labourers Ordinance 1902; Master and Servant Ordinance 1904; Registration of Domestic Servants Ordinance 1910; Native Registration Ordinance 1914 (which began to introduce the *kipande* system); and the Native Registration Ordinance 1915 and from 1919 onwards (4–6). This exhaustive (and exhausting) list is interrupted at the penultimate ordinance by a slide bearing a quotation from the "Bishops' Religious Declaration of 1919 in Support of Forced Labour" (5). The quotation reads:

> The country has been thrown open to settlers. They have poured in, are pouring in and will pour in in increasing numbers ... All of them depend, for their existence as farmers on native labour ... We do not believe that there is the least intention on either side, of exploiting natives for private ends ... Compulsory labour is not in itself evil, and we would favor some form of compulsion ... We are therefore strongly of the opinion that compulsory labour so long as it is clearly necessary should be definitely legalised. (5)[28]

Slavery is in itself evil, as the 1800 decree and Britain's well-documented campaign against slavery in the eighteenth and nineteenth centuries indicate. Compulsory labor, on the other hand, is not only acceptable, but favored—an essential part of the "gospel of labor" that built and drove the Kenyan economy in its early years. Furthermore, compulsory labor brings our attention back to the fact that labor laws were conditioned by a jurisprudence of emergency—in order to bring about a certain orderly state of affairs, exceptional powers were required to obtain and control native labor.

The long series of laws following the Anti-Slavery Decree establishes a genealogy of colonial law that dates back to slavery—"the slides show the history of the colonial labor laws," as Ngũgĩ writes, but, he claims, they also "bring out the difference between WORDS and REALITY, between what the law states and the reality of brutality, repression, theft and robbery, racism, say the oppression hidden by the words" (qtd. in Ndĩgĩrĩgĩ 97–98). Gĩchingiri Ndĩgĩrĩgĩ agrees that the slides highlight "the ironic gap between words and reality" (98), as do I, at least to an extent. Justification for the

28 The full declaration of which this is an excerpt was originally printed in the *East African Standard* on November 1, 1919 as a response to a circular distributed by Kenya's then-governor Sir Edward Northey. Northey's circular called upon the government to "encourage" African men, primarily, but even women and children, to supply the labor needs of settler farms and "Other Undertakings" (qtd. in Okia). Widely perceived as advocating forced labor, the circular received significant criticism from missionary and humanitarian societies, and, to their credit, the Bishops' declaration contributed to this rebuke, condemning "the outlines of Northey's circular as an apparition of slavery," something the slide in *Mother, Sing for Me* leaves out (Okia). However, it was ultimately a "half-hearted" critique as the Bishops still reiterated their position that "some form of compulsion" in making Africans work is good and necessary as long as it is legalized. See chapter 4 of Okia, *Communal Labor in Colonial Kenya* (2012).

Registration Ordinance, for example, insisted that the *kipande* system would actually enhance the freedom and protection of Kenya's workers, but, in reality, the passbooks were highly restrictive. The language of the law was often the language of equity, equality, and justice, but, in reality, colonialism created conditions of inequality and injustice. However, I would argue that the words of the law do more than hide reality: the law plays a constitutive role in creating and legitimating that reality. Injustices and inequalities are often permitted in the name of the law, not in spite of it, and this, I argue, is actually one of the key ideas conveyed by the play's use of the slides during both the colonial and postcolonial moments represented in the play—by comparing the laws with the reality of worker's lives, we see that colonial law, and its postcolonial counterpart, structures in a very fundamental way the reality of labor conditions. The law does not hide theft and racism—it gives theft and racism legitimacy This theme is repeated, not just in the slides, but throughout the play, in various references in the songs and dialogue to law and to labor laws in particular. Labor law is *the* central concern of the play, at least on an explicit thematic level.

In addition to the slides and other references to colonial labor laws, the play's legal preoccupations are also clear from trial scenes, executions, and conversations that echo the language of *Kimathi* (at one point, for example, the farm clerk tells Nyathira to "Obey the law," and, like Kimathi, she replies, "Whose law?" The clerk answers in the dissembling language of Kimathi's judge: "Law is law. Everybody is equal before the law" [26]). However, the play is interested in the competing forms of indigenous law as well. Okot p'Bitek's claim that the African poet "sings and dances his laws" is applicable to the many songs in this play, which provide an authoritative cultural counterpoint to colonial law. In particular, the songs formally and thematically explore what is required for the emergence of new forms of law and justice to rival those of the state. It is not surprising then to find repeated references to the Iregi generation, which recalls the memory of *itwika*, a revolutionary moment in Kenyan history "charged with time of the now" (Benjamin 261) that offers an imaginative roadmap for establishing the conditions needed for the resolution of current crises and the emergence of new "regimes of [normative] intelligibility" (Mbembe 339). After Kariuki finds the KCA paper in his overalls and has begun to emerge into the role of revolutionary leader, he introduces a song. The leaders of a Christian sect endorsed by Kanoru have been leading the workers in a religious hymn, but, at a certain point, Kariuki injects the tune with new words from a Kikuyu song called "mitugo iitu." He fills the Christian song with "new content," or at least content new to the tune, but not new to the workers. Kariuki sings:

> Even if you reject
> Our traditions
> The traditions
> Of us workers

From the times of revolutionaries
I decided:
I'll never forsake our traditions. (56)

Nyathira then joins Karuki in singing the next verse, which talks about the need to tell the children about "The traditions of us workers," because, they sing, clarifying the identity of the revolutionaries, "from the times of *Iregi*-revolutionaries / We decided / We'll never forsake our traditions" (57; emphasis added). Other verses continue and more and more people join Kariuki until all of the workers sing together in unison.[29]

This is one of sixteen references to the Iregi in *Mother, Sing for Me*. To return repeatedly to the Iregi in this way is not simply to find inspiration in revolutionary figures from the past, but to invoke a specific legal tradition that was created to protect the Kikuyu people against despotism and oppression. The Iregi were considered "revolutionary heroes," writes Peter Kagwanja, and thus over time "became iconic of the Kikuyu past, *driven by a collective search for a new moral order, equity and justice*" (61; emphasis added). It is not insignificant, of course, that Ngũgĩ and his co-authors set the first part of the play at the exact time when the *itwika* ceremony would have been performed had it not been banned. Furthermore, as noted earlier, the next *itwika* ceremony would have been performed in the 1950s when the latter part of the play is set, corresponding to the revolutionary moment of the Mau Mau war. Indeed, historians have noted that the revolutionary mythology surrounding the Iregi and *itwika* "exercised an immense influence on the Mau Mau fighters" (Kagwanja 60). Finally, had *itwika* been performed in the 1950s, the next ceremony would have been performed in the 1980s, precisely when *Mother, Sing for Me* was written and performed. Despite the colonial government's declaration of *itwika* as illegal, Kenyatta claimed that "The spirit of *itwika* [...] is still ingrained in the minds of the Gikuyu people" (189), and it seems that in the 1980s this was still the case. *Mother, Sing for Me* does not depict the specific procedures and rituals of the ceremony, but its structure and repeated invocation of the Iregi revolutionaries keep the memory of that ceremony, and the democratic, collectively written laws that were its product, alive.

29 The insertion of revolutionary words into the Christian tune is important. This is, in fact, what Mau Mau and members of the Kenya African Union often did, either appropriating a colonial tune and concealing within it subversive words, or, alternatively, retaining a traditional or revolutionary tune while giving it the appearance of legitimacy to colonial listeners by singing acceptable words. In Kenyatta's trial, for example, a number of "hymn books" containing such songs were discussed at length and the Prosecution held them up as evidence of Kenyatta's involvement with Mau Mau. In a number of the songs, the form and tune conformed to known Christian hymns, but the words were rewritten with nationalist messages and, often, Kenyatta's name was substituted for God's or Christ's. See Slater 86–92 and 172–73.

Although *Mother, Sing for Me* invests much of its performative power in the living memory of the Iregi, it also questions the power of orature, by itself, to bring about necessary change. Songs are sung and celebrated, they mediate and sustain the oppressed characters' process of challenging colonial rule, but a contrast emerges between speaking (or singing) and doing. A little over halfway through the play, before Kariuki and the workers overthrow Kanoru, Kariuki participates in a symbolic ritual signifying his maturation and rebirth. (The name "Kariuki," in fact, means one who is reborn, not unlike "abiku" in Nigeria.) Once he awakes from his rebirth, Kariuki articulates a new realization: "To sing songs of courage is not enough / To sing songs demanding our rights is not enough / To have unity among us workers is not enough" (79). These are all good things, he says, but "That courage and that unity / In demanding all our rights / Should be given a new power." "What new power?" Nyathira asks. He replies, "The power of the Decider." We learn that the "decider" is the gun. Kariuki is advocating armed resistance, in other words. Words are not enough.

This is curious for several reasons, but largely because, generally speaking, the play is invested in the power of words and language to make a difference and to function as or according to a legitimate form of authority. The play includes three epigraphs, two of which are poems by Bertolt Brecht. The second, called "The Anxieties of the Regime," is about the Nazi regime's fear of "the open word," and ends with the following stanza:

> But their Third Reich recalls
> The house of Tar, the Assyrian, that mighty fortress
> Which, according to the legend, could not be taken by any army, but When one single, distinct word was spoken inside it
> Fell to dust.

This image of a single, spoken word capable of bringing down something that could not be brought down by physical force clearly contradicts Kariuki's assertion that songs are not enough. That physical force is the superior act of resistance. Both claims bring to mind Derrida's statement that "What the state fears [...] is not so much crime or *brigandage* [...] The state is afraid of fundamental, founding violence, that is, violence able to justify, to legitimate, or to transform the relations of law, and so to present itself as having a right to law" ("Force of Law" 34–35).

Mother, Sing for Me asks, however, if violence able to present itself as having a right to law can come through language alone or if it must be backed by or transformed into physical violence. Despite the ambiguity, the play ultimately favors the power of the word over the power of the gun. Kariuki's rebirth and epiphany about the "decider" results in the violent overthrow of Kanoru and promises a new beginning for the workers on the farm. However, as described earlier, the power vacuum is filled by an African character who represents the kinds of power-hungry political leaders that simply filled colonial shoes after independence. In a sense, the revolution fails. The workers have to start over, and by the end of the play some of the same images, songs, and motifs of resistance return, the cyclicality suggesting that another armed revolution will be necessary.

By concluding in this way, *Mother, Sing for Me* extends its temporal preoccupations to the level of form. References to the Iregi and portrayals of the crisis of colonial modernity as manifest in the history of labor law signal an awareness of the fundamental nature of narratives of time in debates about law and justice. It could be argued, in fact, that the cyclical temporality of the play reinforces the effort to blast apart colonial time. In contrast to colonialism's "denial of coevalness" (Fabian 31), scholars in recent decades and across a range of disciplines have maintained that indigenous or "traditional" time in Africa is cyclical in contrast to Western linear time.[30] The cyclical structure of *Mother, Sing for Me*, therefore, could, arguably, reflect or be structured upon traditional modes of temporality as a way of unsettling the "homogeneous, empty time" of the colonial system (Benjamin 261). Furthermore, *itwika* follows, also arguably, a cyclical temporality as one generation succeeds another, and perhaps the play's cyclical structure is also supposed to reinforce or echo the idea of generational succession. Kariuki succeeds Kange'the, the deaf-mute old man, and the Iregi when he becomes a revolutionary leader, and with the help of his fellow workers leads a successful revolt against Kanoru that results in (temporary) liberation. The second part of the play, which parallels the play's opening, makes it clear that their revolution was thwarted by neocolonial interests and that the same laws and abuses workers experienced under colonialism are found in the postcolonial state. The play ends with Kariuki (disfigured now like the old man) returning and encouraging the workers with the stick-symbol, asserting that if they are unified, they cannot be broken. The cyclical theme and structure leave the audience expecting and hoping that the workers (and the audience members themselves, Kenyan citizens under a neocolonial regime) can once again follow the lead of the Iregi revolutionaries and carry out "a collective search for a new moral order, equity and justice" (Kagwanja 61).

However, I see a potential problem with this message: if the play and its model of temporality are truly cyclical, then the logical implication is pessimistic rather than optimistic. The first half the play demonstrated a failed revolution—the workers overthrew the old colonial masters, but they fell almost immediately into the hands of neocolonial masters. The play ends with the suggestion that revolution can begin again, but cyclicality dictates that new masters will follow, that this revolution will, ultimately, fail just as

30 See, for example, Belgrave and Allison's *African American Psychology: From Africa to America* (2010), in which they assert, simply, "Time in African cultures is cyclical rather than linear" (40). Perhaps most famously, John S. Mbiti, in his seminal *African Religions and Philosophy* (1989), writes, "The linear concept of time in western thought, with an indefinite past, present and infinite future, is practically foreign to African thinking," which focuses more on the past and present, the "experience" of time, and the "rhythm of natural phenomena" (16–17).

the previous revolution did. If A leads to B which leads back to A, will not the back and forth continue ad infinitum? Logically, yes. However, the play seems to recognize this complication and, therefore, refuses dramatic closure (or at least full cyclical return). The play is, in other words, open-ended. There is suggestion of a potential future revolution with the return of the stick motif, but the play ends there. We do not see that revolution; indeed, we do not even see any concrete beginnings beyond Nyathira picking up the bundle of sticks and wielding it like a gun. *The Trial of Dedan Kimathi* ends in a similarly open-ended way. In both cases, one of the purposes of this sense of non-ending is to open the "boundaries between formal and infinite time" without falling into the trap of cyclical time. I would argue, in fact, that the cyclicality of *Mother, Sing for Me* is less a reflection of the stereotype of African cyclical time than it is an effort to tangle with the contradictory temporality of colonial modernity. Just as characterizations of African time as cyclical are oversimplifications, so too are characterizations of Western time as linear. I have demonstrated that the linear temporal narrative of colonial modernity was contradicted by its atavistic (or cyclical) yearnings: colonialism claimed to promote modernity in Africa, but actually resisted and even feared modernization. The language of linear time (progress) justifies claims to power but because real progress would logically lead to progress (i.e., away from oppression toward modernization, democratization, etc.), those in power tended to revert to forms of governance and control that allowed them to remain in power. Colonial temporality, in other words, was both linear and cyclical, and this, I argue, is the model of temporality that *Mother, Sing for Me* seeks to disrupt. This is one reason why the play refuses closure or full return and one of the reasons why the play's use of orature is so significant. Orature belonged to that part of African culture seen as pre-modern by colonialism, but by demonstrating orature's vitality in the play—by bringing the past into the present in a very tangible way—Ngũgĩ and his co-authors disrupt colonial time; they shatter the barrier between formal and infinite time. Basically, they make a mess of time: they shatter, blast apart, and constellate the fragments of past, present, and future on a horizontal plane in such a way that will allow innovative ways of defining, or exploring definitions of, modernity that do not depend upon or take part in a discourse that opposes "tradition" and "modernity." This is a messier and even riskier approach to time (and social order) than either linearity or cyclicality, but at least it is inclusive, pluralistic, and, ultimately, democratic.

Mother, Sing for Me's formalization of "not yet" suggests the potential of and need for revolution without restricting or prescribing the form that that revolution should take. If something was wrong with the previous revolution (e.g., because it was caught up in the contradictory logic of colonial temporality), then the next revolution needs to be different. Suspending the cycle before the revolution could take shape gives the audience an opportunity to rethink revolution and modernity and define them for themselves. Furthermore, the fact that the play ends where it does reinforces the parallel with the present—it reinforces the audience's experience of Benjaminian *Jetzzeit*, or the "time of the now" (261). The play ends with a depiction that reflects (or is intended to represent) the current lives and conditions of Kenya's workers and peasants, leading the audience to ask, with the characters in the play, "What now?" Although the play is formally open-ended, I argue that there is actually an answer to the question, which can be found in the mode of the play's production.

The plot leads up to the present, leads us to search for a new form of revolution, and it was in the present that a group of people came together and developed a revolutionary movement whose defining feature was the democratic practice of collaborative authorship. The revolutionary achievement of *Mother, Sing for Me* resides in the fact that it answers the question "What now?" in the very act of asking it. The medium—performance, song, orature, in other words—is the message, but so also is the mode of the medium's production. What now? This: what you have just seen, *Mother, Sing for Me*, Kamĩrĩĩthũ, a democratic vision of Kenya's future. Not only do the oral appropriations of the play explore what conditions are needed for the emergence of law, but the collaborative authorship actually demonstrates that the regimes of intelligibility made available through orature are practical, not just theoretical or utopian. *Mother, Sing for Me* is a tangible product of the very ideas of collective work and democratic participation that it advocates.

Ngũgĩ thought of his experience with the Kamĩrĩĩthũ peasants and workers in terms of labor and democratic collaboration. Work, he claimed, "was the great democratic equalizer" during Kamĩrĩĩthũ's activities (*Detained* 76). The creation of *Mother, Sing for Me* continued to demonstrate the power of these ideas. As one of Björkman's interviewees, a man named Gikonyo states, "[Ngũgĩ] has said that he should not be considered the sole author of the plays. It is the peasants as a group that finally came up with what it is" (14). Ngũgĩ himself said "that *Mother, Sing for Me* is definitely not a work of one man. The final script is a result of all this participation by peasants and workers from Kamĩrĩĩthũ, Limuru and, in this case, from Nairobi" (qtd. in Björkman 56). Another of Björkman's interviewees added to this, saying:

> We don't look up to individuals and we cannot close the centre if the Ngũgĩs are not here. If they stopped writing we would come together and write something. Group scripting is not something strange and we would do it. These two individuals are not the centre; the centre is the members. We appreciate an individual's talents but attempt to curb any feeling of self-importance in the individual. (56)

Adding to the play's formal and thematic critiques of colonial temporality, the practice of collective work brings so-called "pre-modern" forms of social order into the present. The principles of democratic participation conveyed through *itwika* mythology and other aspects of Kenyan orature were put into practice in the authorship of *Mother, Sing for Me*. While theorizations of democracy and utopian forms of participatory social order are often articulated in the abstract, Kamĩrĩĩthũ demonstrated that people of different social and ethnic backgrounds can come together and *work* productively toward a common aim. Their activities put the past into a critical relationship with the present in a very concrete way, suggesting that there are ways of structuring society and practicing labor that are not dependent upon (neo)colonial forms of progress and modernity, which perpetuate oppression and exploitative models of labor.

Unfortunately, the momentum of Kamĩrĩĩthũ did not last, confronted as it was with the neocolonial anti-modernism that pushed the democratic project back into the territory of "not yet." This was a tragedy, of course, but it does not change the power of the workers' achievement in demonstrating a form of un-coerced, non-compulsory labor that functioned successfully according to sets of rules and regulations determined by the people themselves and derived from their culture and experience rather than from the will of the State. Their culture simultaneously provided the guiding principles of Kamĩrĩĩthũ's activities and the substance of their creative product: *Mother, Sing for Me*, in other words, both thematizes the issues of labor, collectivity, and revolution and, more importantly, is a concrete demonstration of these principles as they were—and could be again—put into practice in the work of collaborative authorship.

Mother, Sing for Kenya's Tea Workers

Mother, Sing for Me and Ngũgĩ's other plays have not been part of an apocalyptic reception in recent years in any way comparable to Okot's reception in scholarship on the LRA. In many ways, Okot's is a unique situation, but this does not mean, of course, that the work of other East African writers cannot be brought into conversation with contemporary legal issues. To illustrate this in Ngũgĩ's case, I want to conclude with some brief remarks on how *Mother, Sing for Me* and a recent legal case might be "cross-examined," as Brook Thomas would say (16), each one yielding insights into the other. If we imagined the workers in *Mother, Sing for Me* deciding against a second revolution in the end and choosing, instead, to file a lawsuit against the Anglo-American Fruit Storage Company, it would no doubt have looked something like *Kenyan Tea Workers* v. *Unilever plc and Unilever Tea Kenya Ltd* [2015].

In 2015, a group of 218 tea plantation workers in Kenya filed a lawsuit in England alleging negligence on the part of their employer, the multinational corporation Unilever. Represented by Leigh Day, the same UK-based law firm that represented the former Mau Mau fighters in *Mutua & others* v. *The Foreign & Commonwealth Office*, the tea workers claimed that Unilever failed to comply with its duty of care to protect employees from foreseeable violence after the 2007–8 general election in Kenya. The massive Unilever tea planation near Kericho in Western Kenya employed a number of Kisii and Kikuyu laborers who were minorities in the area and were perceived as supporting Mwai Kibaki's presidency. In the violence following the election, many of these workers were targeted by local Kalenjin residents—some also Unilever employees—who opposed Kibaki. In the end, the assailants injured hundreds in violent attacks, raped 56 women, and killed 7 people on the Unilever plantation. The claimants alleged that Unilever was fully aware that violence toward its laborers was possible but did nothing to protect them, although it took steps to protect its properties and management.

Alongside two other recent (and still developing) cases in which African workers are seeking to hold overseas corporations responsible for negligence on the part of their subsidiaries,[31] the *Unilever* case draws attention to complex questions of liability and care with respect to multinational corporations. Given how widely multinational corporations employ laborers throughout the global south, their power to alleviate or cause great harm is significant. Unilever directly employs 155,000 people, for example, and their tea operations alone support an additional "workforce of more than 1 million people in 21 different countries," the majority of which are in regions of the global south ("Time for Tea"). The highest concentration of Unilever employees worldwide, in fact, is in Kenya: the tea plantation workers account for 11 percent of Unilever's global workforce ("Unilever Kenya"). What responsibility do corporations like this have toward employees, contractors, and others when their safety is threatened? If workers were harmed in unsafe conditions because of faulty machinery, for example, or poor management, the corporate "person" would likely be held accountable—but what if the conditions are caused by politics and social unrest? Such questions were implicit in those raised during the *Kenyan Tea Workers* case, namely, given the proximity between the parent company, Unilever plc, and the employees of its subsidiary, Unilever Tea Kenya Ltd., is England or Kenya the more appropriate jurisdiction for a lawsuit? And was the violence truly foreseeable?

The case made its way through the English justice system, first in the London High Court where the judge ruled in 2015 that Unilever was not negligent toward its employees because violence on the plantation was not foreseeable even if violence throughout Kenya more widely was. This was surprising as the claimants had provided evidence that they received threats and then reported the threats to Unilever management prior to the attacks. The judge also ruled, however, that England was the appropriate jurisdiction for hearing the case because doing so in Kenya could expose the claimants to additional violence. Three years later, the Court of Appeal responded only to the question of proximity, overturning the High Court's ruling on jurisdiction because "there was insufficient evidence that Unilever Plc was actively responsible for the alleged crisis management failings of its Kenyan subsidiary" ("Unilever Kenya").[32] The claimants then appealed to the Supreme

31 See *Okpabi & others* v. *Royal Dutch Shell plc and Shell Petroleum Development Company of Nigeria Ltd* [2018] EWCA Civ 191 and *Vedanta Resources plc and another* v. *Lungowe and others* [2019] UKSC 20.

32 *AAA & others* v. *Unilever plc and Unilever Tea Kenya Ltd* [2018] EWCA Civ 1532.

Court, which refused their request in July of 2019, not because it agreed with the lower court's ruling but because the appeal "did not raise an arguable point of law of general public importance which ought to be considered by the Supreme Court" (Owen and Bristow).

This marked the end of the case, but certainly not the end of the questions it raised, particularly because none of the court rulings truly answered the question of Unilever's responsibility toward its employees. Rather, the parent company succeeded in hiding behind its subsidiary and behind the technical question of jurisdiction which the parent–subsidiary relationship raised. This was a disappointing outcome for the claimants, of course, but one that highlights laborers' complicated struggle for rights in the global south: rights as citizens but also as employees of supranational corporate entities. In *Mother, Sing for Me*, after the revolution against Kanoru, the plantation is taken over by such an entity: the Anglo-American Fruit Storage Company. One of Ngũgĩ's most powerful critiques in recent years has been that neocolonial governments are propped up, directly and indirectly, by foreign interests—particularly corporate interests. He explores this most explicitly in the satirical *Wizard of the Crow* (2006), coining the term "corporonialism" to refer to recurring patterns of colonial exploitation in corporate garb (760). *Mother, Sing for Me* offered a similar critique, albeit somewhat more subtly, over two decades earlier, as a Kenyan manager oversaw a farm and its abused workers, all controlled from afar by a foreign corporation. As in the Unilever case, Ngũgĩ's play asks whether the farm manager or the larger corporation is responsible for the workers' suffering: the subsidiary or the parent company. In the end, although the brewing revolution seems directed at Mwendanda, perhaps it is not carried out because the actions of the subsidiary are more symptom than cause. The deeper structural problem that would doom another revolution to failure is traceable to the parent and its corporate form of indirect rule.

This suggests that Kariuki's new revolution should direct its efforts not against the subsidiary, then, but the parent, the Anglo-American Fruit Storage Company, a possibility left open by the play's formal lack of closure. We can try to imagine what this would look like, and the *Kenyan Tea Workers* case gives us a hint as workers joined together and appealed to a higher legal power. Unfortunately, the case also tells us that there is no guarantee that English or international law will succeed in holding corporations accountable for negligence or other abuses. It is to be hoped that the other cases like *Kenyan Tea Workers* (including *Okpabi* [2018] in Nigeria and *Vedanta* [2019] in Zambia) will be more successful and thereby contribute to greater protections for workers throughout Africa and beyond. However, justice remains open-ended for Kenya's tea workers and we must ask what else *Mother, Sing for Me* and the model of collaborative work that created it could offer them in seeking justice and healing their communities. I wish to leave this question open for now, with the hope that other scholars will take it up and continue the conversation, especially once *Mother, Sing for Me* is published. There is fascinating potential for much more work on this prescient text in relation to the ongoing problems of labor and law in Kenya, East Africa, and the global south; labor's relationship to global capitalism; and the seemingly endless challenge of fulfilling the "future democratic vision" of which Kamĩrĩĩthũ was a compelling glimpse.

CHAPTER FOUR

Time Heals All Regimes: Temporality, Somali Oral Law, and the Illegality of African Dictatorships

The bitter-tasting aloe sometimes shoots forth flowers
And you can drink its sweet nectar
I am both sweet and bitter-tasting
My right and left hands are twins
One gives succor to travelers and to the weak
and the other one is sharp knives.

Ahmed Ismail Diriye, "I Am"[1]

And it ought to be remembered that there is nothing more difficult to take in hand, more perilous to conduct, or more uncertain in its success, than to take the lead in the introduction of a new order of things.

Machiavelli, *The Prince* (1532)

—yes, time was ultimately a decider.

Nuruddin Farah, *Sardines* (1981)

At the center of "the crisis" that has characterized African history and politics since independence we find the figure of the dictator. Inheritor of colonial power, grandiose author of personal rule, the dictator in Africa has often been the cause, or if not the cause then at least an enabling agent, of "the chain of upheavals and tribulations, instabilities, fluctuations and ruptures of all sorts" that have been the all-too-common lot of African nations in the postcolonial period (Mbembe 324). Of course, not every nation has been the

1 Translated by Mohamed Diriye Abdullahi and quoted in *Culture and Customs of Somalia* (2001), p. 78.

victim of authoritarian rule to the same extent or in the same manner, but the phenomenon has been sufficiently widespread that it must be seen as part of and even central to the crisis "as a constitutive site of particular forms of subjectivity" (323). The poor, refugees, victims of war crimes and genocide, activists-as-criminals, etc.—all are forms of subjectivity often constituted by or within the context of authoritarian regimes that privilege power over peace, despotism over democracy. Some of the more striking critiques of such regimes have, in recent years, come from works of fiction; specifically, from the emerging genre of the African dictator novel. Numerous authors satirize, counter, and otherwise undermine the myths surrounding figures such as Idi Amin, Robert Mugabe, Daniel Arap Moi, Omar al Bashir, Mobutu Sese Seko, and Siyad Barre, among many others.[2] Throughout both fictional and scholarly responses to dictatorships we find a common set of claims about the colonial origins of authoritarian rule. This is a key theme in the work of Ngũgĩ wa Thiong'o, for example, as we have already seen: the despotism of colonialism put particular structures of governance in place that were not replaced or truly repealed at independence, but rather filled by new rulers—dictators—who perpetuated the crisis of colonial modernity and the political subjectivity of "not yet."

One of the most influential literary responses to dictatorship in Africa has been Nuruddin Farah's trilogy *Variations on the Theme of an African Dictatorship*, written during and as a response to the military regime of Siyad Barre in Somalia (which lasted from 1969 to 1991). In the third novel of the trilogy, *Close Sesame*, Farah makes an important claim about the origins of authoritarian power in Africa. Two characters speak at length about colonial history, democracy, and rights, lamenting that "We Africans did not struggle against the white colonialists only to be colonized yet again by black nincompoops" (101). However, the narrative goes a step further to identify one of the specific colonial mechanisms that made dictatorships possible:

> Then they spoke of the fact that the first threats to the democratic institutions came from the colonial governments which imposed unconstitutional and untraditional dictatorships on the African or the non-European peoples. With informed tolerance and scientific detachment, they talked of the two forms of government the colonial powers employed: one for their own people, the other for the sub-human African. (101)

What they talked of, in other words, was indirect rule. One of the many ironies or contradictions of indirect rule was the fact that administration through

2 There have been rich scholarly conversations on this topic in recent years. See, for example, Colson, "Arresting Time, Resisting Arrest: Narrative Time and the African Dictator in Ngũgĩ wa Thiong'o's *Wizard of the Crow*" (2011); Spencer, "Ngũgĩ wa Thiong'o and the African Dictator Novel" (2012); Ndĩgĩrĩgĩ, *Unmasking the African Dictator: Essays in Postcolonial African Literature* (2014); and Armillas-Tiseyra, *The Dictator Novel: Writers and Politics in the Global South* (2019).

"native institutions" was supposed to be more suited to the "traditional" sensibilities of Africans and, therefore, less despotic than conventional direct rule. The aim of indirect rule was pacification through the prevention of social disorder and unrest. As we have seen in previous chapters, however, indirect rule was far more disruptive than colonial administrators assumed it to be. Among other things, colonial-appointed chiefs were given extensive power within their local jurisdictions, power that was easily abused. "The authority of the chief," Mamdani observes, "thus fused in a single person all moments of power: judicial, legislative, executive, and administrative. This authority was like a clenched fist" (*Citizen* 23). Writing of British rule in northern Somalia, Raphael Chijioke Njoku notes that under the indirect rule system, "the newly appointed Somali traditional official began to assume unusual despotic powers" (57). It is not the case that every African dictator can be traced directly to some figure or provision of indirect rule, but in many countries, including those of East Africa, indirect rule at the very least fertilized the ground in which the seeds of dictatorship flourished.

This fact invites a number of questions, the most important of which, given the concerns of this book, is: if African dictatorships owe something of their form to indirect rule, what is the dictator's relationship to the deeper narratives of time and modernity—and of the crisis of modernity—that made indirect rule possible? This leads, of course, to a second question: if dictatorships are one of the continued manifestations of (or variations on) colonial crisis, what strategies does oral jurisprudence offer for confronting the dictatorship-as-crisis?

This chapter pursues answers to these questions through a reading of the legal and oral contexts of Somalia in relationship to Farah's dictatorship trilogy, which aims widely at dictatorships throughout the African continent even as it takes the Somali context as its immediate point of reference. As in Okot and Ngũgĩ's work, "time" is also one of the dominant motifs of all three books in Farah's trilogy (e.g., immediately following the above reference in *Close Sesame* to indirect rule is an extended meditation on time [103]), but Farah's interest goes beyond thematics as temporality adheres to the long, narrative form itself, or what Peter Hitchcock calls the "long space," which is "a logic of form that pins time to the space and place of postcolonial narration" (42). In terms of form, Farah also, again, like Okot and Ngũgĩ, draws heavily on oral conventions in his work. Born in colonial Somalia in 1945, Farah "grew up in a genuinely oral world which communicated in a virtually unwritten language, his imagination nourished by the legendary oral poets of his Ogaden childhood" (Wright 345). Literary critics have connected this nourishment to Farah's extensive appropriations of and comments on Somali orature in his fiction, though none have noted the unique relationship between law and orature in Somali society.[3]

3 On Farah's orality, see, for example, Sparrow, "Telling the Story Yet Again: Oral Traditions in Nuruddin Farah's Fiction" (1989); Hawley, "Nuruddin Farah: Tribalism, Orality and Postcolonial Ultimate Reality and Meaning in Contemporary Somalia"

I say "unique" because although the ligature connecting law and orature is comparable to that found in Uganda, Kenya, and other African nations, it is much stronger and runs far deeper in Somalia. As we will see, orature and law are, for a large segment of Somali society, essentially indistinguishable, and this encourages us to read Farah's appropriations of orature as drawing on the authority of indigenous legal paradigms and discourses in order to interrogate the myths of time and crisis that lie under the authoritarian regime to which the *Variations* trilogy is a response.

However, I say "unique" also because oral jurisprudence in Somalia is available not only to the revolutionaries who oppose the dictator; it is also available to the dictator himself. Just like Siyad Barre upon whom he is based, "the General" in Farah's novels draws heavily on the forms and authority of Somali orature in the performance of authoritarian power. As one of the above epigraphs suggests, the oral can be "both sweet and bitter-tasting." This leads to some interesting complications. Of course, if orature can serve injustice as easily as justice, can it really be effective in countering the myths of dictatorial power? Furthermore, although Farah seems, at times, to blur the conventional line separating "tradition" from "modernity," at other times, he seems to reinforce it. When the dictator and his agents firmly ground their authority in the myth of "tradition," for example, is one required to embrace the binary in order to enact an effectual form of resistance? If so, what is the point of Farah's extended motif of time and temporality if the outcome of resisting dictatorial power is to restore the tradition/modernity binary that was so essential to colonialism and indirect rule? Can the binary, despite its history, actually provide an imaginative framework for revolution and just action?

The answers we will find to these questions, at least as offered by Farah's fiction, are hardly straightforward, and, in fact, each novel and the trilogy as a whole perform formal open-endedness. Once again, we encounter an absence of closure and the persistence of "not yet." When understood in the context of Somalia's legal history, however, including the complex normative and aesthetic world of *Xeer*, or Somali traditional law, this open-endedness provides a more definite, though perhaps not entirely satisfying, solution to the problem of colonial/postcolonial crisis than we have seen in previous examples: as one of Farah's characters observes, "time was ultimately a decider" (*Sardines* 285). This suggests that however indefinite a dictator's rule may seem to be, however indefinite the crisis, time will eventually outlive

---

(2002); Wright, "Orality and Power in *Sweet and Sour Milk*" (2002). In "A Postcolonial Perspective: Law and the Literary World" (2016), Amanda Ruth Waugh Lagji does offer a reading of Farah's novel *Maps* (1986) in relationship to Somali "customary law," or *Xeer*, but her focus is on Farah as a case study in postcolonial law and literature methodology, and she does not ultimately address the aesthetic dimensions of *Xeer*—i.e., the deep interconnectedness of orature and law for Somalis.

each injustice. Dictators will die. Regimes will pass on. And people are left to invent for themselves a "future without obstacles, a future beyond the future of a future" (45). This may not be particularly comforting in the context of an immediate crisis, and we might reflect that such invention is a luxury of the "modern," middle-class status of Farah's protagonists (doctors, dentists, law professors, students) who form the bulk of the movement that challenges the dictator, but if current debates about "deep time" and efforts to take the "long view" in understanding human history have taught us anything, it is that change, for better or for worse, will eventually come.[4]

In this chapter, I first provide an overview of key aspects of Somali legal history, focusing in particular on the variety of conflicting legal systems in Somalia, the legacies of indirect rule, and the importance of orature both in the *Xeer* system and Barre's dictatorship. I then turn to Farah's trilogy, which was written during the Barre regime and, thus, can be read as a running fictional commentary on Barre's explicit injustices as well as the deeper, implicit assumptions and myths that made such injustices possible. I conclude with some brief thoughts on how this particular trilogy, in addition to Farah's several other trilogies, can enable important ways of thinking about time in relationship to authoritarianism and other crises that continue to plague efforts globally to promote and protect peace, rights, and prosperity.

Legal Pluralism in Somali History

When Somalia gained its independence on July 1, 1960, it was left with a complex and contradictory system of law. In fact, it is perhaps inaccurate to call it a singular "system," as there were multiple legal systems that the newly independent government tried to reconcile. Great Britain had maintained a colony in the northern region, Italy a colony in the south. Britain had established its system of indirect rule alongside Islamic sharia and aspects of European law, but they also incorporated elements of Indian law as they did in Uganda, Kenya, and elsewhere.[5] In the south, Italy monitored the

4 See, for example, Chakrabarty, "Postcolonial Studies and the Challenge of Climate Change" (2012). Also see the conclusion of this book in which I take up Chakrabarty's argument and consider how my own approach to law and literature in East Africa might be brought to bear on questions of climate change.

5 The history of colonial rule in Somalia is fascinating and complex, with multiple European *and* African powers vying for control of the strategically located area bordering the Red Sea in the Horn of Africa. As such, I admit that my representation of that history here is necessarily selective and simplified. The Somalis constitute one of the largest ethnically homogenous blocs in all of Africa, and at one time they were divided into five somewhat arbitrarily designated regions: French Somaliland, British Somaliland, Italian Somaliland, Ethiopian Somaliland (the Ogaden), and the Northern Frontier District (NFD) of Kenya. In 1960, independent Somalia was comprised of the former British and Italian colonies,

courts of customary law and sharia to ensure that all laws and decisions were "compatible with the fundamental principles of Italian law" (Hess 109).

When Italy declared war on Great Britain in 1940, Italian forces invaded and seized British Somaliland and the Ethiopian-controlled area of the Ogaden. Italian control was short-lived, however, when Britain staged a counter-attack in 1941 and seized not only its own colony, but also the Ogaden and Italian Somaliland. From 1941 to 1948, Britain established a military administration over both regions, taking particular care to develop a local military wing, the Somalia Gendarmerie, to oversee police functions—thus, in addition to *Qadis'* courts established to administer sharia, "native" courts established to administer customary law, and both British and Italian laws, the administrative mode of military rule left an imprint on the Somali landscape. In 1948, Britain returned the Ogaden to Ethiopia, and in 1949 the United Nations General Assembly "voted to make southern Somalia a trust territory to be placed under Italian control for ten years, following which it would become independent" (Metz). In 1960, that objective was realized, and in the many years since there has yet to emerge a satisfactory system of law that reconciles the pluralistic imperatives (or contradictions) left by colonial history (although popular representations of present-day Somalia as "lawless" and anarchic do tend to be oversimplified and, at times, incorrect).[6]

The period from 1960 to 1969 witnessed various changes to the Somali constitution and the newly independent government's struggle to develop a functioning parliamentary democracy. Several different political parties formed over time, vying for control of the government's National Assembly, and democratic elections were held with some degree of success, but clan politics began to interfere as some perceived nepotism and cronyism among the government leaders. Alice Hashim observes, "The importance of clan identity and loyalty in Somalia cannot be overstated," and in the years leading up to the end of Somalia's first independent government clan loyalties began to color government choices and elections such that clan affiliations increasingly became more important than party affiliations (9). Somalia's clan system based on kinship is highly complex and beyond any simplified explanation that I can offer here, but suffice it to say that the various clans

with Ethiopia maintaining control of the Ogaden (an area that has led to years of war and conflict between Somalia and Ethiopia); Kenya maintaining control of the NFD; and French Somaliland, now known as Djibouti, gaining independence.

6 For example: in 1991, with the end of Barre's regime, the former British Somaliland seceded and declared itself the independent Republic of Somaliland. Although the international community has yet to recognize officially their sovereignty, Somaliland has developed a system of law and administration that, to some extent, has been able to function democratically and with a relative degree of stability while Somalia to the south continues to struggle. One of the reasons for Somaliland's success is that it has found a way of reconciling a centralized government with the Somali clan system by limiting the government's role to a few necessary areas. See Mark Bradbury, *Becoming Somaliland* (2008).

and sub-clans into which the Somali people are divided are simultaneously valued as institutions and vehicles of tradition (including indigenous law) and reviled as a hedge to modernization.[7] The conflict over the status of the clan system with respect to contemporary politics has its roots, in part, in the British approach to indirect rule in Somaliland. In many ways similar to administrative procedures in other parts of British Africa, indirect rule in Somaliland went through multiple phases as it struggled to take form. At the center of that struggle was the repeated failure of British authorities to understand Somali political and social systems. As one might expect, they assumed Somali society to be "tribally" organized and, thus, identified as tribal chiefs those they perceived to be figures of authority. However, both the assumption and the identification were mistaken, and they inadvertently gave substantial authority to individuals with no significant traditional status in Somali culture. Particularly in the early colonial period, writes Jama Mohamed, "indirect rule created 'artificial political positions' that sowed jealousies and rivalries among the elders and thus weakened the stability of kinship groups" (230).

The debate over whether to preserve tradition or promote modernity intensified in the late colonial period and, as Mohamed explains, there was an effort to create institutions that were "supposed to be modern, yet they were to be built on a 'traditional' basis" (231). What this meant, exactly, remained unclear, and while some policies of modernization appeared to work in urban areas, they were "a total failure in the rural areas" because they were based on mistaken assumptions about the nature of Somali social organization (232). According to Mohamed, the British obsession over questions of kinship (misidentified as "tribal' relations) led them to overlook the more fundamental issue of the rules, embodied in the concept of a "social contract" (or *Xeer* in Somali), that governed Somali kinship structures. The relations themselves, in other words, were important, but so too were the rules and principles that gave meaning to those complex and dynamic relations. The emerging Somali elite adopted the British attitude toward traditional society, identifying it as a "backward system" that "weakened the nationalist movement" (245). At the same time, however, they wished to exploit clan relations for political ends. Hashim claims that the emergence of clan politics during the pre-Barre era was evidence that the "governing formulas" of parliamentary democracy "proved to be inadaptable to local conditions" (77), but, in fact, the ruling elites who rose to power during this time were simply uninterested in "a democratic system. They wanted the kinship relation but not the burden of the rules and ethics of kinship" (Mohamed 245). In order to gain power, in other words, the ruling elite simultaneously advanced and undermined modernization, claiming to offer a mode of progress away from

7 For a detailed discussion of Somalia's clan system, see I.M. Lewis, *Blood and Bone: The Call of Kinship in Somali Society* (1994).

"backward" Somali customs, but also manipulating clan politics for political ends. This perpetuation of the colonial narratives and assumptions central to indirect rule led to "virtual anarchy" (Hashim 69) and, unsurprisingly, to dictatorship. Into the anarchy "stepped Mohamed Siad Barre, military man, nationalist, pan-Somalist, with an agenda that included the dual objectives of freeing Somalis from traditional structures which could no longer serve them and liberating them from the legacy of colonial rule" (77). Barre called his new government the "Supreme Revolutionary Council" (SRC), which took power in 1969.

In her study of the Barre regime, Hashim draws on Robert Jackson and Carl Rosberg's categories of personal rule to argue that at different times Barre exemplified all four, including Prophet, Prince, Autocrat, and Tyrant (79). In the beginning, as Prophet, Barre was the leader of the revolution. He demonstrated exceptional promise and was extremely successful in convincing the public of his ability to overcome Somalia's problems, which, he argued, were a combination of colonialism and clan-ism. He "attempted first to end the corruption and abuse of the parliamentary regime and later through 'Scientific Socialism' attempted to reorganize society by eliminating clan consciousness." From the beginning, however, Barre's "prophetic" style was carried out, in part, through the mechanisms of emergency rule. For although there were seemingly progressive elements to his government, particularly in the early years, the legal instrument that served him most throughout his transition from Prophet to Tyrant was emergency law. Furthermore, it has become commonplace to depict dictatorships in the popular imagination as "lawless" regimes because of their human rights abuses and frequent violations of international law. However, I would argue the opposite: although dictatorships do come into conflict with international law, they are often defined by an excess, rather than lack of, law. Dictators are often obsessed with legality, "dictating" laws in abundance and using the mechanisms of the law to carry out their objectives. At their worst, dictatorships are driven by little more than the autocratic whims of the head of state, but as the government publicly carries out those whims, the law plays a significant role. There were two areas of law in particular that Barre used which are important for our understanding of Farah's trilogy: the first, as noted, was emergency law; the second was customary law.

Almost immediately after taking power, Barre's Supreme Revolutionary Council "banned political parties, abolished the National Assembly, *and suspended the constitution*" (Metz; emphasis added). These actions were no doubt done in the name of wiping the slate clean of the corruption and failures of the previous government, thereby promising a new beginning, but, as we have seen previously, the act of suspending the law in the name of restoring law and order is undone by its contradictory temporality: the exceptional measures claim to be temporary, but they tend to become permanent. Technically, Barre declared official States of Emergency at particular times, so there were temporary breaks between actual emergencies: in 1974, in response to a severe drought in the rangelands (Hashim 88); in 1977, as Barre prepared to go to war with Ethiopia over the Ogaden (101); and from 1980 to 1982 as a result of conflicts with the Issaq clan in the northern region of the country. However, in 1988, Amnesty International reported that since 1982 "the northern regions have been under virtual military rule by the northern sector army commander" (qtd. in Hashim 112). To be fair, the first and second of these declarations were motivated by the desire to protect and defend Somalis. Furthermore, as Hashim discusses, Barre instituted social programs in the first part of his regime that "resulted in important achievements," including effective vaccination campaigns, increased school enrollments, and an increased literacy rate (90). Additionally, in an effort to eradicate patriarchal lineage structures and improve the status and political participation of women, Barre passed an extremely progressive family law, declaring, "As from this date [January 11, 1975] the Somali man and woman are equal. They have the same equality, the same rights, and the same share of whatever is inherited from their parents" (qtd. in Hashim 89).

However, although some of these accomplishments were admirable, "they came at a high cost to civil liberties and human rights" (Hashim 90). Barre would not tolerate any form of dissent or disagreement and "those who persisted in pointing to problems or difficulties were summarily imprisoned" or executed. In response to the 1975 family law, for example, a group of ten Islamic sheikhs voiced their concerns, insisting that the reforms contradicted sharia on the issue of inheritance. Barre had all ten of them executed. (A fictional version of this event appears in Farah's *Sweet and Sour Milk*.) The progressive, socialist reforms that the family law supposedly embodied (which some claim were actually intended to impress the international community)[8] were damaged by Barre's heavy-handed, murderous reaction to the sheikhs, who had done little more than disagree with him openly. Barre also targeted people in his government and in the military, who dared voice concerns, and he created an intelligence arm, the National Security Service (NSS), which aided him in listening for and responding to murmurings among the general citizenry. As Hashim explains, noting the key markers of an environment in which "special powers" have become the norm:

> With the creation of the National Security Service, harassment, arbitrary arrest and imprisonment, denial of a fair public trial, and invasion of the home were common features in the life of the Somali citizen. *By 1978* habeas corpus, *freedom of political association, personal liberty and movement, public expression, and the right to form unions and strike were either highly circumscribed or non-existent.* (90; emphasis added)

These were the common features in the lives of Somali citizens during Barre's rule and they are, therefore, also common features in the lives of the

8 See, for example, Mohamed-Rashid Sheik Hassan, "The 1969 Military Coup in Somalia." Part 13. *Wararka Maanta.* March 1, 2010.

characters in Farah's trilogy. The novels depict a world in which a paranoid dictator, who initially used his power to serve the "revolution," has begun to view all citizens as potential threats and, therefore, potential criminals.

Emergency law is only part of the picture. The other area of law that Barre exploited in consolidating power was one that he initially claimed to supplant. Like the ruling elite whom he displaced in 1969, Barre insisted that Somali customs were a barrier to progress. He opposed customary law and, in particular, the practice of *diya*, or the payment of blood-compensation from one clan to another for wrongs committed. Within the system of *diya*, an entire group may be held responsible for the actions of a single member and an entire group entitled to seek justice—if someone commits murder, for example, the victim's kinship group is entitled to seek compensation or even retribution. Barre condemned such practices and attempted to replace *diya* with a "state judicial system" that would handle all disputes (Hashim 89). As time wore on, however, and as Barre's tactics became increasingly harsh and support for his regime waned, he turned to his own clan networks for support, surrounding himself with what Farah calls an "incestuous circle" of relatives and sycophants (*Sardines* 98). Not only did Barre appoint members of the Marehan, Ogadeni, and Dulbahante clans (respectively, his paternal, maternal, and son-in-law's clans and sub-clans) to positions of power, but, like the ruling elite who came before him, he "reverted to a more 'traditional' political game of manipulating 'the tangled web of kinship relations'" for his benefit (Hashim 105). And although Barre had initially sought to end the practice of *diya*, "the laws of group obligation and responsibility [were] called upon" as Barre built "[r]ings of security around his regime" (9). When anyone offended him, Barre was able to portray it as an offense against his kinship groups and then use that network to carry out acts of retribution. Furthermore, in addition to the laws of clan obligation, Barre relied heavily upon one other significant aspect of indigenous law: orature. Barre was "reputedly versed in the poetry and oral literature for which the Somali people are justly famed, and he was an accomplished orator" (Hashim 77). As in the Acholi and Kikuyu cultures, orature and law are intimately related in Somali society, and to grasp fully the significance of Barre's appropriations of orature in his regime (and as represented in Farah's novels), we need to examine briefly the integral role that orature plays in Somali law.

Somalia has an amazingly rich and sophisticated oral tradition and, as in other cultures, orature plays a significant socio-political, and not simply aesthetic, role. Eloquence in oratory is one of the most highly valued abilities, particularly among "traditional" pastoral-nomadic Somalis, but even in urban areas. As Alexander Stille writes in an essay on oral poetry in contemporary Somalia, "in an oral society—even a postmodern oral society—the poet is king" (183). When Richard Burton wrote of his travels to Somalia in the 1850s, he observed that "the country teems with 'poets'" (82); and Canadian novelist Margaret Laurence famously described Somalia as "a nation of poets" (23). Alice Hashim argues that the importance of the clan for an understanding of

Somali society "cannot be overstated," but I would add that neither can the importance of poetry and oratorical skill (9). Said S. Samatar states it well:

> The Somalis think of their verse as more than just an artistic enterprise whose sole aim is to enlarge the imagination and to inspire men towards the lyrical and the beautiful. When they talk of poetry, Somalis have in mind something which embodies the totality of their culture and to which they attach the highest measure of importance. In the words of one elder, "*Poetry is the central integrating principle without which harmonious relationships in society would be unthinkable.*" (55; emphasis added)

The elder whom Samatar quotes does not state it explicitly, but when he refers to the necessity of poetry for maintaining harmonious relationships he is talking about the central role of poetry in Somali law. This is *Xeer* or the rules of "social contract," that Mohamed argues give meaning to Somali kinship structures. Poetry serves a variety of functions in Somali society—poetry "is resorted to in the formalization and execution of almost every public act of importance" (Samatar 56)—but it has a particularly significant place in the administration of *Xeer.*

Within a clan, large-scale decisions are made, and disputes are resolved through lengthy public consultations during which various concerned parties can present their ideas and perspectives to those (typically elders) designated to weigh options and recommend courses of action. Given the "pre-eminence of the spoken word" in Somali society, "men who wield influence do so mainly through their powers of persuasion rather than coercion" (Samatar 27). However, as Samatar observes, while Somali society purports to be "egalitarian" and "democratic," not all are equal, because some are more gifted speakers and poets than others, and those who have proven their superior oratorical abilities are favored participants in legal disputes.[9] According to Ali Jimale Ahmed, "The best lawyer a plaintiff (or an accused) could have is a good poet."[10] There are two main types of legal courts or formal assemblies that arise in Somali society, and both are described metaphorically as "trees" (which is where, out on the pastoral grasslands, clan groups would gather to resolve disputes): the first is the "Tree of Justice and Jurisprudence"; and the second is the "Tree of Truth and Justice" (28). The former, which will be our primary concern here, is the assembly over which *Xeer*, or secular customary law, has jurisdiction; the latter assembly convenes over matters of concern to Islamic law. In a *Xeer* assembly, all adult males have the right to participate by sharing their opinions in discussing a dispute that affects the community, but "in practice three types of men dominate the meeting: the orator (*'odkar*), the poet (*gabayaa*) and the expert-in-tradition (*heerbeegti*)" (Samatar 29). There

9 Furthermore, the participants in *Xeer* proceedings are primarily men, and this gender inequality is likely one of the reasons Farah maintains a semi-ambivalent perspective on the value of oral culture.

10 Personal correspondence with the author, April 17, 2011.

are typically orator/poet pairs on each side of a dispute acting as advocates of a particular position: the orator speaks first, presenting his case, and then "he usually gives the floor to a poet, who covers the same ground in poetic oration" (30). The *heerbeegti*, usually elders with proven knowledge of precedent and tradition as well as exceptional skill in oration, listen to the presentations and deliberate not only on the basis of the substantive merits of each case, but also their aesthetic merits. A *Xeer* assembly is "a battle of wits and of words," and, for success in the battle, Samatar states,

> Not only is knowledge of history, customs and tradition essential, but also the ability to articulate them into a coherent whole is equally, if not more, indispensable. For although they do not concede it in so many words, Somalis tend to emphasize style over substance in resolving litigation, so that the skill with which a case is presented seems to carry greater weight than its actual merits. (30)

Poets are truly the acknowledged legislators of the Somali world—they are not simply the voices of morality and wisdom whose expressed principles form the basis of codified laws, but their poetry and skill with words in oral performance play a fundamental, constitutive role in legal procedures.

The interconnectedness of orature and law is such that, according to Ali Moussa Iye, there is an entire corpus of orature/literature that he calls "la littérature du Xeer" (277). Not only do orators and poets use literary techniques in presenting cases to the *heerbeegti*, but because of poetry's role in legal procedures, there are poems, proverbs, and prose texts of different kinds dealing directly with *Xeer*-related themes. Iye enumerates these different forms and their characteristics in his study of the laws of the Issa clan (in Djibouti), devoting an entire chapter to "*Xeer* literature." He conducted interviews with a number of Somali elders in an effort to collect examples of this literature, but he said it was difficult because often even the elders could not make a distinction between what might be considered literary versus what was legal.

Most often, *Xeer* was both. As an example, here is a translation of one of the poems he recorded, which is basically a judge's prologue offered at the beginning of a case:

> One convenes, the other presents the case
> One opens the meeting, the other explains the facts
> One presides and the other decides
> One loses and one wins.
> The case is discussed
> By those who have faith
> Without intrigue and without ulterior motives.
> Hear, those who have ears!
> See, those who have eyes!
> When the testimonies are taken
> When oaths are taken

Let the reporters report!
Let the experts evaluate!
Let the arbitrators advise!
And may the just watch over the law.
Against amalgams and failures,
Against the biased and ignorant,
Against liars and the corrupt,
Always, before taking a decision, separate
Facts which are due to the coincidence of circumstances
And those due to human malevolence.
The judgment of the dead is left to God
The living is the business of the old. (283)[11]

Iye observes that such a poem reveals the extent to which poetic techniques are used by *Xeer* lawyers and judges not only to make their arguments more effective, but to appeal to the Issa's sensitivity to "la beauté du Verbe" (284). In Somali society, in short, we see the strongest connection yet between orature and law—the two, indeed, are indistinguishable in the *Xeer* tradition.

Just because orature is law, however, does not necessarily mean that orature is also equivalent to justice. One of the refrains of Somali poetry, particularly in discussions of its legal function, emphasizes the fact that orality can be both "sweet and bitter-tasting" (qtd. in Abdullahi 78). While skill in poetry can bring honor to the poet and his clan and can be used to persuade others toward justice and fairness in a dispute, the same skill can be used to attack others and bring about evil and injustice. Samatar identifies four types of orators, all ranked according to their skill: The least skillful is the "afgaroo," which means "mouth deformed," or the speaker who has absolutely no oratorical skill whatsoever; the afgaroo is "Hashiisa ma da'sade," or "he who cannot defend his camel" (31). The most skillful is the "afmaal," which means, literally, "mouth wealth," or the speaker whose words are like wealth, the orator of "towering prestige who has the reputation of never having lost a case in which he has argued." The second is the "aftahan," which means "mouth generous," or the speaker who lacks the prestige of the afmaal, but who still commands some respect for his skill. The third orator is called "afmiishaar" and has skill comparable to the first two types, certainly exceeding the last, but uses it for negative and destructive purposes. Literally meaning "mouth saw," the afmiishaar is "the man of universal scandal and provocation, trafficking in malice and insidious rumors and inciting clans to feud" (30). The afmiishaar's vocabulary is drawn from the "bitter-tasting" dimensions of Somali orature. "He has powerful instruments for persuasion," states a Somali elder, "but always uses them to create mayhem" (qtd. in Samatar 30). Significantly, while afmiishaars have played a role in rural, pastoral Somali

11 Iye records the poem in both Somali and French. This is my translation of the French version.

society, urbanization and "modernization" created a new niche in which the mouth-saw poets flourished (31). Reviled and feared in rural Somalia, the afmiishaar became a commodity in the politics-driven environment of the city. With the erosion of "collective kinship accountability," afmishaars exploited the "impersonal society of the city" and began in particular to lend their services as "propagandists and public relations men" to politicians and others in positions of power. As Samatar explains, afmiishaars demonstrated "unprincipled readiness to sell their talents to the highest bidder," and "nowhere was this more obvious than in their intimate attachment to the powerful in the politics of pre- and post-independence Somalia."

Siyad Barre, though he initially sought to do away with certain aspects of *Xeer* law, fully understood and appreciated the necessity of oratorical eloquence in achieving and maintaining power in post-independence Somalia. As noted earlier, Barre knew the Somali oral tradition extremely well and "was an accomplished orator" (Hashim 77). However, Barre also employed poets, some of whom, we can safely assume, would no doubt be considered afmiishaars. "In the early years of his regime," writes Ali Jimale Ahmed, "Barre managed to lure the support of many oral poets to his cause. [...] The traditional intellectual or artist—the poet, the oral historian, etc.—gave moral and intellectual justifications for Barre's rule" (12).[12] We see these phenomena in the fictionalized version of Barre's regime in Farah's *Variations* trilogy. In fact, the title of the first novel, *Sweet and Sour Milk*, gestures toward the very problem of orature's duality: sweet one the one hand, capable of promoting justice and attacking injustice; sour on the other, able to stir up malice and suspicion, to propagandize, to sing the praises of that which is unjust. However, not only is Barre, or "The General," able to appropriate orality for unjust purposes, but he also mobilizes the other side of the oral performance—*aurality*—in order to attain ubiquitous control over the Somali soundscape. Barre was an excellent orator, but, particularly through the ears of his National Security Service, he was also an excellent listener, attuned to voices of dissent and ready to employ the law (whether emergency or the clan-based laws of group obligation) to suspend such voices. In an environment such as this, how is resistance possible? What role can the sweet or just dimensions of Somali orature play when the conditions for oral performance (i.e., the freedom to speak publicly to an audience, with an interlocutor, etc.) are severely restricted and controlled? These are among the key questions Farah explores in his *Variations* trilogy, drawing upon narratives and motifs of temporality in addition to orality to address the crisis that was the Barre dictatorship.

12 The poet Abdullahi Waranle, for example, was an early supporter and, later, witnessing Barre's faltering regime, wrote, "O Allah, can anyone help the elder [i.e., Barre] [...]?" (Ingriis 232). Poets critical of Barre include figures such as Abdulkadir Hersi Yamyam (Ingriis 94) and modern Somalia's best-known poet, Mohamed Ibrahim Warsame, or "Hadrawi," whom I discuss in more detail below.

Inventing a Future beyond the Future of a Future: *Variations on the Theme of an African Dictatorship*

A common cliché, often cited in popular characterizations of Benito Mussolini's regime, holds that whatever else dictatorships get wrong, at least they make the trains run on time. Hardly a justification for authoritarian rule, the cliché is instead typically a tongue-in-cheek (or selectively nostalgic) recognition that although dictatorships are largely destructive and unjust, they can also be highly efficient. The top-down mode of dictatorial rule is a simpler form of governance that, while easily abused, has a tendency to get things done. In *Sweet and Sour Milk*, the first novel in Farah's *Variations* trilogy, one of the protagonists references this cliché, saying that he once asked an older Italian man what he remembered about Mussolini and what connotations the name held for him. "When Mussolini was here," the man replies, "the trains arrived exactly on time" (247). The narrator then observes that the same was true of Stalin's Russia and Hitler's Germany. And, we presume, it might be said of the Somali dictatorship to which these are being compared. Although, as Hashim demonstrates, Siyad Barre went through several phases in his time as head of state, we see the General only in the tyrannical phase.

Farah's critique, obviously, is most concerned with Barre's abuses rather than his (moderate and early) successes, and, as a result, the time period and the normative world we encounter in the novels are conditioned by the authoritarian law of the dictator. Indeed, one character observes that they have been in an official state of emergency for over five years (*Sweet* 179), and the General himself declares, "I am the constitution!" (251) Despite this, we do not see the trains running on time, and, in fact, the first novel portrays the failures of bureaucracy: a delayed funeral van is described as "the height of this régime's inefficiency" (38). What we do see is efficiency in other areas of the dictator's influence. The trains (and funeral vans) may not run on time, but the General's systems of propaganda and surveillance, both of which rely heavily on Somali oral culture, are highly efficient and lead to frequent arrests and abductions. In both of these expressions of power—apprehensions and surveillance—we find key aspects of the regime's relationship to and reliance upon myths of temporality.

In terms of arrests, abductions, and detention without trial, the dominant temporal refrain in *Sweet and Sour Milk* is expressed in the question, "When will your turn come?" (36). In other words, when will the General's security forces come for you, just as they have come for others who are taken and interrogated, tortured, and who often disappear and are never seen again? The specter of "your time," or the moment when the General's gaze turns to you, haunts every character in *Sweet and Sour Milk* and encapsulates the normative universe of the General's regime. The General possesses the power over life and death, and through the mechanisms of emergency rule he produces a particular kind of subject: the citizen-as-potential-criminal. States of emergency are declared in the face of an internal or external threat of some kind, but authoritarian regimes (including colonialism) perpetuate the "temporary" provisions of emergency law and treat all citizens as potential criminals. In this way, the dictator is, according to the law, justified in restricting public gatherings, banning subversive material, detaining suspects indefinitely, and executing detractors. As potential criminals, every character throughout Farah's trilogy has a "time," or a moment when the general will come for them.

Loyaan, the main protagonist of *Sweet and Sour Milk*, spends much of the novel investigating the mysterious death of his twin brother Soyaan, and, in the process, he begins to uncover his brother's subversive activities. The General's gaze turns toward Loyaan, and at one point he is told the exact moment when his turn will come: on the following day at "Seven in the evening, precisely" (224). The following day is the "seventh-day commemoration of Soyaan's death"; and after the commemoration the time finally comes and there is nothing Loyaan can do to escape. The last lines of the novel are: "It was seven in the evening. There was a knock on the outside door" (263).

This efficiency in making the abductions run on time, so to speak, turns the General into a point of temporal reference. In *Sardines*, Sagal, a student and nationally recognized swimmer who sympathizes with the clandestine movement, observes:

> Nomads name their years and seasons "the year of the drought," "the season of waterlessness and famine," "the year of the child-killing measles" or "the rainy month in which the Sultan died." We date our memory differently; we think of the General as an institution and date and name things accordingly. I remember such-and-such happened when Dheel, Gavere, and Caynaanshe were killed [...]. I remember that was when Soyaan was mysteriously eliminated and made a hero. (266)

Just as a large part of the world began measuring time with reference to Greenwich, England, at the height of the British Empire, the Somali world in the novel measures time with reference to the General.[13] This manipulation of time grows out of the colonial narratives of temporality that sought to invent and manipulate the temporal character of its subjects. Similarly, the General wields temporality as a mechanism of control, not only becoming a calendrical reference point and exerting power over the lives and deaths of his subjects, but also controlling their afterlives. As Loyaan tries to solve the mystery of his brother's death, he watches helplessly as the regime co-opts Soyaan into the machinery of its propaganda. Hiding all details of his revolutionary activities, the General and his "Supreme Revolutionary Council" turn Soyaan into a hero of the revolution, naming streets after him and falsely claiming that his last words were "LABOUR IS HONOUR AND THERE IS NO GENERAL BUT OUR GENERAL" (*Sweet* 107). Loyaan is told that the regime is "re-writing your

13 See Barrows, *The Cosmic Time of Empire: Modern Britain and World Literature* (2011).

family's history" even as it fabricates and controls his family's future, erasing the memory of Soyaan's true character and activities and, in the end, coming for Loyaan (115).[14]

In addition to controlling time, the General attempts to drown out voices of opposition by controlling space: specifically, the oral soundscape. He is the ultimate *afmiishaar* who uses his remarkable powers of persuasion to provoke and propagandize. Through emergency powers, for example, the General has made it illegal "to have an assembly of more than five persons," and through orality he leaves an exception: more than five can gather if they "sing the General's praises" and "chant the chorus of the General's ninety-nine good-names" (*Sweet* 95). The General fills the newspapers and billboards with quotations of his wisdom, and the radios broadcast songs "of the General's praise names" sung by poets and performers recruited, or coerced, into supporting the regime (10). Furthermore, the General has filled his National Security Service with

> illiterates, men and women who belong to an oral tradition and who neither read nor write but report daily, report what they hear as they hear it, word by word. They report verbatim what they think they heard when they walked into the shop. [...] Everything is done verbally. Instructions are given on the phone: "Before dawn arrest So-and-so." Most of these are not even traceable to their origin, for there are no written warrants. (148)

By only speaking orders and reporting orally, the General's security forces are able to carry out their activities in a way that leaves very few traces of their actions, aside from their fatal effects. With "no written warrants," those involved in carrying out the regime's violence are difficult to identify, and concrete evidence of orders from the General are difficult to obtain. It is in this way that, according to Derek Wright, "the oral tradition [acquires] darker dimensions" because it is "effectively allied with the reactionary forces of tribal authoritarianism and obscurantism, thus polarizing oral despotism and written revolution, unalphabeted tyranny and textual subversion" (347). I disagree with Wright that the oral is necessarily opposed to the written—the General after all does control print media as much as oral, and the written word is both a strength and a liability for the opposition. (Soyaan's

14 The General's control of time is comparable to that of another larger-than-life fictional dictator, the Ruler in Ngũgĩ wa Thiong'o's *Wizard of the Crow* (2006). For example, when the Ruler's wife begins to question him about rumors that he is ill, he responds angrily by imprisoning her in a house full of clocks all frozen to the exact time she raised her question. His objective is to show his wife "that he, the Ruler, had power, real power over everything including ... yes ... Time" (7). Farah's portrayal of the General's control over time is, perhaps, more realistic and less satirical, but in many ways it is just as surreal. For an excellent reading of the temporal themes and formal structures of *Wizard of the Crow*, see Colson, "Arresting Time, Resisting Arrest."

death, for example, can be partly attributed to the fact that he *wrote* several secret memoranda criticizing the regime.) However, Wright's point that oral culture becomes something "darker" in *Sweet and Sour Milk*, is certainly true. In this way, "Farah seeks neither to rehabilitate the traditional forms [...] nor to discredit and repudiate them [...] but rather to show how indigenous traditions, both oral and domestic, have themselves been implicated in the new political tribulations and terrors of the independent state" (Wright 346).

The passage about the General's security service also illustrates the leader's appropriation of *aurality* in addition to orality. Spoken to Loyaan by a man named Ibrahim, a member of Soyaan's underground movement, the description of the General's network of illiterate security personnel comes during a discussion of Soyaan's secret memoranda that the General is aware of and desperately wants to obtain. The one Ibrahim describes, which is never found, is titled "Dionysius's Ear" (*Sweet* 147). Loyaan correctly guesses that Dionysius refers to the "Syracusan tyrant," and Ibrahim explains: "The Syracusan tyrant had a cave built in the shape of a human ear which echoed to him in polysyllables whatever the prisoners whispered secretly to one another. Soyaan and I saw a similarity between this and the method the General has used so far" (148). In other words, not only does the General graft the oral tradition onto his regime as a way of manipulating and monopolizing what is spoken, but he dominates the *aural* dimensions of the soundscape as well, listening through his network of NSS officers and others loyal to him. The General listens for voices of dissent and when they are heard, he silences them.

This control of the soundscape is related to the General's manipulation of temporal narratives, in a sense, because it is part of his turn to "tradition." The "illiterate" agents are often described as "(tribal) upstarts," or members of clans with close ties to the General (*Sweet* 36; parentheses in original). The General, like Barre, tried to do away with clan-based politics and the *diya* system to impose a "progressive" socialist regime, but his dictatorial tactics lost him support and he retreated into the safe house of tradition in order to protect his power. However, this is a framework of tradition without the content of *Xeer* that Jama Mohamed says provides the ethical principles that should govern kinship relations (227). Thus, in addition to his tribal upstarts, the General also employs traditional singers and poets, and he manipulates traditional figures of familial authority. A quotation from Wilhelm Reich provides an epigraph for Part Two of *Sweet and Sour Milk*: "In the figure of the father the authoritarian state has its representative in every family, so that the family becomes its most important instrument of power" (103). Loyaan's father Keynaan is the General's representative in their family, for example, willingly supporting the regime's revision of Soyaan's life and legacy. An even more dramatic example appears in *Sardines* along with and as part of an expanded examination of the concepts of tradition and modernity in relationship to orality and temporality. The

General's representative, Idil, is a matriarch rather than a patriarch, but her authority is no less threatening.[15]

Sardines marks an interesting "variation" on the various themes of the General's dictatorship. Focusing primarily on female characters, the novel continues to portray the day-to-day violence of life under an authoritarian regime; but in the process of doing so it also seems to reinforce the tradition/modernity binary. Simon Gikandi has written that in Farah's novels, "terms such as *modern* and *tradition*, which have been the central paradigms in some of the most powerful commentaries on African literature, are constantly blurred and deauthorized" ("Nuruddin Farah" 753). This seems to be the accepted wisdom about these novels, but I would trouble that wisdom and argue that there is a sense in which Farah does the opposite, reinforcing the line between tradition and modernity; or, more properly, exploiting the more clearly established line that the General and his representatives have drawn around the concept of tradition. The line perhaps becomes somewhat blurred in the final novel of the trilogy, as we will see, but in *Sardines* there is a clear distinction between the representatives of traditional authority and the modern, cosmopolitan characters who oppose that authority. The main protagonist of the novel, Medina, for example, is well-educated, a writer and newspaper editor, and also a mother. Her husband, Samater, works in the General's ministry, and together they have a young daughter, Ubax. One of the tensions that emerges early in the novel is between Medina and Idil, Samater's mother, who wishes the traditional procedure of infibulation to be performed on Ubax. "Idil," we are told, "represents traditional authority, and it is in the old and not the young that society invests power" (26–27). Medina resists Idil's authority, even going so far as to leave Samater and protect Ubax from the demands of tradition. Idil bitterly believes the younger generation to be incapable of finding "any substitute with which to replace the traditional culture they appear to have discarded" (9), and later she criticizes her weak-willed son, saying, "I am a product of a tradition with a given coherence and solidity; you of confusion and indecision" (88). Reflecting on the conflict between Medina

15 Farah's treatment of gender is fascinating and important and has been the subject of much discussion. It is not my intention to examine or contribute to those particular debates in this chapter, but I do find it interesting that as progressive as *Sardines* is in many ways in terms of its representations of gender (e.g., the debate about infibulation carried on throughout the novel, Sagal's desire to determine her own future, etc.), Farah still makes the villain a woman. Farah is clearly not interested in romanticizing women in a simplistic way to counter patriarchal authority, but the matriarchal tyrant also seems to draw attention, in a sense, away from the gender dynamics to the dynamics of traditional authority. For discussions of the gender question in Farah's work, see, among others, Juraga, "Nuruddin Farahs' *Variations on the Theme of an African Dictatorship*: Patriarchy, Gender, and Political Oppression in Somalia" (1997); Brown, "Bleeding for the Mother(Land): Reading Testimonial Bodies in Nuruddin Farah's *Maps*" (2010); and Gagiano, "Farah's *Sardines*: Women in a Context of Despotism" (2011).

and Idil, the narrator asks, "Did Medina not realize that a confrontation with Idil meant a direct challenge to tradition, to the General's generation?" (112). For Idil, as for the General and his followers, tradition is stable, a source of authority, a foundation from which social order and power can be enacted. It is, furthermore, timeless. "Unlike the seasons, the years, the men, the women and children," Idil tells her son, "unlike all these, tradition stays and wins in the end" (199).

The antagonists in *Sardines* are not the only ones to reinforce this concept of tradition. As noted, the protagonists are mostly "modern," cosmopolitan, future-oriented characters (it is Sagal, Medina's protégé, who desires to invent for herself "A future without obstacles" [45]), but they also use terms that place them in opposition to tradition and, therefore, seemingly in the position that European colonialists held in the past. In describing the General, Medina calls him "primitive," "backward," and an "uneducated imbecile" (52). Nasser, another member of the movement, converses with Dulman, a traditional singer, about her use of cassette tapes to collect and distribute subversive poetry. I will discuss Dulman in more detail below, but at one point Nasser observes that Dulman, who must listen to the tapes to memorize new poems because she is illiterate, is "dependent on the twentieth century's advanced technology" (184). He clearly places her in the realm of tradition, catching her in an apparent contradiction as she relies upon modern technology. Lastly, following an evening conversation between Medina and a friend, the narrator turns our attention to a lit candle on the table between them. A moth has flown into the flame and killed itself, and the narrator describes the other moths "that revolved around the light frenziedly like Cherokee Indians preparing a tribal assault on the technology of this century when armed with the weapons of another epoch" (240). Why does Farah choose this particular simile? Given the themes of the novel, and the trilogy as a whole, it hardly seems coincidental, but it also seems strange given the novel's critique of colonialism and the unquestioning use here of characteristically colonial language. Native Americans and moths are compared in terms of their assumed naivety and technological inferiority.

One might defend Medina's description of the General as "primitive" because she acknowledges that it is an "aggressive, violent term" (52)—a nod, apparently, to its colonial history—and, further, because she is criticizing the General's fascism. Nasser might be excused because he is asking Dulman questions about how she reconciles the traditional and the modern, a process that may blur the boundaries between the two. But the reference to the futile "tribal assault" of the Cherokee Indians seems, to me, to be inexcusable. Farah is rarely ironic, preferring a stylistic earnestness that verges, at times, on the sentimental and the falsely profound, and, whatever this unexpected simile is supposed to convey, it most certainly serves to clarify rather than blur a line between tradition and modernity. Rather than simply fault Farah for this, it is worth considering whether or not there is a political strategy behind this delineation, even if it seems discordant from a conventional postcolonial perspective. In short, if tradition has become a source of oppression, as it clearly has in the hands of the General, does modernity offer a solution, or a "regime of intelligibility" for making sense of and resisting tradition (Mbembe 324)? If so, what form does this modernity take? Must one return to colonial modernity (as Farah seems to in the reference to the Cherokee), or are there alternative modernities that might counter an essentialized and authoritarian tradition without reinforcing the paradigms of colonial crisis?

To answer these questions, it is first necessary to consider the relationship between the General's concept of tradition and colonialism's. On the one hand, within the colonial economy of time and modernity, tradition is a mark of temporal lag, of inferiority and an inability to cope with the demands of the modern world. For the General, tradition is a source of power and control, and, according to Idil, it is far superior to the "confusion and indecision" of modernity (88). On the other hand, the colonial concept of tradition was central to indirect rule, and just as the "tribal chiefs" of indirect rule used traditional authority in the exercise of "despotic powers" (Njoku 57) so too does the General in the exercise of his despotic powers. As established earlier, the character of Deeriye in *Close Sesame* suggests that the General's authoritarian tradition is directly traceable to the tradition of indirect rule, and we saw how in late colonial and early postcolonial Somalia the ruling elite manipulated the concept of tradition for political purposes, something Barre himself also does. One strategy for minimizing this authority, therefore, would be to adopt the colonial binary in order to return tradition to a position of inferiority. This may be Farah's intention, at least in *Sardines*, although doing so would clearly risk repeating the cycle of crisis that colonial modernity initiated. It seems to me that Farah's reference to the Cherokee, which describes a people in terms that were historically used to facilitate their oppression and even genocide, is guilty of taking that risk. Although not applied to the General or the segment of Somali society committed to his form of tradition, the Cherokee comparison can clearly be seen in relationship to the confrontation between tradition and modernity taking place in the novel.

And even if Farah did not intend the simile to be a commentary on Somali politics, the fact that he used it at all, and without apparent irony, demonstrates the danger of adopting modernity, or at least the colonial-induced form of modernity, as a strategy for opposing tradition.

This returns us to the question of whether or not there are other forms of modernity available for the struggle against dictatorships. Although Medina's modern, future-oriented views, and the views of her protégé Sagal, seem to be privileged throughout *Sardines*, we find a possible model of modernity tempered or qualified by a just use of tradition in the figure of Dulman. As noted earlier, Dulman is a traditional singer, illiterate, and situated precariously between the world of the General and the world of the resistance. Publicly, Dulman sings the General's praises and might be, therefore, characterized as an *afmiishaar*, or an opportunistic "mouth saw" poet who sells her abilities to the highest bidder. There are brief references to Dulman in this capacity in *Sweet and Sour Milk* (see pp. 10–11), but we learn in *Sardines* that she secretly supports the resistance by recording and distributing subversive poems on cassette tapes. Like many poets and artists in Somalia in the 1970s, Dulman has her reasons for selling her services to the regime. Some did so willingly, others did so out of necessity, and yet others were coerced against their will. One of those who was open to the initial promises of Barre's regime is Mohammed Ibrahim Warsame, contemporary Somalia's most famous poet who is better known by his nickname, "Hadrawi." Hadrawi and Dulman have much in common and, in fact, I would go so far as to suggest that Dulman is based in part on Hadrawi, so it would benefit our analysis to look briefly at his experience.[16]

Because of the chaos that had overwhelmed the Somali government by 1969, many were elated when Barre took control, including Hadrawi, who admits, "I welcomed the revolution like everyone else. We were nationalists" (qtd. in Stille 190). Hadrawi even "went to work for the government's information office but became increasingly disillusioned" as Barre's true nature became evident (191). Barre tried to control all public media, written, oral, and electronic, and Hadrawi joined the ranks of those who sought ways of safely criticizing the government. Given poetry's central function in Somali society, problems facing the community are traditionally debated and worked out through poetic duels or "chains" in which one poet would compose a poem on a particular theme and use an *alliterative* scheme (rather than a rhyme scheme) that subsequent poets would follow in a competitive, call-and-response fashion. Two such poetic duels broke out during Barre's regime, the first called "Siinley" (or S-alliterated poems) in 1969, and the second "Deeley" (D-alliterated) in 1979 (Ahmed 14–15). These duels were an effective form of public debate in the face of government censorship for two reasons: first, the poems used highly metaphorical and allusive language which made the precise meaning ambiguous and therefore difficult to identify as seditious. As Stille writes, "the standard tropes of Somali poetry—a bitter drought or a cleansing storm—might either have a subversive meaning or just be about the vicissitudes of nomad life" (192). Second, the poems were recorded and distributed on cassette tapes, which made the poetic duels simultaneously and paradoxically both public and private.

Cassettes had become a "staple of Somali life in the early 1970s" as many Somalis traveled abroad for work and brought cassette players home with them so that, "in the absence of writing, families could exchange oral 'letters'" (Stille 192). The new technology flourished, and continued to flourish for many years, because of the ease with which it adapted to and blended with oral culture. Furthermore, the low cost and widespread availability of

16 Although she is likely based on or inspired by Hadrawi, Hadrawi himself is actually mentioned in the novel several times, and at one point Dulman mentions that the General accused her of "having collaborated with Hadraawi on an underground play" (187).

cassette technology made it universally accessible, unlike writing, which is accessible only to the few members of an educated elite. As Barre's dictatorial power became increasingly evident and as he took control of all public media, the cassette was a promising form of alternative communication. People began to "copy or rerecord poetry cassettes and circulate them" (192). These poems contained powerful expressions of dissent, particularly in the extensive poetic chains that emerged in response to Barre's regime. Hadrawi initiated and was a leading participant in the "Siinley" and "Deeley" poetic duels, the second of which he started with a fellow poet specifically "to confront the regime" (196). Hadrawi recalls, "We said to each other: 'History will not forgive us if we don't respond.' That was the beginning of the end. From that day on, we made war on the regime" (qtd. in Stille 196). Hadrawi's poems were particularly popular in the cassette market, and Barre himself was "said to have amassed a formidable collection of tapes" (194). Barre placed Hadrawi under house arrest at one point (in part for refusing to change his play *The She-Camel* after it was reviewed by the censorship board), and even tried banning the Deeley poems, but he ultimately "proved powerless to stop the underground cassette traffic" (184). Anyone could listen to a poem in the privacy of his or her home, share the cassette directly with someone else, or re-record it themselves (sometimes with the poem altered in a way that made listeners active participants in shaping the chain) and pass it on, thus continuing the fluid growth of the cassette-poem genre. Furthermore, the cassettes facilitated the development of an Andersonian "imagined community," or a community of dissent that allowed members to share views and feel unified with one another in their stance against the dictator. Abdulrahman Youssef, a former soldier in the Somali National Movement, observed:

> These songs opened up discussion for people. They were becoming educated and informed. They would sit around listening to the songs and talk. People generally didn't listen to these songs alone. They listened with other people and they had to screen the people whom they were listening with and so these were the basis of political groupings. So Siad Barre was not wrong to be afraid of the poets. (qtd. in Stille 198)

Hadrawi has lamented technology's effect on the culture of Somali poetry, feeling that it weakens an individual poet's skill with memory and therefore knowledge; his own poetry, he says, "is an expression of a world that is coming to an end" (qtd. in Stille 188). However, as Youssef makes clear, during Barre's regime the cassette served a necessary function. In times of peace, it is certainly lamentable that the cassette tape would replace the in-person interaction between poet and audience, but its mediatory function made it a powerful weapon in the time of emergency. A single poet could be in multiple places at once, speak simultaneously to multiple households through cassettes, and thus bring people together from across Somalia, and indeed across the world, as cassettes were frequently copied and sent to relatives and supporters abroad. The cassettes helped create a public forum within the protected spaces of people's private homes and lives.

Although Dulman, like Hadrawi, has become disillusioned with the regime in *Sardines*, she maintains a public persona that supports the General. Dulman's proximity to the regime requires her to perform in public as a supporter, but in private she works to undermine the General by recording and distributing subversive cassette tapes. In effect, Dulman is an *afmiishaar* in public and an *afmaal* in private. The issue that worries Hadrawi—about technology marking the end of the oral world—comes up in a conversation between Nasser and Dulman. Nasser discovers that Dulman cannot read or write and notices an open cassette recorder on the table. He begins to ask her, in an almost accusatory tone, what it means for her as a performer of oral traditions to rely on technology. "Since you can't write and you don't read, you use this, tape everything straight from the poet's mouth and then learn your part, is that it?" (184). The reason for Nasser's frustration is unclear, but he seems to be upset or confused by the apparent incongruity in the image of tradition depending upon modernity for its survival. He continues, "You're dependent upon this machine and not on your own memory to learn your parts? ... You are dependent upon the twentieth century's advanced technology, do I understand?" Dulman does not respond immediately, but, when she does, she draws attention to the anachronism that she represents and the necessary adaptations that life under the General's regime has forced upon her and those like her. "Some of us," she says, "have been catapulted into the centre-stage of a century we actually don't belong in and have nothing in common with" (185). "Some of us," she continues later, "belong only partly to the twentieth century [...]. And I believe we have the right to use its technology as much as an African dictator makes the right or the wrong use of a given ideology" (186). Returning thus to the theme of the "sweet and bitter-tasting," Dulman insists on her right to use modern technology despite belonging to a cultural tradition that is associated with the past. This particular intersection and tension between the traditional and the modern becomes not a contradiction, as Nasser assumes, but a productive site of resistance to the General's model of tradition. Dulman recognizes that orature, technology, and ideology can be put to both good and evil uses, and she chooses to align a form of tradition, made whole through the ethics of *Xeer*, with modern technology in a way that supports the necessary struggle at hand. Dulman's conversation with Nasser ends as she implores him to take the cassettes she has recorded and "distribute [them] as cheaply as possible" (193). Nasser asks if the tapes are good, and she replies: "Rich as the Russian underground literature. Russians read, Somalis don't, for our tradition is oral. One can communicate with the hearts of Somalis only through their hearing faculties."

Later in the novel, we learn that both Nasser and Dulman are arrested for their activities. As happened with other members of the movement, Nasser and Dulman's time finally came. And, we are told, "According to law, both Nasser and Dulman, if found guilty, would be sentenced to death"

(276–77). The specific law they violated is actually provided in the text at the end of the novel. Medina is thinking about all that has happened, and the narrator describes "the National Security Law of 10 September 1970 (Article 18) which would sentence both Nasser and Dulman to death for having 'spread, disseminated, or distributed reading, spoken or broadcast matter or information aimed at damaging the sovereignty of the revolution of the Somali nation'" (284). This emergency regulation is one of the few instances where the actual text of a law makes it into the narrative. The law becomes explicit, more concrete, and its effects painfully real as Medina recognizes the likely fate of her co-conspirators. Like *Sweet and Sour Milk*, *Sardines* thus ends on a negative note, depicting the disheartening reality of the General's power as exercised through the oppressive mechanisms of emergency law. However, *Sardines* has its suggestions of hope and optimism in the fact that the cassettes, the hybrid form of tradition and modernity, are out there in distribution, as they were under Barre's regime, promoting dissent, building community, and offering an alternative form of authority through the legal poetics of Somali orature. Furthermore, as Medina suddenly recognizes that she is no longer an outsider in Somalia but "a full and active participant in the history of her country," she thinks to herself, "yes, time was ultimately a decider" (285). Time has decided her status within Somalia, and the trilogy's preoccupations with temporality suggest that time may decide other things as well. Medina also thinks that "There wasn't time to tie up the loose ends of the story," meaning it is not yet time for a decision about the larger problems facing Somalia as a whole, and this open-endedness propels us into the third and final novel.

The explicit appearance of one of the General's laws at the end of *Sardines* links it formally to the beginning of *Close Sesame*, when Deeriye, the aged patriarch and former anti-colonial fighter from whose perspective the story is told, recalls a conversation with his son Mursal from the night before. Musral is a professor of constitutional law at the National University of Somalia in Mogadishu, and Deeriye, we are later told, is one of the respected elders "experienced with the art of litigation at clan gatherings" (108). He is, in other words, a *heerbeegti*. Their conversation followed "no order or logic, their colloquy about internal politics intriguing and at the same time ambiguous: jumping from a theological subject to one of no political or religious relevance and then moving on to something more pertinent—like the concept of *lex talionis*, and what it implies in a modern Islamic state" (9). The ambiguous, exploratory form of their conversation—an act of *oral* collaboration—suggests an affinity with Somali oral culture and law, which are characterized by dialogue, openness, and ambiguity in exploring the various positions on a particular issue. Mursal and Deeriye continue the open-ended conversation until the father makes a decisive move when "his son point-blank asked him whether or not he would consider the use of violence or condone it if one close to him were involved." Instead of answering, Deeriye asks with equal directness, "You are yourself involved in overthrowing the state?

Are you?" Mursal evades the question, indicating that his own question was hypothetical, but Deeriye persists, asking if Mursal himself is involved in such activities or his friend Mahad, a "jurist" who works for the government (83).

Mursal continues to avoid the question and Deeriye insists that he provide an answer. Mursal finally responds by resuming their discussion of *lex talionis*:

> The question is, Father, whether or not there is any legal sense in finding a logical link between the aspects of traditional (i.e., private) justice and state (i.e., public) justice; and if we understand that there is, whether or not we too should work out an amalgam whose final result and aim will offer the same kind of exaction. (10)

Deeriye interrupts by saying that he has not understood, so Mursal continues his explanation, which is worth quoting in full:

> Let me see. You agree—don't you?—that traditional justice is private justice in so far as the kith and kin of the aggrieved person, in order that the family or clan not be dishonoured, uses what is known as the *lex talionis* system of justice: a life for a life, an eye for an eye and that sort of thing. All right?
>
> Embedded in public justice is that sense of an all-encompassing justice. The victim's family need not worry about taking revenge, need not worry whether they will receive a hundred or so camels in blood-money compensation for the relation killed or fifty camels for a clanswoman, for no one would accuse them of drinking the milk of the blood-wit instead of the blood of the person who had killed their relation. Embedded in public justice is the consensus of the community, their trust in public justice, hence in the constitution. It is the state which acts as the arbiter here, the state which represents this consensus or what we may call the constitution.

And then, later: "My [...] most essential point is simply this: does the state in Somalia as we know it have a traditional base in Somali thought? Does the régime of Somalia today have any Islamic legitimacy?" (11).

I quote Mursal's words at length here because, like the National Security Law quoted at the end of *Sardines*, Mursal's profound questions about the legitimacy of the Somali state ground the third novel, and the entire trilogy, in a way, in the very fundamental question of law's status in this society (and, by implication, in any society similarly oppressed by a dictatorship). A successful struggle against the General and the future success of the Somali state, Mursal suggests, are deeply contingent upon working within, rather than outside of or against, a framework of law. We learn later that Mursal is, in fact, involved in an effort to overthrow the State, as his father suspects, and Mursal, Mahad, another member of their group named Jibriil Mohamed-Somali, and, eventually Deeriye himself (after much deliberation, as we will see), actually carry out assassination attempts on the General's life, though all are unsuccessful. In this conversation with his father, Mursal is attempting to explore possible justifications for violence against the General, and his methods and reasons for doing so are crucial. In terms of his methods, Mursal, as a "modern" legal thinker and practitioner, recognizes the distinction between traditional and state (or private and public) forms of justice; he then considers the implications of a link between the two and the possibility of "work[ing] out an amalgam" that combines both. As discussed earlier, when Siyad Barre took power in 1969, he attempted to do away with private forms of justice and developed a public form of justice in a "state judicial system" that would handle all disputes (Hashim 89). Mursal compares the forms of obligation and consent inherent in the two systems: on the one hand, according to private justice, any wrongs committed against a person oblige that person's relatives to seek compensation or retribution (the *diya* system, which Mursal identifies with *lex talionis*, or the "law of retribution" ["Lex"]); on the other hand, because the State has taken over the responsibility of dispute resolution, it assumes the consent of the community—in other words, it presumes to remove the obligations that traditionally bind clan members, and takes upon itself the responsibility to act on behalf of the aggrieved. By assuming all Somalis consent to this arrangement, the State radically alters deeply embedded notions of normativity and obligation, and this leads Mursal to wonder if the State, therefore, has any traditional or Islamic (Mursal uses the terms somewhat interchangeably) legitimacy. The key implication is that if the State lacks this legitimacy, then the State is illegal, and persons who do possess traditional legitimacy are justified in passing a judgment and carrying out a sentence fitting the crime. Mursal does not make this point explicit in this conversation with Deeriye, but it becomes clear later in the novel when Mursal and his companions begin to act on the principle of *lex talionis* and seek retribution.

One might assume that culturally and legally specific justifications for deposing a dictator would be unnecessary. Most people would likely see a dictator's corruption, political excesses, and human rights abuses as justification enough for removal, whether or not a particular legal system can provide technical justification. In fact, it might be argued that removing a dictator would effectively require one to go outside legal norms in order to restore a normal rule of law.

However, this, I argue, is precisely what Mursal is trying to avoid, and this is why he searches for a *legal* justification for political violence. As a professor of law, Mursal believes firmly in the law and recognizes that acting outside of or in defiance of it would only result in anarchy and further crisis. By following the principle of *lex talionis*, as defined by Somali thought, Mursal would be able to act in a way that would be seen as legitimate and, therefore, as resulting in a logical and necessary outcome. Killing the General, in other words, would not be an attack on law and order, nor an exceptional action outside of the law, but a validation of the legitimate forms of law and order grounded in Somali thought. If Mursal were to justify retribution as a suspension of law and order, he would only be repeating the General's illegitimate practices and would be in danger of perpetuating his forms of governance. In his conversation with Deeriye, Mursal is not overtly committing to a particular course of action, but his questions indicate his desire to find a way of acting within an "amalgam" of private and public justice that will make retribution against the General fully legal and be perceived as legal by the larger Somali community. This point does become overt, however, with later discussions of *lex talionis* in relationship to the actual attempts to kill the General.

Mahad is the first to carry out an attack. The General has just finished his "annual speech to the Judiciary," and Mahad is among those in attendance (83). When the General walks down among the diplomats and jurists to shake hands and receive congratulations, Mahad steps forward, quickly steals a handgun from one of the bodyguards, and then tries but fails to shoot the General. The General captures Mahad who then disappears into the void of detention. Mursal describes all of this to his family, claiming to have learned it from eyewitness accounts, and asserts that the attack was not premeditated and that he was not involved in its planning. Throughout the novel, however, Mursal maintains strict secrecy about his plans and involvement with the underground movement, so it is possible to assume that he planned the attack with Mahad. Either way, the attack's location is significant: in his speech the General "made a great ado about justice, socialism and democracy," but Mahad and others know this to be little more than mystifying political rhetoric; killing the General *in front of* Somalia's legal professionals after the leader's mendacious speech would have had great symbolic significance, pitting the legitimacy of retribution against the illegitimacy of the General's "constitution" (i.e., himself). The assassination would have constituted the act of "founding violence" capable of proving itself "as having a right to law" (Derrida 34). After Mursal relates the story of Mahad's attempt, Deeriye asks Mursal where he was when it happened. Mursal's location is also significant: he was at the university, teaching his class on constitutional law. Just as Mahad was removing (or attempting to remove) the illegitimate "constitution" from power in a setting of symbolic legal significance, Mursal was helping to put in place a legitimate constitutional order through the training and instruction of future legal professionals. Although Mursal denies involvement in the attack, Deeriye understands from their previous conversations that Mursal, Mahad, and others have decided to act on their justification for political violence. Later in the novel, when speaking to his brother-in-law about his suspicions of Mahad and the others' plans, Deeriye states:

> Mursal and Mahad came to me and talked day in day out of what they referred to as public and private justice. They explained justifiably, to me at any rate, that a clansman whose brother is executed in public because he has broken one of those laws decreed by the General's régime can traditionally, instead of exacting blood compensation for the dead brother from government pension schemes, take the law into his own hands, *lex talionis*, kill: kill the General. (166)

In these terms, Mursal and Mahad not only provided a justification for killing the General, but they discovered they had a responsibility to do so.

The General has carried out various executions in public, and Mursal argues that the relatives of those killed have a right and responsibility according to the laws of clan obligation to seek "blood compensation." The system that the General used to replace *diya* provided financial compensation through "pension schemes," but if "private law" retains any legitimacy, as Mursal and others insist it does, then relatives of the aggrieved can legally seek retribution against the General himself. In effect, this is what Mursal and Mahad attempt to do, although, as mentioned, they are unsuccessful. After Mursal's attempt, he disappears for a time, and then his family receives confirmation that he has been killed. Deeriye is left finally to "vindicate justice" (222).

Deeriye is a fascinating character, particularly in terms of the issues that are the concern of this book: the threads of time, orature, and law converge in his person. Not only is he a sounding board for (and eventual participant in) his son's legal strategies, but, as a respected elder, he is a representative of the authority of the Somali oral tradition and the revolutionary history of which it was a part. In contrast to Keynaan in *Sweet and Sour Milk* and Idil in *Sardines*, the dominant figure of traditional authority in this novel refuses to represent the General in his household. Deeriye does not immediately engage in the revolutionary activities of his son, but it is significant that the fate of his son's movement, which has been led throughout the trilogy by the younger generation of modern, educated professionals, eventually falls into the hands of a *heerbeegti*. It is because of Deeriye's expertise in Somali orature and history that Jacqueline Bardolph sees *Close Sesame* as, ultimately, "a meditation on time and history" and "a dramatization of human consciousness of the past and of time fleeing" (416). Deeriye invokes the past through both historical and legendary references, and he becomes the source or focal point of multiple appropriations of Somali orature in the novel, demonstrating a form of tradition that, in contrast to the dictator's, has not abandoned its ethical content. Deeriye frequently tells Samawade, his grandson, stories drawn from history or Somali orature, and three of these stories are included in their entirety in the text. Although aspects of orature are incorporated into the form of the two earlier novels to a limited extent and often indirectly, they are directly included in *Close Sesame*. The stories are typically parables, demonstrating Deeriye's commitment to using the past to shape the future generation.

Deeriye is a source of the oral tradition, but he is not anti-modern. In fact, not only is Deeriye literate (he learned to read and write in Italian and Arabic while in prison where he had "more time" for education [56]), but he frequently sits by himself listening to the Qur'an or his favorite poets on cassette tapes. Like Dulman, Deeriye embraces the intersection of orality and technology, demonstrating a productive amalgam of the traditional (again, made whole by *Xeer*) and the modern that could provide a challenge to the dictator's reified form of tradition emptied of ethical content. One of Deeriye's favorite poets is the famous Somali revolutionary Sayyid Mahammad 'Abdille Hasan, who led the 1912 Dervish movement against colonialism and was popularly known by the British as the "Mad Mullah." Deeriye considers himself a "Sayyidist" and sees (or creates) parallels between his life and the Sayyid's. Deeriye does not know the exact year of his own birth, for example, but he claims it was 1912, which was the year the Sayyid "defeated the British imperialists" in Somalia (14). Throughout his 20-year struggle against the British and Ethiopia, the Sayyid frequently composed poetry and many of his poems were taken up by nationalists in subsequent years. Deeriye's favorite poem, and the one he most frequently listens to on cassette, is called "The Death of Corfield," which is addressed to the British officer Richard Corfield, who led forces against the Sayyid in 1913 and was killed.[17] The poem celebrates Corfield's death and is filled with imperatives directed at the officer, telling him what he should say when he is questioned by God on his way to hell. It is a curious poem for Deeriye to treasure; harsh and unforgiving in its treatment of Corfield, the poem would seem to provide a fairly clear justification for political violence, and yet Deeriye, though he fought valiantly in his youth, is undecided on the justification for violence when Mursal presents it to him. For much of the novel, in fact, Deeriye has a moderating effect on those around him, encouraging peaceful action in response to violence. After Mursal has disappeared, for example, the wandering madman Khaliif comes to Mursal's house, where Deeriye and others are gathered, and begins uttering curses against "those who *betray*" (148). Samawade stands in an upper room of the house with Deeriye, looking down angrily at Khaliif and soon begins searching for something to throw at him. What he chooses is significant: "Deeriye watched him go to the window clutching a book in one hand and a cassette in the other" (149). The book is an "edited collection of the Prophet's tradition" and the cassette is a recording of "The Death of Richard Corfield."

Deeriye talks Samawade out of throwing the objects, which the boy grabbed blindly not knowing what they were, but later in the novel Deeriye is thinking about various "mad activities" that have gone on in his life recently, and he sees it all "culiminat[ing] in Samawade's determined wish to use the cassette [...] and the Holy Book as weapons" (238). On the one hand, orature and the written word—or the traditional and the modern, if we accept the larger symbolic economy with which Farah is working—can both provide guidance and can be useful weapons in the struggle against oppression. Texts such as the Sayyid's can remind current freedom fighters of the history of which they are a part. Furthermore, as we have seen, oral jurisprudence can bind communities together and, when adapted to new forms of technology, can be useful in creating public spaces of discussion and dissent in the privacy of people's homes, safe from the General's eyes and ears. The written word is also a weapon that can threaten the General's regime when, as with Soyaan's memos, it is used to demystify his politics. On the other hand, when Samawade picks up the cassette and the book, he threatens to treat the two

17 See Andrzejewski and Lewis, *Somali Poetry: An Introduction* (1964), pp. 70–74.

objects *literally* as weapons—in other words, he demonstrates the danger of oversimplifying or misunderstanding the potential of orature, technology, and the written word in resisting tyranny. As a young man, Samawade represents the ambivalence of the new generation: eager for change but also at risk of reacting with blind force and treating the useful tools of culture and representation as objects with which to bludgeon the enemy rather than as sources of ideology, wisdom, and law that can, and must, guide action and be used carefully if one is to justify political violence. Deeriye and Mursal's discussion of the traditional and modern justifications for political violence connects with this "culminating" moment when Samawade attempts to use the material objects of the cassette and book for an act of political violence. Deeriye fears unprincipled action, and wisely directs Samawade to think about what he is doing and consider the true significance of the objects he has chosen. Shortly after this, Deeriye tells one of the three oral stories to Samawade, clearly as an attempt to provide further guidance and instruction to his grandson.

Mursal, Mahad, and other members of their movement commit themselves to action, but for most of the novel, Deeriye remains uncertain. As a *heerbeegti*, Deeriye must ponder, deliberate, and take care not to act in haste as his grandson does. After Mursal disappears, however, Deeriye thinks about those who have died "heroically" in fighting for their cause, and he thinks about his own fears and the fact that, given his age and poor health, the government considers him "not worth arresting, not worth reckoning with" (221). He then thinks, "Was it not high time he did something heroic to prove them wrong?" This thought betrays a motivation based more on pride than a desire to achieve justice, but Deeriye does not act right away. He continues to deliberate and consider the reasons for and implications of doing something "heroic." Deeriye finds a revolver in his son's study and decides to keep it so that, "if necessary," he can "use it to 'vindicate justice'" (222). Deeriye uses the phrase "vindicate justice" several times in the subsequent pages, and, for him, it articulates a proper justification for action. He considers the possibility of vindicating those who have been lost, but he turns away from political violence as an act of personal revenge or to satisfy his ego. Even after he learns of Mursal's death, Deeriye states, "I could kill to vindicate not my son but justice" (238). Deeriye realizes that to kill to vindicate his son would run contrary to his son's beliefs about justice and law. Although the form of *lex talionis* that Mursal considers and ultimately acts on is based on the idea that one's family or clan-members can exact retribution for a lost relative, the larger motivation is not revenge, but justice and the preservation of a system of justice grounded in Somali thought. Because of his prominence in the community and relationship to Mursal, Deeriye receives a phone call and is invited at one point to meet with the General personally. He hesitates making an appointment, but finally makes the decision and calls the General. The final events of the novel are described in a way that makes it difficult to determine what exactly happens; the details emerge as if through the filter of rumor. However, we do learn that Deeriye takes the revolver and leaves for his appointment with the General, and it is clear that at some point he attempts to assassinate the General, but, like those before him, he fails. It is not yet the General's time.

As a challenge to the dictator's form of tradition, Deeriye brought together the resources of a more malleable tradition and fluid modernity, charting a future-oriented course based on the lessons of the past. His attempt to create an amalgam of past and future, traditional and modern was an attempt both to challenge the dictator and his myths of temporality and use the crisis as an opportunity to produce, with Mursal, a "regime of intelligibility" (Mbembe 324) and a "lexicon of normative action" (Cover, "Foreword" 9) according to which a just society might be formed. As noted at the beginning of this chapter, one of Deeriye's many discussions in the novel focuses on rights and the colonial origins of dictatorships, specifically in the system of indirect rule. In light of his failure to "vindicate justice," it is worth returning to this discussion and, specifically, to the extended meditation on time that immediately follows it. Though written in the third person, the passage presumably gives us privileged access to Deeriye's thoughts, which describe time using ten different metaphors. Mursal's wife, Natasha, is driving him to meet with some friends. Time is first described as "an echo of a purring, revving engine" and then as "the dust which trailed behind them" (103). Then, "time was the sun," "time was the travel," and "Time: a city within a city." Time is "the abyss with the open door; it was human for it had hands [...] Time was also the rest of sleep [...] the photograph whose future print would read like an illuminated manuscript." Finally, and most prosaically, "Time was history," and history is identified as many things, including revolutionary events from the past and the "half-truths" and "intolerable nonsense" of colonialism (104). Coming where this does, essentially in the middle of the novel before Deeriye has decided to act, these metaphors reflect Deeriye's interrogation of the myths of the regime and his imaginative, almost stream-of-consciousness exploration of alternative myths to guide just action. Time is, firstly, associated with forward momentum, technology, and development—in a word, with modernity. But then it is an "abyss," an "open door," without definite direction or concrete form. Deeriye, I argue, recognizes the multiplicity of temporality, or the fact that time can be seen, or constructed, in a variety of ways in contrast, perhaps, to the singular (though contradictory) narrative of colonial temporality. The empty abyss of time thus turns into something human with the arms and hands that break time into discrete and measurable units. The forward-moving, routine-driven form of time leads to sleep and rest and then a photograph, which I see as Deeriye's metaphor for memory, for ways of recording and remembering time past. Finally, Deeriye's thoughts return to time as history, and this metaphor—if we can call it that—receives the most detailed explanation, suggesting perhaps that the most relevant form of time in the present circumstances is that provided by history: the injustices of the past and the revolutionary figures who suffered and fought against those injustices must be remembered. Like the Iregi myths in Ngũgĩ's *Mother, Sing for Me*, Somali history flows into the present and holds out promise for a better future.

However, before Deeriye is able to articulate the full significance of or provide any conclusions about his thoughts on history, an ellipsis appears, indicating Deeriye's shift in attention as he realizes Natasha has brought him to his destination. He never returns to complete his train of thought. We have the freedom to interpret Deeriye's ideas about time and history, but the lack of closure to his interior monologue runs parallel to the lack of closure at the end of the novel. The dramatic events of the trilogy, like his thoughts about time, never reach a satisfying end. Why does Farah do this? Why, if he is opposed to Barre and African dictators in general, does Farah let them win within the fictional world of the novels? The simplest answer is that Farah's refusal to depict the heroic killing of the General is historically realistic: when this novel was published in 1983, Barre was still in power and, though faced with mounting problems of various kinds, showed no signs of giving up. To depict the killing of the General in the novels might seem heroic, but it would jump the gun, so to speak, and fail to offer a solution to Somalia's problems. By portraying the dictator as maintaining power, Farah stays true to Somalia's situation at the time, and successfully conveys the tragedy of life under the Barre regime. At the same time, Farah stays true to the fact that dictators have a tendency to stay in power indefinitely. The term "indefinite" might be said to be one of the keywords of the *Variations* trilogy, not because it is used frequently but because it expresses one of the fundamental temporal characteristics of dictatorships: suspects are detained indefinitely, civil rights are suspended indefinitely, presidential terms are extended indefinitely. Dictators throughout Africa, and the world, tend to linger, to hold on to power for as long as possible, and the open-endedness of the General's regime at the end of *Close Sesame* reflects this.

Ironically, however, that open-endedness also gestures toward a definite solution to such power. Farah's historical fiction of the present ran parallel to the Barre regime, and his choice to end the trilogy without resolving the central conflict was not only realistic but it also yielded the narrative up to time itself. The formal open-endedness effectively reasserts the idea that "time was ultimately a decider" (*Sardines* 285), that however long dictators are able to remain in power, time will eventually decide their fate: the regime will end either through successful violent resistance (as it did for Barre in 1991) or mortality (e.g., Jomo Kenyatta died at the age of 86 after 17 years in office). At the very most, a president can only ever be "President for Life."

Unfortunately, the end of one regime often leads to another, but there are promising signs that the era of the "Big Man" in Africa is waning. In 2007, Daniel Posner and Daniel Young argued that although there are still dictators throughout Africa, political institutions are increasingly more effective in placing restraints on dictators, who often work within rather than outside of those institutions. "Across sub-Saharan Africa," they write, "formal institutional rules are coming to matter much more than they used to, and have displaced violence as the primary source of constraints on executive behavior" (127). Amazingly, ten years later, Robert Mugabe, one of the longest ruling dictators in postcolonial Africa, actually resigned rather than remain in power until death.[18] Hopefully, this trend toward rules rather than rulers will continue, but of course it will take time. And this is Farah's point. As much as we may desire an immediate solution to the immediate crisis, most problems of the kind Farah is interested in take time to resolve. Some myths and crises, like those of colonial modernity, are so deeply entrenched that many years must pass before their influence begins to wear away. Farah's repeated use of the trilogy form in charting and responding to the course of Somalia's postcolonial history from before Barre to long after suggests not only an awareness of this phenomenon but a commitment to the power of fiction, in particular, to bear the weight of the burdens of time, the burden of endlessly waiting for change.

Given this commitment and the commitment of Farah's protagonists to the struggle against injustice, he certainly does not advocate apathetic resignation to temporality. Peter Hitchcock is correct when he says that "Farah's writing does not simply wait out horrors" (133). Rather, through the "long space" of the trilogy, he enables "an enduring public vocation that the last volume does not outlast" (40), creating a sense of purpose that extends well beyond the end of the text itself. But if failure to fulfill that purpose continues, time still offers the promise that even a (temporarily) failed struggle will not (eventually) be in vain. The "future beyond the future of a future" is not much of a consolation to those whose suffering limits their ability to see beyond immediate circumstances; but the long view encouraged by Farah's characters and the open-ended, long form of the trilogy may do much as part of a larger "regime of intelligibility" to help make sense of and give meaning to injustices experienced in the present and the burden of waiting for justice to be done.

As with Ngũgĩ's plays, Farah's dictator novels have not had an apocalyptic reception like Okot's, but the ongoing importance of Farah's ideas for world affairs are no doubt clear: there are still numerous authoritarian regimes (political, corporate, and otherwise) in and beyond Africa to which we might compare Farah's General, and Farah himself invites such comparisons not only through the trilogy's title that identifies this as a variation on a theme, but also through numerous references in the text to Stalin, Lenin, Hitler, Mussolini, and other non-African dictators. Elsewhere, I have examined the implications of such comparative gestures in detail,[19] but here I would simply say that as culturally and historically specific as the *Variations* trilogy is, the larger questions Farah raises and the temporal solution he proposes can be brought to bear on all forms of authoritarianism, including those we witness

18 See McKenzie et al., "Robert Mugabe Resigns after 37 Years as Zimbabwe's Leader" (2017).

19 See "Like a Corpse Resurrected: The Politics of Living Death in Nuruddin Farah's *Sweet and Sour Milk*" (forthcoming in *NOVEL: A Forum on Fiction*).

today in oppressive regimes worldwide and in the emboldened reemergence of right-wing populism in Europe and the USA.[20] Again, Farah would certainly advocate resistance to any form of injustice, but the prospect or experience of failure in fighting injustice is tempered, however minutely, but the idea that time will heal all regimes. However, this idea is complicated today by a temporal crisis that stands above all others and in which the injustices of global authoritarian rule and corporate negligence are deeply implicated: climate change. In my conclusion to this book, therefore, I offer some parting observations about how Okot, Ngũgĩ, and Farah's approaches to law and futurity might help us think through and respond to a crisis that the world cannot afford simply to wait out.

20 In terms of contemporary relevance, there is another intriguing question raised by Farah's discussion in *Close Sesame* of private vs. public law and Somali practices of paying blood compensation. Mursal makes the argument that according to *diya* the families of those killed by the General could legally seek retribution, but what about the families, in recent years, of those killed by air strikes under the Obama and Trump administrations? Somali private law does not, of course, have international jurisdiction and legitimacy, but it is worth asking whether there are resources within that system (like those within the Acholi and Kikuyu justice systems) that might be adapted to an international claim in some way. This is an increasingly pertinent question given the extent to which Donald Trump's administration has quietly and somewhat secretively increased air strikes in Somalia, presumably for the purpose of fighting Al Shabaab, although many others are being killed. See Schmitt and Savage, "Trump Adminstration Steps Up Air War in Somalia," *New York Times*, March 10, 2019, and Sperber, "Report: U.S. Airstrikes Are Killing Civilians in Somalia in Wave of Attacks under Trump," *Intercept*, March 20, 2019.

Conclusion: Temp/orality and Law in the End Times

One problem with Nuruddin Farah's formulation of time as the only certain solution to dictatorial rule is that time, in a sense, may be running out. A constant stream of studies, filtered into panic-inducing headlines by the media, remind us daily that humans are destroying the planet and, ultimately, themselves. One hundred years, fifty years, twenty years, eighteen *months*[1]—the predictive timescales grow frighteningly small, leaving us deprived of the luxury of waiting out authoritarianism or misrule or bad policies with a hopeful eye on "a future beyond the future of a future" (*Sardines* 45). The time to act is not simply now—it may, in fact, be *then*. In the past. When we had a chance to make a difference. How does one wait or hope or sing in such a moment?

A book about the relationship between normative worlds and temporality must, at some point, address itself to the problem of time's end. A book about, in particular, the significance of open-ended, legalistic narratives that confront the temporal narratives of colonial law with orality and futurity must, at some point, grapple with the limits of futurity itself and the limits of placing hope and trust in the future. Robert Cover defined law as "the projection of an imagined future upon reality," suggesting that the limits of futurity may also mark the limits of law ("Violence" 1604). How might a book—*this* book—begin to confront and account for such limits? Dipesh Chakrabarty offered a possible answer when he asserted the following in his influential 2012 article "Postcolonial Studies and the Challenge of Climate Change":

> However we come to the question of postcolonial studies at this historical juncture, there are two phenomena, both topics of public debate since the early 1990s, that none of us can quite escape in our personal and collective

1 See McGrath, "Climate Change: 12 Years to Save the Planet? Make That 18 Months" (2019).

> lives at present: globalization and global warming. All thinking about the present has to engage both. (1)

The force of Chakrabarty's imperative—i.e., that *all* thinking about the present must do this—has sparked debate, but there is no denying that in the years since this was first published, the latter topic, in particular, has become inescapable (although, clearly, the two topics are deeply interrelated). In a sense, globalization is something I have addressed throughout this book: the global south's challenge to the north in terms of the "world-historical processes" that generated modern law can be read through the local narratives of East Africa, narratives that employ oral conventions oriented toward problems of time in order to critique the legacies of colonial law and imagine new forms of law and order suited to the needs of particular historical moments, including those yet to come. To be just, modern law in the era of globalization must take account of its evolution in conjunction with places like East Africa and the perspectives that East African oral artists, writers, and legal thinkers can offer.

The second topic, climate change, is something I feel I cannot conclude without touching on, at least tentatively. My approach in this book has obviously not been ecocritical or otherwise directly attentive to environmental issues, and I realize that to do the topic justice I would need to write another book, if not several. However, my hope is that this book as a whole will contribute to an ongoing conversation within postcolonial studies, law, and literature, and any effort to better understand human history and the universal imperatives placed upon us by our centuries of collective misdeeds and misuses of lives and resources in the names of empire and progress. Going ahead, climate change will come to dominate that conversation, and I believe areas like East Africa will have much to contribute in helping the world think through the implications of our inaction and possible future actions and, also, develop a form of courage necessary to keep fighting, literally, for our lives and the life of our planet even if we have no hope of succeeding.

Despite the absence of environmental questions in this book to this point, climate change does connect with some of my central thematic and theoretical concerns: namely, that the reality of climate change and the alarming possibility of animal and human extinction have everything to do with our sense of, and, therefore, narratives about, time. Temporal experience in recent years has been inescapably altered by warnings about climatological crisis and by the crisis itself. Not only is time running out, but we are currently living through what scientists call the "sixth extinction"—there have been five major mass extinction events throughout the Earth's 4.5 billion-year history and the sixth is underway, with species dying off at 1,000 times the natural rate, primarily due to human-related causes ("The Extinction Crisis"). For this and other reasons, we have transitioned out of the geological era of the Holocene into the Anthropocene, or the era in which humanity has collectively begun to function like a "geophysical force" (Chakrabarty 11). Climate change has marked our era with major turning points in Earth's geological and environmental history, but it is also forcing us to think differently about time and about ourselves in relation to time. To think, in other words, in terms of millions of years rather than centuries, geological epochs instead of historical eras. Some have used the term "deep time" to describe such immense forms of temporality when looking back into the geological record,[2] and Chakrabarty himself is ultimately interested in what it would mean "to think of human agency over multiple and incommensurable scales at once"—scales of both size (i.e., individual vs. collective) and time (1).

Climate change also poses unique challenges to the law. Legal scholars have, of course, written about the climate for some time, particularly in the field of Environmental Law. Others are deeply engaged in discussions about what role law must play in our new geological era: Nicholas A. Robinson's "Fundamental Principles of Law for the Anthropocene?" (2014) and Eric Biber's "Law in the Anthropocene Epoch" (2017) are illustrative of such approaches, both recognizing that just as law had to respond to the social and political changes of the Industrial revolution, for example, so too must law respond and adapt to those created by climate change. The prospect of an end should provoke us to question whether law as we now know and practice it is suited to the demands of a global crisis. One of the questions this book has posed is: if colonial law depended upon temporal narratives, and modern law owes its form to colonialism, what would modern law look like were it founded upon different models of time, temporalities of the global south, postcolonial futurity, etc. rather than colonial or neoliberal modernities? Similarly, we might ask: in the era of climate change, what would law look like were it founded upon the new conceptions of time that climate crisis has forced upon us? Can we think law over "multiple and incommensurable scales at once"? If law is the "projection of an imagined future upon reality," what happens to law when there may be no future to imagine or when our likely future is substantially worse than it is now? Would a form of emergency law that suspends our current norms in order to address an immediate threat be the only path forward? States of emergency are often declared in response to natural disasters—does the world need a global form of emergency, or something like "Lawino's curse" on a global scale that would force action to save the larger community? How would that even be possible?

Different nations have responded differently to this crisis, with some taking radical steps to reduce carbon emissions through stricter regulations, some pushing for greater consensus within the international community, and others actually granting legal personhood to entities in the natural world as a strategy of protection. The Whanganui River in New Zealand, for example, was granted legal personhood in 2017 and a national park followed.[3]

2 See, for example, Dimock, *Through Other Continents: American Literature across Deep Time* (2006).

3 See Warne, "National Geographic: A Voice for Nature" (2019).

Some nations have embedded new environmental rights into their constitutions. Kenya's famously progressive 2010 constitution, for example, includes detailed statements about the environment, something the previous constitution, instituted by the exiting colonial government in 1963, left out entirely. Article 42 of the 2010 constitution declares:

> Every person has a right to a clean and healthy environment, which includes the right—a. to have the environment protected for the benefit of present and future generations through legislative and other measures.

The attention here to future generations reveals a long-term vision that many other nations lack, including the USA under the current administration (as of early 2020). Climate activists frequently point to the horrors we are setting up for future generations unless we make drastic changes to our ways of life, but so many of those with the power to enact necessary change at a global level are corrupted by the short-term, profit-driven visions of capitalism. The long-term effects of deforestation and burning fossil fuels mean little to those in power if massive profits accumulate in the moment. This highlights the significance of Kenya's new constitution and its importance as a standard for others to follow—it offers a model for a law that seeks to compel action in the present that will have consequences for the far future. However, it also begs the question: what is to be done if others do not follow? What if those with the most power to act continue to refuse? Can the optimistic futurity of one environmentally conscious constitution make a real difference?

At this time, it is natural to look beyond any one nation's laws to international law. If we are to mitigate the effects of climate change and extend the timeline for human survival, it will take the cooperation of many, if not all, nations, and international law is one mechanism for facilitating that cooperation. However, climate change is one of the global phenomena that has contributed to what some call the "crisis of international law," or the inadequacy of the Westphalian paradigm of international law when problems such as climate change, globalization, human rights, etc. exceed the limits and jurisdictional capacities of sovereign nations. The birth of the nation-state is generally located in the 1648 Treaty of Westphalia, which ended the Eighty Years War and the Thirty Years War in Europe and, in the process, codified national sovereignty, allowing only a weak form of international law to govern relations among states. The substance and institutions of international law have grown significantly since that time, but the authority has remained weak. According to Joel Trachtman, the current crisis of international law is akin to a Kuhnian scientific revolution in that "the existing paradigm has grown increasingly unable to explain what we do, or to give us the tools to devise solutions to our problems" (408). Westphalian international law is unequal to the challenges of climate change, unable to do more than invite and weakly coerce nations into acting. We need a new paradigm, clearly, and the general impulse of alternatives will inevitably be toward a stronger international law, which, again, hints at the possibility of an international emergency law. I am not interested in proposing another paradigm like this, however. In fact, I am largely skeptical that any practical alternative to the existing paradigm will be of any use given the rapidly advancing deadlines dictated by our changing environment. The wheels of the law, international or otherwise, tend to move slowly, and, even if we can accelerate them somehow, their efficacy on a global scale still depends upon such a variety of factors that success *in time* seems unlikely, if not impossible.

Climate change has thus thrown global interdependencies into sharp relief. Not only are rising temperatures, extreme weather patterns, deforestation, species extinction, etc. in some parts of the world caused by environmental and political choices in others, but the ability to enact real solutions on a large scale requires the consent and participation of multiple actors. The USA's planned withdrawal from the Paris Climate Agreement (announced in 2017) will not wholly stall the Agreement's capacity for change, but it will certainly make it more difficult. If the largest contributors to CO_2 levels refuse even to acknowledge the reality of climate change, to say nothing of actually working to mitigate it, what hope do other countries, particularly those in the global south, have for enacting change or even surviving? It appears that it has become necessary for anyone who is willing or able to act to do so without assuming others will do their part. Too many, from individuals who refuse to recycle to governments who refuse to regulate fossil fuel industries, are not doing their part and, frankly, probably never will. I want to believe that the arc of the moral universe bends toward justice, but when it comes to the environment it appears to be slouching toward self-destruction. (As I write this, Brazil's president is refusing international aid to fight fires in the Amazon.) What is any individual or community to do in times like these? How does one act in the face of likely failure?

Every postcolonial author in this book has asked a version of this second question. Whatever their suggestions of hope or optimism about the future, Okot p'Bitek, Ngũgĩ wa Thiong'o, and Nuruddin Farah all end on notes of uncertainty and even despair. All are quite bleak, in a sense, even tragic. Lawino employs every word, tactic, and emotion in begging Ocol to repent, but he refuses her and rejects his community. Kariuki in *Mother, Sing for Me* prepares for a new revolution against the neocolonial ruler, but the action of the play stops short, implying that if the cycle repeats, this revolution will also fail. Every effort to stop the General in Farah's *Variations* trilogy fails—every hero dies or is lost. All of these texts and authors are, rightly, held up as giants of postcolonial African literature whose critiques of colonialism, neocolonialism, and authoritarian power are necessary steps in the struggle for authenticity, equality, and liberty. Less often do critics dwell on the strange tragedy of these texts that verge nearly on pessimism. Even I, in my analysis above, argue that the visions of these and other authors not only challenge colonial injustice but lay the groundwork for new forms of law, new normative worlds. I stand by this potentially utopian argument, but at the same time I am forced to question it because these texts are also about failure. The failure of justice in the face of superior power. The failure of action in the face of a world unwilling to change. But failure in these texts does not necessarily mean closure and surrender. Because all are formally open-ended, pausing narration or performance in ambiguity, they offer a question rather than an answer: what, if anything, can we do now?

This question is similar to those central to tragedy, both the performative genre and the mode of experience defined by grief and suffering. In his book, *Tragedy, the Greeks, and Us* (2019), Simon Critchley contests the traditional exclusion of tragedy from the discipline of philosophy, arguing instead that tragedy "articulates a philosophical view that challenges the authority of philosophy by giving voice to what is constricted about us, what is precarious about us, and what is limited about us." Whereas Plato preached the "idea and ideal of a noncontradictory psychic life," tragedy "gives voice to what suffers in us and in others" (9). As a result, tragedy tends not to produce clear, singular, and hopeful outcomes, but provocative confrontations with ambiguity and uncertainty. Similarly, David Scott, in *Conscripts of Modernity: The Tragedy of Colonial Enlightenment* (2004), notes that tragedy reveals how, despite our ambitions or pretensions to the contrary, humans are deeply susceptible to forces beyond our control. Tragedy, he says, attends to the human capacity "to reason and plan, to order values and ends and make decisions between their relative worth," but, in doing so, it reveals that rationality ultimately cannot protect us from uncertainty, chance, *contingency* (182). "In short, tragedy sets before us the image of a man or woman obliged to act in a world in which values are unstable and ambiguous" (13). This is particularly necessary, according to Scott, in the postcolonial world where "anticolonial utopias have gradually withered into postcolonial nightmares" (2).

For Critchley, tragedy is, thus, "thinking *in* action, thinking *upon* action, *for the sake of* action"; and this thinking, ultimately, "takes the form of a radical questioning: How do I act? What shall I do?" (5; emphasis in original). These are precisely the questions Okot, Ngũgĩ, and Farah ask at the conclusions of their texts, and precisely the questions we must ask as both causes and casualties of the Anthropocene. Critchley then points to a subjectivity or affective agency that results from such questions and that, I argue, enables us to understand more fully how East African writers similarly grapple with uncertainty in ways that may offer some insight into how to approach the experience of climate change and (human) time's possible end. Critchley writes:

> In opposition to forms of vapidly hopeful idealism that leads only to despair, I see tragedy's philosophy as offering a bracing, skeptical realism that heavily qualifies what we think of as hope, but perhaps also deepens it into a form of courage. (29)

A pessimistic reading of Okot, Ngũgĩ, and Farah would say that they simply give up hope after failing to overcome the brutalities and injustices of oppression. Hence, the defiantly unrepentant Ocol, the unfinished revolution against

Mwendanda, the victorious General. Any serious reader would balk at such claims, of course, but even if these authors are not fatalistic, they are also not particularly hopeful, especially in a vapidly idealistic sense. I believe Critchley's formulation of hope vs. courage more usefully explains the outcome of their confrontation with failure: they offer a "bracing, skeptical realism that heavily qualifies" the idealistic hope that many people had after independence, deepening it instead "into a form of courage." Hope, like international law, is a weak force that, on its own or in certain forms, does little practical work in the world, particularly when it comes to climate change. We might speak of a crisis of hope like a crisis of international law in that neither is sufficient for altering the course, or even mitigating the phenomenal experience, of a global, existential problem like climate change. Hopelessness would seem to be the true Anthropocenic condition, at least for those who are willing to adopt a longer view of human history and a bracingly realistic view of human futurity.

Hopelessness, however, does not have to mean finality or surrender. It does not have to mean simply giving up. As Critchley says, the "bracing, skeptical realism" that comes from tragedy's philosophy can deepen "what we think of as hope" into a form of courage. Courage without or in place of hope, at least hope in a superficial sense, outlines a different kind of orientation toward the future. It motivates one to act despite the likelihood, or even certainty, of failure. Scientists and environmental activists are the new prophets crying in the wilderness, projecting the future of humanity upon reality—the difference now is that a particular version of the future is becoming inevitable. Religious prophets said, "Change before it is too late." Prophets of the Anthropocene will soon say, or are already saying, "It is too late." But do we resign, give up, allow the world, or parts of the world, simply to end if there is no hope of stopping it? Lawino failed but we can be sure she did not give up. There were still options, but they required courage rather than hope. And this is the lesson, perhaps the most critical lesson, of the authors I have studied (setting aside, as we must in times like these, the postmodern distaste for didacticism in literature). Their orature-infused texts are open-ended in the face of failure, suggesting, paradoxically, that failure is not the end. In fact, I would argue that their open-endedness constitutes an invitation—as if in a song, a call and response—to complete the texts through real action in the world. After all, these were never academic arguments for these authors—they were concerned with practical, day-to-day, existential realities; they also suffered real consequences for their work, including harassment, censorship, imprisonment, and exile. Their solutions, then, which are framed in and through tragedy, should be understood as being oriented toward the world, toward real people and real conditions. They call upon readers and viewers and listeners to act despite the uncertainty of success, to respond with courage even if they are unable to hope and others are unwilling to act.

We see such courage in those former Mau Mau fighters who succeeded in suing the British government in *Mutua & others* v. *The Foreign & Commonwealth*

Office even though the idea of holding a former empire accountable seemed absurd and impossible. We see such courage in those rebuilding their communities in the wake of unimaginable tragedy in Northern Uganda, Rwanda, Sudan, Somalia, and elsewhere. We see it in the workers who sued a global corporation in *Kenyan Tea Workers* v. *Unilever plc*. And we see it in those willing to attempt the impossible in fighting to protect the environment. There are important and inspiring environmental activists across the globe, but Kenya, again, offers a compelling example: the late 2004 Nobel Peace Prize winner Wangari Maathai, founder of the Green Belt Movement (GBM), which, since 1977, has planted over 50 million trees throughout Kenya.

This movement, primarily driven by networks of rural women, emerged not simply in response to deforestation, which had devastated Kenya since the colonial era,[4] but in response to the fact that ecological security and sustainability go hand-in-hand with economic security, democratic governance, and peace. Given the wide-reaching implications of their work, Wangari and her fellow activists have been targeted by those in power, suffering "violence and incarceration; Maathai herself was jailed several times and badly beaten by police and hospitalized in 1992" (Taylor 184). Many of us would quit after such treatment, but Wangari continued to struggle, refusing to surrender and accept failure. "This led to the *reputation for courage* that Maathai and her movement enjoy, both domestically and internationally" (184; emphasis added). Through such courage, the GBM grew in its influence. Wangari was elected to the Kenyan parliament in 2002 and appointed Assistant Minister for Environment and Natural Resources, for example. In that position, Bron Taylor observes, "she helped shape Kenya's Forest Act of 2005. This was a very progressive policy—compared with other environmental laws around the world—which was designed to promote environmental sustainability, reduce greenhouse gasses, preserve biodiversity, and meet human needs" (185). In fact, Wangari was instrumental in ensuring that Kenya's 2010 constitution included the articles protecting the right to a clean environment for current and future generations. What began as a simple effort to fight deforestation and lift rural women out of poverty became a leading movement in Kenya, with global influence—a movement that ultimately transformed the normative world of East Africa, projecting *its* imagined future upon reality.

No doubt falling within the inspiring shade of Wangari's environmental legacy, news of a significant tree-planting feat went viral in the summer of 2019 when a government-led project in Ethiopia claimed to have planted over 350 million trees in one day. The aims of the project, dubbed "Green Legacy," included reversing years of deforestation (at the turn of the century, 30 to 35 percent of Ethiopia was covered by forests; today it is less than

4 "Estimates of deforestation found in Forestry Ministry publications indicate that about 98 percent of Kenya's original primary forests have been destroyed or converted to agro-ecosystems, human settlements, and commercial zones" (Taylor 184).

4 percent ["Economic incentives"]) and fighting climate change.[5] The project received significant news coverage—in part, because it seemed to be a practical response to a study published just weeks earlier that claimed a global reforestation effort has the potential to cut atmospheric CO_2 levels by 25 percent.[6] Almost immediately, popularized versions of this argument hit media outlets, with some claiming that planting 1 trillion trees was the key to finally stopping climate change.[7] This apparently simple and practical solution appealed to many, but critics quickly spoke out, including a number of scientists who challenged the study's methods and painted a somewhat more complex picture of the role of reforestation in addressing climate change. Among their criticisms was that although tree planting is certainly a good idea, forests typically take decades to grow and, under the circumstances, we need more immediate, fast-acting solutions.[8] This would seem to imply that widespread reforestation would have been more effective had it started years ago. However, in some places it did. In Kenya, for example. The Green Belt Movement has promoted this kind of work for years; but even with the global recognition that came when Wangari received the Nobel Prize, the international community failed to follow her lead.

In humanity's search for answers to the ongoing problems of modernity, including globalization and climate change, the global south has repeatedly led the way, but the north has too often lacked the courage, wisdom, and humility to follow. It may be too late. Failure may be inevitable. But, like Lawino, Karikuki, Somali revolutionaries, aged Mau Mau fighters, abused tea plantation workers, Wangari Maathai, and so many others, the prospect of failure should not stop us. With realism and courage, we must take action as individuals and communities whether or not those "in power" choose to follow.

5 See Daley, "Ethiopia Plants 350 Million Trees in 12 Hours—A New Record" (2019). There have been some doubts cast on the number of trees Ethiopia claims to have planted and whether such a feat is even possible without vast amounts of land and millions of volunteers, but, whatever the case, Ethiopia does appear to have planted a significant number of trees, with a goal, ultimately, to plant 4 billion in total in 2019.

6 See Bastin et al., "The Global Tree Restoration Potential" (2019).

7 See Lewis, "Planting A Trillion Trees Could Be the 'Most Effective Solution' to Climate Change, Study Says" (2019).

8 See Daley, "Trees Alone Can't Save Us from Climate Change" (2019).

Bibliography

Abdullahi, Mohamed Diriye. *Culture and Customs of Somalia*. Westport, CT: Greenwood Press, 2001.

"About the Court." International Criminal Court, n.d. www.icc-cpi.int/test-new-master. Accessed May 2, 2015.

Abrahams, Ray. "A Modern Witch-Hunt among the Lango of Uganda." *Cambridge Anthropology* 10.1 (1985): 32–45.

Adjaye, Joseph K. "Modes of Knowing: Intellectual and Social Dimensions of Time in Africa." *KronoScope* 2.2 (2002): 200–24.

Agamben, Giorgio. *State of Exception*. Trans. Kevin Attell. Chicago: University of Chicago Press, 2005.

"Agreement for the Prosecution and Punishment of the Major War Criminals of the European Axis, and Charter of the International Military Tribunal." *Charter of the International Military Tribunal*. August 8, 1945. International Committee of the Red Cross. https://ihl-databases.icrc.org/ihl/INTRO/350. Accessed June 15, 2016.

Ahmed, Ali Jimale. *Daybreak is Near: Literature, Clans, and the Nation-State in Somalia*. Lawrenceville, NJ and Asmara, Eritrea: Red Sea Press, 1996.

——. Personal correspondence with the author. April 17, 2011.

Aiken, Susan Hardy. *Isak Dinesen and the Engendering of Narrative*. Chicago: University of Chicago Press, 1990.

Akpan, Ntieyong U. *Epitaph to Indirect Rule: A Discourse on Local Government in Africa*. London: Frank Cass & Co., 1967.

Allen, Tim. "The International Criminal Court and the Invention of Traditional Justice in Northern Uganda." *Politique Africaine* 3.107 (2007): 147–66.

——. *Trial Justice: The International Criminal Court and the Lord's Resistance Army*. London: Zed Books, 2006.

Aluchio, L.P.A. *Trade Unions in Kenya: Development and the System of Industrial Relations*. Nairobi: Jomo Kenyatta Foundation, 1998.

Amin, Shahid. *Event, Metaphor, Memory: Chauri Chaura, 1922–1992*. Berkeley: University of California Press, 1995.

Anderson, David. *Histories of the Hanged: The Dirty War in Kenya and the End of Empire*. New York: Norton, 2005.

——. "Kenya, 1895–1939: Registration and Rough Justice." *Masters, Servants, and Magistrates in Britain and the Empire, 1562–1955*. Ed. Douglas Hay and Paul Craven. Chapel Hill: University of North Carolina Press, 2004: 498–528.

Andrews, J.A. "The Aberystwyth Law School 1901–1976." *Cambrian Law Review* 7 (1976): 7–10.

Andrzejewski, B.W. and I.M. Lewis. *Somali Poetry: An Introduction*. Oxford: Oxford University Press, 1974.

Anghie, Antony. *Imperialism, Sovereignty and the Making of International Law*. Cambridge: Cambridge University Press, 2007.

Anker, Elizbeth. *Fictions of Dignity: Embodying Human Rights in World Literature*. Ithaca, NY: Cornell University Press, 2012.

Armillas-Tiseyra, Magalí. *The Dictator Novel: Writers and Politics in the Global South*. Evanston, IL: Northwestern University Press, 2019.

Asein, Samuel Omo. "Okot p'Bitek: Literature and the Cultural Revolution in East Africa." *Journal of African Studies* 5.3 (1978): 357–72.

Atwell, David. *Rewriting Modernity: Studies in Black South African Literary History*. Athens: Ohio University Press, 2005.

Bakhtin, Mikhail. *Rabelais and His World*. Trans. Hélène Iswolsky. Bloomington: Indiana University Press, 1984.

Bal, Anjali S., Chris Archer-Brown, Karen Robson, and Daniel E. Hall. "Do Good, Goes Bad, Gets Ugly: Kony 2012." *Journal of Public Affairs* 13.2 (2013): 202–08.

Balogun, F. Odun. *Ngũgĩ and African Postcolonial Narrative: The Novel as Oral Narrative in Multigenre Performance*. Saint-Hyacinthe, Quebec: World Heritage Press, 1997.

Bardolph, Jacqueline. "Time and History in Nuruddin Farah's *Close Sesame*." *Emerging Perspectives on Nuruddin Farah*. Ed. Derek Wright. Trenton, NJ: Africa World Press, 2002: 399–418.

Barrows, Adam. *The Cosmic Time of Empire: Modern Britain and World Literature*. Berkeley: University of California Press, 2011.

Bastin, Jean-Francois et al. "The Global Tree Reforestation Potential." *Science* 365.6448 (July 5, 2019): 76–79.

Behdad, Ali. "*Une Pratique Sauvage*: Postcolonial Belatedness and Cultural Politics." *The Pre-Occupation of Postcolonial Studies*. Ed. Fawzia Afzal-Khan and Kalpana Seshadri-Crooks. Durham, NC: Duke University Press, 2000: 71–85.

Behrend, Heike. *Alice Lakwena and the Holy Spirits: War in Northern Uganda, 1985–1997*. Trans. Mitch Cohen. Athens: Ohio University Press, 1999.

Belgrave, Faye Z. and Kevin W. Allison. *African American Psychology: From Africa to America*. 2nd ed. Thousand Oaks, CA: SAGE Publications, 2010.

Benjamin, Walter. *Illuminations*. Trans. Harry Zohn. New York: Schocken Books, 1969.

Berman, Bruce. *Control and Crisis in Colonial Kenya: The Dialectic of Domination*. Athens: Ohio University Press, 1991.

——. "Nationalism, Ethnicity, and Modernity: The Paradox of Mau." *Canadian Journal of African Studies* 25.2 (1991): 181–206.

Bhabha, Homi. *The Location of Culture*. London: Routledge, 1994.

Biber, Eric. "Law in the Anthropocene Epoch." *Georgetown Law Journal* 106.1 (2017): 1–68.

Birla, Ritu. "Performativity between Logos and Nomos: Law, Temporality and the Non-Economic Analysis of Power." *Columbia Journal of Gender and Law* 21.2 (2011–12): 90–113.

Bishop, Stephen L. *Legal Oppositional Narrative: A Case Study in Cameroon*. Lanham, MD: Lexington Books, 2008.

Björkman, Ingrid. *Mother, Sing for Me: People's Theatre in Kenya*. London: Zed Books, 1989.

Blishen, Edward. Introduction to Okot p'Bitek. *Song of Prisoner*. New York: Third Press, 1971: 1–40.

Blixen, Karen. *Den afrikanske Farm*. Copenhagen: Gyldendal, 2007.

Boire, Gary. "Symbolic Violence: Law, Literature, Interpretation—An Afterword." *ARIEL: A Review of International English Literature* 35.1–2 (2004): 231–45.

Bradbury, Mark. *Becoming Somaliland*. London: Progressio, 2008.

Branch, Adam. *Displacing Human Rights: War and Intervention in Northern Uganda*. Oxford: Oxford University Press, 2011.

Branch, Daniel. "Footprints in the Sand: British Colonial Counterinsurgency and the War in Iraq." *Politics & Society* 38.1 (2010): 15–34.

Brantley, Susan C. *Understanding Isak Dinesen*. Columbia: University of South Carolina Press, 2002.

Brecht, Bertolt. *Brecht on Theatre: The Development of an Aesthetic*. Ed. and trans. John Willett. New York: Hill & Wang, 1977.

Brown, Michelle Lynn. "Bleeding for the Mother(Land): Reading Testimonial Bodies in Nuruddin Farah's *Maps*." *Research in African Literatures* 41.4 (2010): 125–43.

Burton, Sir Richard Francis. *First Footsteps in East Africa, or, An Exploration of Harrar*. vol. 1. London: Tylston and Edwards, 1894.

Cannadine, David. *Aspects of Aristocracy: Grandeur and Decline in Modern Britain*. New Haven, CT: Yale University Press, 1994.

Carothers, J.C. *The African Mind in Health and Disease: A Study in Ethnopsychiatry*. 1953. New York: Negro Universities Press, 1970.

——. *The Psychology of Mau*. Nairobi: The Government Printer, 1955.

Cartwright, Samuel A. "Report on the Diseases and Peculiarities of the Negro Race." *Health, Disease, and Illness: Concepts in Medicine*. Ed. Arthur L. Caplan, James J. McCartney, and Dominic A. Sisti. Washington, DC: Georgetown University Press, 2004.

Castillejo-Cuéllar, Alejandro. "Historical Injuries, Temporality and the Law: Articulations of a Violent Past in Two Transitional Scenarios." *Law and Critique* 25.1 (2014): 47–66.

Cavaleri, David P. *The Law of War: Can 20th-Century Standards Apply to the Global War on Terrorism?* Global War on Terrorism Occasional Paper 9. Fort Leavenworth, KS: CSI Press, 2005.

Center for Biological Diversity. "The Extinction Crisis." n.d. www.biologicaldiversity.org/programs/biodiversity/elements_of_biodiversity/extinction_crisis/. Accessed December 7, 2019.

Chakrabarty, Dipesh. "Postcolonial Studies and the Challenge of Climate Change." *New Literary History* 43.1 (2012): 1–18.

——. *Provincializing Europe: Postcolonial Thought and Historical Difference*. Princeton, NJ: Princeton University Press, 2000.

Chanock, Martin. *Law, Custom, and Social Order: The Colonial Experience in Malawi and Zambia*. Portsmouth, NH: Heinemann, 1998.

Churchill, Winston S. *My African Journey*. London: Holland Press, 1962.

Civil Evidence Act 1968 (Chapter 64). London: Her Majesty's Stationery Office, 1968.

Clayton, Anthony and Donald C. Savage. *Government and Labour in Kenya: 1895–1963*. London: Frank Cass, 1974.

Cole, Teju. "The White-Savior Industrial Complex." *The Atlantic*. March 21, 2012.

Collier, Paul and Deepak Lal. *Labour and Poverty in Kenya, 1900–1980*. Oxford: Oxford University Press, 1986.

Colson, Robert. "Arresting Time, Resisting Arrest: Narrative Time and the African Dictator in Ngũgĩ wa Thiong'o's *Wizard of the Crow*." *Research in African Literatures* 42.1 (2011): 133–53.

Colvin, Brenda. "In Praise of Kenya." *Times Literary Supplement*. December 18, 1937, Issue 1872.

Comaroff, Jean and John L. Comaroff. *Theory from the South, or How Euro-America is Evolving Toward Africa*. Boulder, CO: Paradigm Publishers, 2012.

"Composition of Macro Geographical (Continental) Regions, Geographical Sub-Regions, and Selected Economic and Other Groupings." United Nations Statistics Division. September 26, 2016. https://unstats.un.org/unsd/methodology/m49/. Accessed December 7, 2019.

Conrad, Joseph. *Heart of Darkness*. Ed. Paul B. Armstrong. 4th ed. New York: W.W. Norton & Co., 2006.

Cover, Robert M. "Foreword: *Nomos* and Narrative." *Harvard Law Review* 97.1 (1983): 4–68.

——. "Violence and the Word." *Yale Law Journal* 95 (1986): 1601–29.

Crang, Mike and Nigel Thrift, eds. *Thinking Space*. London: Routledge, 2000.

Critchley, Simon. *Tragedy, the Greeks, and Us*. New York: Pantheon, 2019.

Cronin-Furman, Kate and Amanda Taub. "Solving War Crimes with Wristbands: The Arrogance of 'Kony 2012.'" *Media and Civil Society in 21st Century Conflict*. Ed. E.L. Gaston. New York: International Debate Education Association, 2014: 101–04.

Daley, Jason. "Ethiopia Plants 350 Million Trees in 12 Hours—A New Record." *Smithsonian Magazine*. July 30, 2019. www.smithsonianmag.com/smart-news/ethiopia-plants-350-million-trees-12-hours-180972760/.

——. "Trees Alone Can't Save Us from Climate Change." *Sierra*. The national magazine of the Sierra Club. July 17, 2019. www.sierraclub.org/sierra/trees-alone-can-t-save-us-climate-change. Accessed December 7, 2019.

Davies, Mary Llewelfryn. Personal correspondence with the author. September 19, 2006.

Derrida, Jacques. "Force of Law: The 'Mystical Foundation of Authority.'" *Deconstruction and the Possibility of Justice*. Ed. Drucilla Cornell, Michael Rosenfeld, and David Gray Carlson. New York: Routledge, 1992: 3–67.

——. *Of Grammatology*. Trans. Gayatri Chakravorty Spivak. Baltimore, MD: Johns Hopkins University Press, 1977.

Dimock, Wai Chee. *Through Other Continents: American Literature across Deep Time*. Princeton, NJ: Princeton University Press, 2006.

Dinesen, Isak (Karen Blixen). *Letters from Africa, 1914–1931*. Chicago: University of Chicago Press, 1981.

——. *Out of Africa* and *Shadows on the Grass*. 1937. New York: Vintage, 1989.

——. *Shadows on the Grass* London, Michael Joseph, 1960.

"Documentary Evidence." *Kenya Legal Resources*. 2011. www.kenyalawresourcecenter.org/2011/07/documentary-evidence.html. Accessed August 2, 2016.

Douglas, Lawrence. "Film as Witness: Screening Nazi Concentration Camps before the Nuremberg Tribunal." *Yale Law Review* 105.2 (1995): 449–81.

Drumbl, Mark A. *Atrocity, Punishment, and International Law*. Cambridge: Cambridge University Press, 2007.

——. "Child Soldiers and Clicktivism: Justice, Myths, and Prevention." *Journal of Human Rights Practice* 4.3 (2012): 1–5.

"Economic Incentives Help Stem Deforestation in Ethiopia." *Farm Africa*. July 7, 2015. www.farmafrica.org/media/press-releases/post/720-economic-incentives-help-stem-deforestation-in-ethiopia. Accessed December 7, 2019.

Edgerton, Robert B. *Mau Mau: An African Crucible*. New York: Free Press, 1989.

Ehrenberg, Suzanne. "Embracing the Writing-Centered Legal Process." *Iowa Law Review* 89 (2004): 1159–99.

Elias, T. Olawale. *British Colonial Law*. London: Stevens, 1962.

Elkins, Caroline. *Imperial Reckoning: The Untold Story of Britain's Gulag in Kenya*. New York: Henry Holt and Co., 2005.

"Enact." *verb* I. 2. *Oxford English Dictionary*. Online.

Engelhart, Katie. "40,000 Kenyans Accuse UK of Abuse in Second Mau Mau Case." *Guardian*. October 29, 2014. www.theguardian.com/world/2014/oct/29/kenya-mau-mau-abuse-case. Accessed December 7, 2019.

English, F.M. "Admissibility of Sound Recordings in Evidence." 58 A.L.A.2d. (Originally published in 1958.)

Fabian, Johannes. *Time and the Other: How Anthropology Makes Its Object*. New York: Columbia University Press, 1983.

Fanon, Franz. *Black Skin, White Masks*. 1952. Trans. Charles Lam Markmann. New York: Grove Press, 1967.

——. *The Wretched of the Earth*. 1961. Trans. Richard Philcox. New York: Grove Press, 2004.

Farah, Nuruddin. "Celebrating Differences: The 1998 Neustadt Lecture." *Emerging Perspectives on Nuruddin Farah*. Ed. Derek Wright. Trenton, NJ and Asmara, Eritrea: Africa World Press, 2002: 15–24.

——. *Close Sesame*. Saint Paul, MN: Graywolf Press, 1983.

——. *Sardines*. Saint Paul, MN: Graywolf Press, 1981.

——. *Sweet and Sour Milk*. Saint Paul, MN: Graywolf Press, 1979.

——. "Why I Write." *Emerging Perspectives on Nuruddin Farah*. Ed. Derek Wright. Trenton, NJ and Asmara, Eritrea: Africa World Press, 2002: 1–13.

Finnegan, Ruth. *The Oral and Beyond: Doing Things with Words in Africa*. Chicago: Chicago University Press, 2007.

Finnström, Sverker. "'KONY 2012,' Military Humanitarianism, and the Magic of Occult Economies." *Africa Spectrum* 47.2–3 (2012): 127–35.

——. *Living with Bad Surroundings: War, History, and Everyday Moments in Northern Uganda*. Durham, NC: Duke University Press, 2008.

Fitzpatrick, Peter. "Marking Time: Temporality and the Imperial Cast of Occidental Law." *Birkbeck Law Review* 1.1 (2012): 63–79.

——. *Modernism and the Grounds of Law*. Cambridge: Cambridge University Press, 2001.

——. *The Mythology of Modern Law*. London: Routledge, 1992.

Foucault, Michel. "Of Other Spaces: Utopias and Heterotopias." 1967. Trans. Jay Miskowiec. *Architecture/Mouvement/Continuité* (October 1984): 1–9.

Gagiano, Annie. "Farah's *Sardines*: Women in a Context of Despotism." *Africa Today* 57.3 (2011): 2–20.

Gakaara wa Wanjau. *Mau Mau Author in Detention: An Author's Detention Diary*. Nairobi: East African Educational Publishers, 1988.

Gauvin, Lara Rosenoff. "In and Out of Culture: Okot p'Bitek's Work and Social Repair in Post-Conflict Acoliland." *Oral Tradition* 28.1 (2013): 35–54.
Gee, Henry. *In Search of Deep Time: Beyond the Fossil Record to a New History of Life*. New York: The Free Press, 1999.
Ghai, Y.P. and J.P.W.B. McAuslan. *Public Law and Political Change in Kenya: A Study of the Legal Framework of Government from Colonial Times to the Present*. London: Oxford University Press, 1970.
Gikandi, Simon. *Ngũgĩ wa Thiong'o*. Cambridge: Cambridge University Press, 2000.
——. "Nuruddin Farah and Postcolonial Textuality." *World Literature Today* 72.4 (1998): 753–58.
——. "Pan-Africanism and Cosmopolitanism: The Case of Jomo Kenyatta." *English Studies in Africa* 43.1 (2000): 3–27.
——. "The Postcolonial Wizard: A Review of Ngũgĩ wa Thiong'o's *Wizard of the Crow*." *Transitions* 98 (2008): 156–69.
Gikandi, Simon and Evan Mwangi, eds. *The Columbia Guide to East African Literature since 1945*. New York: Columbia University Press, 2007.
Gilroy, Paul. *The Black Atlantic: Modernity and Double Consciousness*. Cambridge, MA: Harvard University Press, 1993.
Girling, F.K. *The Acholi of Uganda*. London: Her Majesty's Stationery Office, 1960.
Gogineni, Roopa. "Mau Mau Ruling Sets Legal Precedent." October 8, 2012. *Voice of America*. www.voanews.com/africa/mau-mau-ruling-sets-legal-precedent. Accessed May 11, 2015.
Greenhouse, Carol J. "Just in Time: Temporality and the Cultural Legitimation of Law." *Yale Law Journal* 98.8 (1989): 1631–51.
Gregory, Sam. "Kony 2012 Through a Prism of Video Advocacy Practices and Trends." *Journal of Human Rights Practice* 4.3 (2012): 463–68.
Grogan, Ewart and Arthur H. Sharp. *From the Cape to Cairo: The First Traverse of Africa from South to North*. New and revised ed. London: Hurst & Blackett Ltd., 1902.
Gulick, Anne. *Literature, Law, and Rhetorical Performance in the Anticolonial Atlantic*. Columbus: Ohio State University Press, 2016.
Gunner, Liz. "Africa and Orality." *The Cambridge History of African and Caribbean Literature*. vol. 1. Ed. Abiola Irele and Simon Gikandi. Cambridge: Cambridge University Press, 2004: 1–18.
Gusfield, Joseph R. "Tradition and Modernity: Misplaced Polarities in the Study of Social Change." *American Journal of Sociology* 72.4 (1967): 351–62.
Gyekye, Kwame. *Tradition and Modernity: Philosophical Reflections on the African Experience*. Oxford: Oxford University Press, 1997.
Hague, William. "Statement to Parliament on Settlement of Mau Mau Claims." June 6, 2013. www.gov.uk/government/news/statement-to-parliament-on-settlement-of-mau-mau-claims. Accessed May 11, 2015.
Harlacher, Thomas et al. *Traditional Ways of Coping in Acholi*. Gulu, Uganda: Thomas Harlacher and Caritas Gulu Archdiocese, 2006.
Hartmann, Ivor W., ed. *AfroSF: Science Fiction by African Writers*. n.p.: StoryTime, 2012.
Hashim, Alice Bettis. *The Fallen State: Dissonance, Dictatorship, and Death in Somalia*. Lanham, MD: University Press of America, 1997.
Hassan, Mohamed-Rashid Sheik. "The 1969 Military Coup in Somalia." Part 13. *Wararka Maanta* (March 1, 2010). Online. Accessed April 4, 2011.

Hawley, John C. "Nuruddin Farah: Tribalism, Orality and Postcolonial Ultimate Reality and Meaning in Contemporary Somalia." *Emerging Perspectives on Nuruddin Farah.* Ed. Derek Wright. Trenton, NJ: Africa World Press, 2002: 67–94.

Heberer, Patricia and Jürgen Matthäus, eds. *Atrocities on Trial: Historical Perspectives on the Politics of Prosecuting War Crimes.* Lincoln: University of Nebraska Press, 2008.

Heerey, Peter. "Aesthetics, Culture, and the Whole Damn Thing." *Law and Literature* 15 (2003): 295–311.

Hemingway, Ernest. *Green Hills of Africa.* New York: Charles Scribner's Sons, 1935.

Henderson, Ian. *The Hunt for Kimathi.* London: Hamish Hamilton, 1958.

Heron, G.A. "Introduction." *Song of Lawino / Song of Ocol.* By Okot p'Bitek. Oxford: Heinemann, 1972: 1–33.

——. *The Poetry of Okot p'Bitek.* London: Heinemann, 1976.

Hess, Robert L. *Italian Colonialism in Somalia.* Chicago: University of Chicago Press, 1966.

Heywood, Annemarie. "Modes of Freedom: The Songs of Okot p'Bitek." *Journal of Commonwealth Literature* 15 (1980): 65–83.

Hill, M.F. *Cream Country: The Story of Kenya Co-operative Creameries Limited, Twenty-Five Years of Progress.* Nairobi: Kenya Co-operative Creameries Limited, 1956.

Hirsch, Susan F. *In the Moment of Greatest Calamity: Terrorism, Grief, and a Victim's Quest for Justice.* Princeton, NJ: Princeton University Press, 2006.

Hitchcock, Peter. *The Long Space: Transnationalism and Postcolonial Form.* Stanford, CA: Stanford University Press, 2010.

Hobsbawm, Eric and Terence Ranger, eds. *The Invention of Tradition.* Cambridge: Cambridge University Press, 1992.

Hochschild, Adam. *King Leopold's Ghost: A Story of Greed, Terror, and Heroism in Colonial Africa.* Boston: Houghton Mifflin, 1998.

Hopwood, Julian. "We Can't Be Sure Who Killed Us: Memory and Memorialization in Post-Conflict Northern Uganda." *Justice and Reconciliation Project.* New York: International Center for Transitional Justice, 2011.

Horsley, Kate. "Our Lives, Our Stories: Storytelling Workshops in Uganda's Refugee Camps." *Short Fiction in Theory and Practice* 1.2 (2011): 147–61.

Hussain, Nasser. *The Jurisprudence of Emergency: Colonialism and the Rule of Law.* Ann Arbor: University of Michigan Press, 2003.

Huxley, Elspeth. *The Flame Trees of Thika: Memoirs of an African Childhood.* London: Chatto & Windus, 1959.

——. *Settlers of Kenya.* Nairobi: Highway Press; London: Longman's Green and Co., 1948.

Ibbetson, David J. *A Historical Introduction to the Law of Obligations.* Oxford: Oxford University Press, 2000.

"ICC Prosecutor Presents Case against Sudanese President, Hassan Ahmad Al Bashir, for Genocide, Crimes against Humanity and War Crimes in Darfur." International Criminal Court Press Release. International Criminal Court. July 14, 2008. www.icc-cpi.int/Pages/item.aspx?name=a. Accessed May 15, 2015.

Imbo, Samuel Oluoch. *Oral Traditions as Philosophy: Okot p'Bitek's Legacy for African Philosophy.* Lanham, MD: Rowman & Littlefield, 2002.

The Indian Contract Act (IX. of 1872). 4th ed. Calcutta: Thacker, Spink, 1883.

The Indian Evidence Act (I. of 1872). London: Macmillan and Co., 1872.

Ingiriis, Mohamed Haji. *The Suicidal State in Somalia: The Rise and Fall of the Siad Barre Regime, 1969–1991.* Lanham, MD: University Press of America, 2016.

International Criminal Court, "President of Uganda Refers Situation Concerning the Lord's Resistance Army to the ICC." International Criminal Court Press Release. January 29, 2004. The Hague: ICC.

Invisible Children. "KONY 2012." Online video. www.youtube.com/watch?v=Y4MnpzG5Sqc. Accessed March 5, 2012.

——. "KONY 2012 Part II: Beyond Famous." Online video. www.youtube.com/watch?v=c_Ue6REkeTA. Accessed April 6, 2012.

Irele, Abiola. "Orality, Literacy, and African Literature." *African Literature: An Anthology of Criticism and Theory*. Ed. Tejumola Olaniyan and Ato Quayson. Malden, MA: Blackwell Publishing, 2007: 74–91.

Iye, Ali Moussa. *Le verdict de l'arbre (Go'aan Kii Geedka): Le Xeer Issa, Etude d'une "Democratie Pastorale."* Djibouti: International Printing Press, 1990.

JanMohamed, Abdul R. *Manichean Aesthetics: The Politics of Literature in Colonial Africa*. Amherst: University of Massachusetts Press, 1983.

Japhet, Kirilo and Earle Seaton. *The Meru Land Case*. Nairobi: East African Publishing House, 1967.

Julien, Eileen. *African Novels and the Question of Orality*. Bloomington: Indiana University Press.

Juraga, Dubravka. "Nuruddin Farahs' *Variations on the Theme of an African Dictatorship*: Patriarchy, Gender, and Political Oppression in Somalia." *Critique* 38.3 (1997): 205–20.

Kagumire, Rosebell. "My Response to Kony 2012." Online video. www.youtube.com/watch?time_continue=13&v=KLVY5jBnD-E&feature=emb_logo. Accessed March 9, 2012.

Kagwanja, Peter Mwangi. "'Power to *Uhuru*': Youth Identity and Generational Politics in Kenya's 2002 Elections." *African Affairs* 105.418 (2005): 51–75.

Kahn, Liaquat Ali. "Temporality of Law." *McGeorge Law Review* 40 (2008): 1–52.

Kahumbu, Paula. "Kenya Jails Ivory Kingpin for 20 Years." *Guardian*. July 23, 2016. www.theguardian.com/environment/africa-wild/2016/jul/23/kenya-jails-ivory-kinpin-for-20-years. Accessed August 12, 2016.

Kalliney, Peter. "East African Literature and the Politics of Global Reading." *Research in African Literatures* 39.1 (2008): 1–23.

Kanogo, Tabitha. *Squatters and the Roots of Mau Mau, 1905–1963*. London: James Currey; Nairobi: East African Educational Publishers, 1987.

"Kapenguria Trial Transcript." vols. 1–8. Kenya National Archives. Nairobi, Kenya. 1952–53.

Kariuki, Josiah Mwangi. *"Mau Mau" Detainee*. Oxford: Oxford University Press, 1976.

Kennedy, Dane. *Islands of White: Settler Society and Culture in Kenya and Southern Rhodesia, 1890–1939*. Durham, NC: Duke University Press, 1987.

Kenya's Constitution of 2010. Comparative Constitutions Project. August 12, 2019. www.constituteproject.org/constitution/Kenya_2010.pdf?lang=en. Accessed December 7, 2019.

Kenyatta, Jomo. *Facing Mount Kenya*. 1938. New York: Vintage Books, 1965.

——. *Suffering without Bitterness: The Founding of the Kenya Nation*. Nairobi: East African Publishing House, 1968.

Kitson, Frank. *Bunch of Five*. London: Faber & Faber, 1977.

——. *Gangs and Counter Gangs*. London: Barrie & Rockliff, 1960.

——. *Low-Intensity Operations: Subversion, Insurgency and Peacekeeping*. London: Faber & Faber, 1971.

Knipp, Thomas R. "Kenya's Literary Ladies and the Mythologizing of the White Highlands." *South Atlantic Review* 55.1 (1990): 1–16.

Kravits, Mark R. "Written and Oral Persuasion in the United States Courts: A District Judge's Perspective on their History, Function, and Future." *Journal of Appellate Practice and Process* 10 (2009): 247–72.

Kriel, Robyn and Briana Duggan. "'Queen of Ivory' Arrested in Tanzania." *CNN*. October 9, 2015. https://edition.cnn.com/2015/10/09/africa/tanzania-elephant-ivory-queen-arrest/index.html. Accessed August 12, 2016.

"'Lamogi Rebellion against British Rule Was Justified'—President Museveni." News Release. The State House of Uganda. March 22, 2015. www.statehouse.go.ug/media/news/2015/03/22/%E2%80%9Clamogi-rebellion-against-british-rule-was-justified%E2%80%9D-%E2%80%93-president-museveni. Accessed June 19, 2015.

Lang, Maurice Eugen. *Codification in the British Empire and America*. Amsterdam: H.J. Paris, 1924.

Langbaum, Robert. "Autobiography and Myth in the African Memoirs." *Isak Dinesen: Critical Views*. Athens: Ohio University Press, 1993: 38–50.

Lasson, Frans. "Chronology." Karen Blixen Museet. 1997. https://blixen.dk/life-writings/karen-blixens-life/chronology/?lang=en. Accessed April 12, 2013.

Lauer, Helen. "Cashing in on Shame: How the Popular 'Tradition vs. Modernity' Dualism Contributes to the 'HIV/AIDS Crisis' in Africa." *Review of Radical Political Economics* 38.1 (2006): 90–138.

Laurence, Margaret. *A Tree for Poverty: Somali Poetry and Prose*. Toronto and Hamilton, Ontario: ECW Press and McMaster University Press, 1993.

Leakey, Louis. *Defeating Mau Mau*. London: Methuen & Co., 1954.

——. *Mau Mau and the Kikuyu*. London: Methuen & Co., 1952.

——. *White African: An Early Autobiography*. Cambridge, MA: Schenkman Publishing Company, 1966.

Lee, Judith. "The Mask of Form in *Out of Africa*." *Isak Dinesen: Critical Views*. Athens: Ohio University Press, 1993: 266–82.

Leigh, Ione. *In the Shadow of Mau Mau*. London: W.H. Allen, 1954.

Leman, "Singing the Law: Okot p'Bitek's Legal Imagination and the Poetics of Traditional Justice." *Research in African Literatures* 40.3 (2009): 109–28.

Lewis, I.M. *Blood and Bone: The Call of Kinship in Somali Society*. Lawrenceville, NJ: Red Sea Press, 1994.

Lewis, Sophie. "Planting A Trillion Trees Could Be the 'Most Effective Solution' to Climate Change, Study Says." *CBS News*. July 8, 2019. www.cbsnews.com/news/planting-a-trillion-trees-could-be-the-most-effective-solution-to-climate-change/. Accessed December 7, 2019.

"Lex talionis." *Oxford English Dictionary*. Online.

Lipscomb, J.F. *We Built a Country*. London: Faber & Faber, 1956.

——. *White Africans*. 1955. Westport, CT: Greenwood Press, 1974.

Liu Institute for Global Issues. *Roco Wat I Acoli. Restoring Relationships in Acholi-land: Traditional Approaches to Justice and Reintegration*. September 15, 2005. http://restorativejustice.org/rj-library/author/2753/. Accessed December 7, 2019.

Lonsdale, John. "Contests of Time: Kikuyu Historiography, Old and New." In *A Place in the World: New Local Historiographies from Africa and South Asia*. Ed. Axel Harneit-Sievers. Leiden: Brill, 2002: 201–54.

——. "Kenyatta's Trials: Breaking and Making an African Nationalist." In *The Moral World of the Law*. Ed. Peter Coss. Cambridge: Cambridge University Press, 2000: 196–239.

——. "Mau Maus of the Mind: Making Mau Mau and Remaking Kenya." *Journal of African History* 31.3 (1990): 393–421.

——. Personal correspondence with the author. October 31, 2013.

Lonsdale, John and Bruce Berman. "Louis Leakey's Mau Mau: A Study in the Politics of Knowledge." *History and Anthropology* 5.2 (1991): 143–204.

Loomba, Ania. *Colonialism/Postcolonialism*. 3rd ed. London: Routledge, 2015.

"LRA Commander Dominic Ongwen Appears before ICC in The Hague." *BBC News*. January 26, 2015. www.bbc.co.uk/news/world-africa-30976818. Accessed July 10, 2015.

Lubwa p'Chong. "A Biographical Sketch." *Artist, the Ruler*. By Okot p'Bitek. Nairobi: Heinemann, 1986: 1–12.

Lugard, F.D. *The Dual Mandate in British Tropical Africa*. Edinburgh: William Blackwood & Sons, 1922.

McClennan, Sophia A. and Joseph R. Slaughter. "Introducing Human Rights and Literary Forms; or, the Vehicles and Vocabularies of Human Rights." *Comparative Literature Studies* 46.1 (2009): 1–19.

McGrath, Matt. "Climate Change: 12 Years to Save the Planet? Make That 18 Months." *BBC News*. July 24, 2019. www.bbc.com/news/science-environment-48964736. Accessed December 7, 2019.

McKenzie, David, Angela Dewan, and Brent Swails. "Robert Mugabe Resigns after 37 Years as Zimbabwe's Leader." *CNN*. November 21, 2017. www.cnn.com/2017/11/21/africa/robert-mugabe-resigns-zimbabwe-president/index.html. Accessed December 7, 2019.

MacKenzie, John M. *The Empire of Nature: Hunting, Conservation and British Imperialism*. Manchester: Manchester University Press, 1988.

Maine, Henry Sumner. *Ancient Law*. 1861. New Brunswick, NJ: Transaction Publishers, 2002.

"MAITU NJUGIRA: A PLAY BY NGUGI WA THIONGO WHICH WAS BANNED BY MOI." *YouTube*. May 24, 2016. www.youtube.com/watch?v=CTQPgbcdvC0. Accessed December 7, 2019.

Mamdani, Mahmood. *Citizen and Subject: Contemporary Africa and the Legacy of Late Colonialism*. Princeton, NJ: Princeton University Press, 1996.

——. *Define and Rule: Native as Political Identity*. Cambridge, MA: Harvard University Press, 2012.

——. *Saviors and Survivors: Darfur, Politics, and the War on Terror*. New York: Doubleday, 2010.

Mantena, Karuna. *Alibis of Empire: Henry Maine and the Ends of Liberal Imperialism*. Princeton, NJ: Princeton University Press, 2010.

"The Manuscript for 'Out of Africa.'" The Royal Danish Library. n.d. www5.kb.dk/en/nb/materialer/haandskrifter/HA/e-mss/karen_blixen/out_of_africa.html. Accessed December 7, 2019.

Markham, Beryl. *West with the Night*. 1942. New York: North Point Press, 1983.

"The Mau Mau Claims." *Leigh Day*. n.d. www.leighday.co.uk/International/Further-insights/Detailed-case-studies/The-Mau-Mau-claims. Accessed February 12, 2015.

Mawani, Renisa. "Law as Temporality: Colonial Politics and Indian Settlers." *UC Irvine Law Review* 4.65 (2014): 65–95.

Mazuri, Alamin and Lupenga Mphande. "Orality and the Literature of Combat: The Legacy of Fanon." *Critical Essays on Ngũgĩ wa Thiong'o*. Ed. Peter Nazareth. New York: Twayne Publishers, 2000: 228–48.

Mbembe, Achille. "Figures of the Subject in Times of Crisis." *Popular Culture* 7 (1995): 323–52.

Mbise, Ismael. *Blood on Our Land*. Dar es Salaam: Tanzania Publishing House, 1974.

Mbiti, John S. *African Religions and Philosophy*. 2nd ed. Oxford: Heinemann, 1989.

Mengistu, Dinaw. "Not a Click Away: Joseph Kony in the Real World." *Warscapes*. March 12, 2012.

Merry, Sally Engle. *Colonizing Hawai'i: The Cultural Power of Law*. Princeton, NJ: Princeton University Press, 2000.

Metz, Helen Chapin, ed. *Somalia: A Country Study*. Washington, DC: Federal Research Division of the Library of Congress, 1992.

Miller, J. Hillis. "Laying Down the Law in Literature: The Example of Kleist." In *Deconstruction and the Possibility of Justice*. Ed. Drucilla Cornell, Michel Rosenfeld, and David Gray Carlson. New York: Routledge, 1992: 305–29.

Mino, Takako. "Dwog Paco: Tackling the Challenges of Reintegrating Ex-LRA in Kitgum District." *Independent Study Project (ISP) Collection*. Paper 814 (2009).

Mnookin, Jennifer L. "The Image of Truth: Photographic Evidence and the Power of Analogy." *Yale Journal of Law & the Humanities* 10.1 (2013): 1–74.

Mohamed, Jama. "Kinship and Contract in Somali Politics." *Africa* 77.2 (2007): 226–49.

Moore, Jennifer. *Humanitarian Law in Action within Africa*. Oxford: Oxford University Press, 2012.

Moore-Gilbert, Bart, Gareth Stanton, and Willy Maley. "Introduction." *Postcolonial Criticism*. New York: Routledge, 2013: 1–72.

Morris, H.F. *Some Perspectives on East African Legal History*. Uppsala: Scandinavian Institute of African Studies, 1970.

Morris, H.F. and James S. Read. *Indirect Rule and the Search for Justice: Essays in East African Legal History*. Oxford: Clarendon Press, 1972.

——. *Uganda: The Development of Its Laws and Constitution*. London: Stevens, 1966.

Morton, Stephen. *States of Emergency: Colonialism, Literature and Law*. Liverpool: Liverpool University Press, 2013.

Mueller, Susanne D. "Kenya and the International Criminal Court (ICC): Politics, the Election and the Law." *Journal of Eastern African Studies* 8.1 (2014): 25–42.

Mugerwa, P.J. Nkambo. "Status, Responsibility and Liability: A Comparative Study of Two Types of Society in Uganda." *Ideas and Procedures in African Customary Law*. Ed. Max Gluckman. Oxford: Oxford University Press, 1969: 279–91.

Mugo, Mĩcere Githae. *African Orature and Human Rights*. Lesotho: Institute of Southern African Studies, National University of Lesotho, 1991.

——. *African Orature and Human Rights in Gikuyu, Shona, and Ndebele Zamani Cultures*. Harare: SAPES Books, 2004.

Mwangi, Evan. "Gender, Unreliable Oral Narration, and the Untranslated Preface in Ngũgĩ wa Thiong'o's *Devil on the Cross*." *Research in African Literatures* 38.4 (2007): 28–46.

Myers, J.C. *Indirect Rule in South Africa: Tradition, Modernity, and the Costuming of Political Power*. Rochester, NY: University of Rochester Press, 2008.

Nanni, Giordano. *The Colonisation of Time: Ritual, Routine, and Resistance in the British Empire*. Manchester: Manchester University Press, 2013.

"Native Courts and Native Customary Law in Africa." *Judicial Advisers' Conference*. Special supplement to the *Journal of African Administration*. October 1953.

Ndĩgĩrĩgĩ, Gĩchingiri. *Ngũgĩ wa Thiong'o's Drama and the Kamĩrĩĩthu Popular Theater Experiment*. Trenton, NJ and Asmara, Eritrea: Africa World Press, 2007.

——, ed. *Unmasking the African Dictator: Essays in Postcolonial African Literature*. Knoxville: University of Tennessee Press, 2014.

Ndiku Mutua et al. "Letter to Gordon Brown." June 24, 2009.

Ngatia, Martin. "Kenya: Will Cholmondeley Walk Away with Another Cold-Blooded Murder?" *Ethiomedia*. May 14, 2006. www.ethiomedia.com/carepress/cholmondeley_murder.html. 2015. Accessed December 7, 2019.

Ngũgĩ wa Thiong'o. *Decolonising the Mind: The Politics of Language in African Literature*. London: James Currey, 1986.

——. *Detained: A Writer's Prison Diary*. London: Heinemann, 1981.

——. *Devil on the Cross*. London: Heinemann, 1982.

——. *Globalectics: Theory and the Politics of Knowing*. New York: Columbia University Press, 2012.

——. *A Grain of Wheat*. London: Heinemann, 1967.

——. "Introduction." *Africa's Cultural Revolution*. By Okot p'Bitek. Nairobi: Macmillan Books for Africa, 1973: ix–xiii.

——. *Matigari: A Novel*. 1989. Trenton, NJ and Asmara, Eritrea: Africa World Press, 1998.

——. *Mother, Sing for Me*. Unpublished play. Nairobi, Kenya, 1982.

——. *Penpoints, Gunpoints, and Dreams: Towards a Critical Theory of the Arts and the State in Africa*. New York: Oxford University Press, 1998.

——. *Weep Not, Child*. Nairobi: Heinemann, 1964.

——. *Wizard of the Crow*. New York: Pantheon Books, 2006.

Ngũgĩ wa Thiong'o and Mĩcere Githae Mugo. *The Trial of Dedan Kimathi*. Oxford: Heinemann, 1976.

Ngũgĩ wa Thiong'o and Ngũgĩ wa Mĩriĩ. *I Will Marry When I Want*. Oxford: Heinemann, 1982.

Njoku, Raphael Chijioke. *The History of Somalia*. Santa Barbara, CA: Greenwood, 2013.

Ntuli, Pitika. "Orature: A Self Portrait." *Storms of the Heart: An Anthology of Black Arts and Culture*. Ed. Kwesi Owusu. London: Camden Press, 1988: 209–18.

O'Brien, Eugene. "The Return and Redefinition of the Repressed: The Construction of Female Identity in the Writings of James Joyce." *Joyce, Imperialism, and Postcolonialism*. Ed. Leonard Orr. Syracuse, NY: Syracuse University Press, 2008: 41–57.

Ochieng, Abiud. "Lawyers Battle It Out for Mau Mau Billions." *Daily Nation*. February 17, 2015. www.nation.co.ke/news/Lawyers-battle-it-out-for-Mau-Mau-billions/1056-2625942-2jk673/index.html. Accessed May 12, 2015.

Ofuani, Ogo A. "The Traditional and Modern Influences in Okot p'Bitek's Poetry." *African Studies Review* 28.4 (1985): 87–99.

Ojaide, Tanure. "Poetic Viewpoint: Okot p'Bitek and His Personae." *Callaloo* 27 (1986): 371–83.

Ojwang, Humphrey J. *Okot p'Bitek on Trial: A Biographical Play*. Nairobi: Lifelong Educational Materials Publishers, 1993.

Okia, Opolot. *Communal Labor in Colonial Kenya: The Legitimization of Coercion, 1912–1930*. Houndmills: Palgrave Macmillan, 2012.

Okot p'Bitek. *Acholi Proverbs*. Nairobi: Heinemann, 1985.

——. *Africa's Cultural Revolution*. Nairobi: Macmillan Books for Africa. 1973.

——. *African Religions in Western Scholarship*. Nairobi: East African Literature Bureau, 1971.

——. *Artist, the Ruler*. Nairobi: Heinemann, 1986.

——. *The Defense of Lawino*. Trans. Taban lo Liyong. Kampala: Fountain, 2001.

——. *Horn of My Love*. Nairobi: Heinemann, 1974.

——. Interview. In Bernth Lindfors. *Africa Talks Back: Interviews with Anglophone African Authors*. Trenton, NJ: Africa World Press, 2002: 289–308.

——. "Oral Literature and its Social Background among the Acholi and Lango." B.Litt. thesis. University of Oxford, 1963.

——. *Religion of the Central Luo*. Nairobi: East African Literature Bureau, 1971.

——. *Song of Lawino/Song of Ocol*. Oxford: Heinemann, 1972.

——. *Two Songs: Song of Prisoner, Song of Malaya*. Nairobi: Heinemann, 1988.

Okpewho, Isidore. *African Oral Literature: Backgrounds, Character, and Continuity*. Bloomington: Indiana University Press, 1992.

Okumu, Charles. "The Form of Okot p'Bitek's Poetry: Literary Borrowing from Acholi Oral Traditions." *Research in African Literatures* 23.3 (1992): 53–66.

"Omar al-Bashir Celebrates ICC Decision to Halt Darfur Investigation." *Guardian*. December 14, 2014. www.theguardian.com/world/2014/dec/14/omar-al-bashir-celebrates-icc-decision-to-halt-darfur-investigation. Accessed May 15, 2015.

Ong, Walter J. *Orality and Literacy: The Technologizing of the Word*. London: Methuen, 1982.

Opalo, Ken. "The Constitutional Devolution of Power in Kenya—Will It Work?" *AfricaPlus*. June 10, 2015. https://africaplus.wordpress.com/2015/06/10/the-constitutional-devolution-of-power-in-kenya-will-it-work/. Accessed July 7, 2015.

Osuagwu, Ndubuisi C. "A Traditional Poet in Modern Garb: Okot p'Bitek." *Literary Criterion* 23.1–2 (1988): 13–29.

Owen, Chris and Adam Bristow. "Mass Torts Case Alert: Supreme Court Refuses Permission to Appeal in Unilever Case." *elexica*. July 19, 2019. Simmons & Simmons. www.elexica.com/en/legal-topics/dispute-resolution-commercial/190719-mass-torts-case-alert-supreme-court-refuses-permission-to-appeal-in-unilever-case. Accessed December 7, 2019.

Paice, Edward. *Lost Lion of Empire: The Life of "Cape-to-Cairo" Grogan*. London: HarperCollins, 2001.

Paradis, Pierre R. "The Celluloid Witness." *University of Colorado Law Review* 37 (1965): 235–69.

Paramaguru, Kharunya. "Justice for the Mau Mau: Court Case in the U.K. Sheds Light on Grim Colonial Past." *Time*. October 10, 2012. http://world.time.com/2012/10/10/justice-for-the-mau-mau-court-case-in-the-u-k-sheds-light-on-grim-colonial-past/. Accessed May 11, 2015.

Patterson, J.H. *The Man-Eaters of Tsavo*. 1908. New York: Pocket Books, 1996.

Peterson, Derek R. *Creative Writing: Translation, Bookkeeping, and the Work of Imagination in Colonial Kenya*. Portsmouth, NH: Heinemann, 2004.

Picart, Caroline Joan S. "Nationalities, Histories, Rhetorics: Real/Reel Representations of the Holocaust and Holocaust Trials and a Poethics of Film and Law." *Dapim: Studies on the Holocaust* 29.2 (2015): 114–33.

Podmore, Will. *British Foreign Policy since 1870*. Philadelphia: Xlibris, 2008.

Poore, Charles. "Book of the Times: *Out of Africa* Remembrance of Things Past." *New York Times*. March 3, 1938.

Posner, Daniel N. and Daniel J. Young. "The Institutionalization of Political Power in Africa." *Journal of Democracy* 18.3 (2007): 126–40.

Pritt, Denis Nowell. *The Autobiography of D.N. Pritt, Parts One to Three*. London: Lawrence & Wishart, 1965–66.

"The Prosecutor v. Uhuru Muigai Kenyatta." International Criminal Court, October 2011. www.icc-cpi.int/kenya/kenyatta. Accessed June 12, 2015.

Rama Rau, Santha. "The Trial of Jomo Kenyatta." *Reporter*. March 16, 1954: 12–23.

Ramazani, Jahan. *The Hybrid Muse: Postcolonial Poetry in English*. Chicago: University of Chicago Press, 2001.

Ranger, Terence. "The Invention of Tradition Revisited: The Case of Colonial Africa." In *Legitimacy and the State in Twentieth-Century Africa*. Ed. Terence Ranger and Olufemi Vaughan. Houndmills: Palgrave Macmillan, 1993: 62–111.

Rawcliffe, D.H. *The Struggle for Kenya*. London: Gollancz, 1954.

Richland, Justin B. "Sovereign Time, Storied Moments: The Temporalities of Law, Tradition, and Ethnography in Hopi Tribal Court." *PoLAR: Political and Legal Anthropology Review* 31.1 (2008): 8–27.

Robinson, Nicholas A. "Fundamental Principles of Law for the Anthropocene." *Environmental Policy and Law* 44.1–2 (2014): 13–32.

Roco Wat I Acoli, Restoring Relationships in Acholi-land: Traditional Approaches to *Justice and Reintegration*. Liu Institute for Global Issues. 2005. Web. http://restorativejustice.org/rj-library/roco-wat-i-acoli-restoring-relationships-in-acholi-land-traditional-approaches-to-justice-and-reintegration/6883/. Accessed September 2006.

Rodney, Walter. *How Europe Underdeveloped Africa*. Washington, DC: Howard University Press, 1974.

Roper, Peter P. "Sound Recording Devices Used as Evidence." *Cleveland-Marshall Law Review* 9 (1960): 523–34.

Rosberg, Carl and John Nottingham. *The Myth of Mau Mau: Nationalism in Kenya*. New York: Praeger, 1966.

Rwegasira, Abdon. *Land as a Human Right: A History of Land Law and Practice in Tanzania*. Dar es Salaam: Mkuki na Nyota, 2012.

Rychlak, Ronald J. "Sound in the Courtroom: Audio Recordings at Trial." *American Journal of Trial Advocacy* 39.1 (2015): 1–23.

Said, Edward. *Culture and Imperialism*. New York: Vintage Books, 1993.

Samatar, Said S. *Oral Poetry and Somali Nationalism: The Case of Sayyid Mahammad 'Abdille Hasan*. Cambridge: Cambridge University Press, 1982.

Samolsky, Russell. *Apocalyptic Futures: Marked Bodies and the Violence of the Text in Kafka, Conrad, and Coetzee*. New York: Fordham University Press, 2011.

Save Darfur Campaign. "Celebrities Speak Out for Darfur." Online video. September 19, 2007. www.youtube.com/watch?v=lAjhRHlYEak. Accessed August 12, 2016.

Schmitt, Eric and Charlie Savage. "Trump Administration Steps Up Air War in Somalia." *New York Times*. March 10, 2019. www.nytimes.com/2019/03/10/us/politics/us-somalia-airstrikes-shabab.html. Accessed December 7, 2019.

Schoenherr, Steven. "The History of Magnetic Recording." Audio Engineering Society. November 5, 2002. www.aes-media.org/historical/html/recording.technology.history/magnetic4.html. Accessed May 1, 2016.

Scott, David. *Conscripts of Modernity: The Tragedy of Colonial Enlightenment*. Durham, NC: Duke University Press, 2004.

Shadle, Brett. "'Changing Traditions to Meet Current Altering Conditions': Customary Law, African Courts and the Rejection of Codification in Kenya, 1930–1960." *Journal of African History* 40 (1999): 411–31.

"Shooting Tragedy at Ngong." *East African Standard*. December 22, 1923. Newspaper Archives, British Library, London.

Simmons, Diane. *The Narcissism of Empire: Loss, Rage, and Revenge in Thomas de Quincy, Robert Louis Stevenson, Arthur Conan Doyle, Rudyard Kipling, and Isak Dinesen*. Brighton: Sussex Academic Press, 2007.

Slater, Montagu. *The Trial of Jomo Kenyatta*. London: Secker & Warburg, 1957.

Slaughter, Joseph. *Human Rights, Inc.: The World Novel, Narrative Form, and International Law*. New York: Fordham University Press, 2007.

Smith, George. *Twelve Indian Statesmen*. London: John Murray, 1897.

"Somali Piracy Exposes Weakness in the UN Law of the Sea." *VOA: Voice of America*. November 2, 2009. www.voanews.com/archive/somali-piracy-exposes-weakness-un-law-sea. Accessed September 15, 2015.

"Somerhough, Anthony George." *Who was Who: A Companion to Who's Who, Containing the Biographies of Those Who Died during the Period 1951–1960*. vol. 5. London: A. & C. Black, 1960: 1023.

Sparrow, Fiona. "Telling the Story Yet Again: Oral Traditions in Nuruddin Farah's Fiction." *Journal of Commonwealth Literature* 24 (1989): 164–72.

Spear, Thomas. *Mountain Farmers: Moral Economies of Land and Agricultural Development in Arusha and Meru*. Berkeley: University of California Press, 1997.

Speke, John H. *Journal of the Discovery of the Source of the Nile*. Edinburgh and London: William Blackwood and Sons, 1863.

Spencer, Robert. "Ngũgĩ wa Thiong'o and the African Dictator Novel." *Journal of Commonwealth Literature* 47.2 (2012): 145–58.

Sperber, Amanda. "Report: U.S. Airstrikes are Killing Civilians in Somalia in Wave of Attacks under Trump." *Intercept*. March 20, 2019. www.theintercept.com/2019/03/19/u-s-air-strikes-in-somalia-kill-civilians-in-wave-of-attacks-under-trump-amnesty-report-says/. Accessed December 7, 2019.

Stanley, Henry Morton. *Through the Dark Continent*. 1878. New York: Dover Publications, 1988.

Stephen, James Fitzjames. "Legislation under Lord Mayo." In William Wilson Hunter, *A Life of the Earl of Mayo, Fourth Viceroy of India*. 2nd ed. London: Smith, Elder, & Co., 1876: 143–226.

Stichter, Sharon. *Migrant Labour in Kenya: Capitalism and African Response, 1895–1975*. Harlow: Longman, 1982.

Stille, Alexander. *The Future of the Past*. New York: Farrar, Straus and Giroux, 2002.

Stoneham, C.T. *Out of Barbarism*. London: Museum Press Limited, 1955.

Stratton, Florence. *Contemporary African Literature and the Politics of Gender*. London: Routledge, 1994.

Taban lo Liyong. *The Last Word*. Nairobi: East African Publishing House, 1969.

——. "On Translating the 'Untranslated': Chapter 14 of *Wer pa Lawino* by Okot p'Bitek." *Research in African Literatures* 24.3 (1993): 87–92.

——. *Popular Culture of East Africa: Oral Literature*. Nairobi: Longman, 1972.

Taylor, Bron. "Kenya's Green Belt Movement." *Civil Society in the Age of Monitory Democracy*. Ed. Nina Witoszek, Lars Tragardh, and Bron Taylor. Oxford: Berghahn Books, 2013: 180–207.

Thomas, Brook. *American Literary Realism and the Failed Promise of Contract*. Berkeley: University of California Press, 1997.

——. *Civic Myths: A Law and Literature Approach to Citizenship*. Chapel Hill: University of North Carolina Press, 2007.

——. *Cross-Examinations of Law and Literature: Cooper, Hawthorne, Stowe Melville*. Cambridge: Cambridge University Press, 1987.

——. *The New Historicism and Other Old-Fashioned Topics*. Princeton, NJ: Princeton University Press, 1991.

Thuku, Harry. *Harry Thuku: An Autobiography*. With assistance from Kenneth King. Nairobi: Oxford University Press, 1970.

"Time for Tea: Unilever Publishes Full Global List of Tea Suppliers." *Unilever*. September 12, 2019. www.unilever.com/news/press-releases/2019/time-for-tea-unilever-publishes-full-global-list-of-tea-suppliers.html. Accessed December 7, 2019.

Trachtman, Joel P. "The Crisis of International Law." *Case Western Reserve Journal of International Law* 44 (2011): 407–21.

Treves, Tullio. "Piracy, Law of the Sea, and Use of Force: Developments off the Coast of Somalia." *European Journal of International Law* 20.2 (2009): 399–414.

Twist, Susan. "Evidence of Atrocities or Atrocious Use of Evidence: The Controversial Use of Atrocity Film at Nuremberg." *Liverpool Law Review* 26 (2005): 267–302.

"Unilever Kenya: Post-Election Violence on Unilever's Kenyan Tea Estates." Leigh Day. n.d. www.leighday.co.uk/International/Corporate-accountability/Security-human-rights/Unilever-Kenya. Accessed December 7, 2019.

Usongo, Kenneth. "Cultural Identity and Literature: A Study of Okot p'Bitek's *Song of Lawino*." *Matatu: Journal of African Culture and Society* 39 (2011): 179–90.

Walcott, Derek. *Collected Poems, 1948–1984*. New York: Farrar, Straus and Giroux, 1986.

Walters, Guy. *Hunting Evil: The Nazi War Criminals Who Escaped and the Quest to Bring Them to Justice*. New York: Broadway Books, 2010.

Warne, Kennedy. "National Geographic: A Voice for Nature." *National Geographic*. April 24, 2019. www.national geographic.com/culture/2019/04/maori-river-in-new-zealand-is-a-legal-person/. Accessed December 7, 2019.

Weindling, Paul J. *John W. Thompson: Psychiatrist in the Shadow of the Holocaust*. Rochester, NY: University of Rochester Press, 2010.

Wilson, Christopher. *Before the Dawn in Kenya*. Nairobi: The English Press, 1953.

——. *Kenya's Warning*. Nairobi: The English Press, 1954.

Wise, Christopher. "Resurrecting the Devil: Notes on Ngũgĩ's Theory of the Oral–Aural African Novel." *Research in African Literatures* 28.1 (1997): 134–40.

Wistrich, Andrew J. "The Evolving Temporality of Lawmaking." *Connecticut Law Review* 44.3 (2012): 737–826.

Wittgenstein, Ludwig. *Philosophical Investigations*. 1953. Trans. G.E.M. Anscombe. Upper Saddle River, NJ: Prentice Hall, 1958.

Woods, Katherine. "Isak Dinesen's Fine Record of Life on an African Farm." *New York Times Book Review*. March 6, 1938.

Wright, Derek. "Orality and Power in *Sweet and Sour Milk*." *Emerging Perspectives on Nuruddin Farah*. Ed. Derek Wright. Trenton, NJ and Asmara, Eritrea: Africa World Press, 2002.

Yakubu, Alhaji Mahmood. *An Aristocracy in Political Crisis: The End of Indirect Rule and the Emergence of Party Politics in the Emirates of Northern Nigeria*. Aldershot and Brookfield, VT: Avebury, 1996.

Referenced Cases

International Criminal Court

The Prosecutor v. *Joseph Kony and Vincent Otti* (ICC-02/04-01/05)
The Prosecutor v. *Uhuru Muigai Kenyatta* (ICC-01/09-02/11)

Kenya

Regina v. *Kenyatta & others* (1952)

United Kingdom

Harry Parker Ltd v. *Mason* [1940] 2 KB 590, CA
Mutua & others v. *The Foreign & Commonwealth Office* [2012] EWHC 2678 (QB)
Kenyan Tea Workers v. *Unilever plc and Unilever Tea Kenya Ltd* [2015]
Okpabi & others v. *Royal Dutch Shell plc and Shell Petroleum Development Company of Nigeria Ltd* [2018] EWCA Civ 191
AAA & others v. *Unilever plc and Unilever Tea Kenya Ltd* [2018] EWCA Civ 1532
Kimathi & others v. *The Foreign and Commonwealth Office* [2018] EWHC 2066 (QB)
Vedanta Resources plc and another v. *Lungowe and others* [2019] UKSC 20

United States of America

Boyne City, G. & A. R. Co. v. *Anderson*, 146 Mich. 328, 108 NW 429 (1906)
Glyn v. *Weston Feature Film Co. Ltd.* 114 LTR (NS) 354 (1915)
United States v. *McKeever*, 169 F. Supp. 426 (SDNY 1958)
United States of America v. *Usama bin Laden, et al.* US District Court for the Southern District of New York, S(7) 98 Cr. 1023 (2001)

Index

Printed and bound by CPI Group (UK) Ltd, Croydon, CR0 4YY

13/09/2026

14961097-0005